"This will be a wonderful addition to our tools as folks go forward in utilizing RTI to improve outcomes for all kids!"

—*Alice Parker, Ph.D.,* former assistant superintendent, California Department of Education; state director of special education; past president, National Association of State Directors of Special Education

"Silvia DeRuvo doesn't just talk the talk, she walks the walk. She's an educator who is grounded in the realities that face teachers and administrators on a daily basis. Because of this, *The Essential Guide to RTI* moves beyond theory into practical ways to meet the needs of all students in a classroom and school. Every teacher and administrator should read this guide!"

—*Erika Benadom,* education technology and assessment coordinator, Lennox School District, Lennox, CA

"*The Essential Guide to RTI* provides school leaders with tools for change with which to meet the challenge of making achievement for all children a priority. This is a must-read for leadership! The book provides school teams with a moving and transforming step-by-step process for the implementation of RTI and powerful change."

—*Meredith Cathcart, M.S.,* special education consultant

"DeRuvo's new book clearly outlines the steps for implementing a thoughtful process for serving struggling learners. This is a must-read for all who care about improving their approach to teaching and learning."

—*Patt Kearly,* professor of special education, California State University, Sacramento

"Implementing the appropriate RTI model at an urban middle school is downright challenging. However, Silvia DeRuvo's book has made implementation sexy, exciting, and inspiring. Achievement for EVERY learner in our current standards-based, high-stakes education era in public schools is attainable!"

—*Yesenia Alvarez,* principal, Lennox Middle School 6, Lennox Elementary School District, Lennox, CA

"Finally, an experienced practitioner with a long track record of RTI implementation tackles the difficult task of defining what RTI truly is and is not, and, step-by-step, takes educators through the process of effective RTI roll-out. If you are to read one book on RTI—this is it."

—*Erik Burmeister,* principal, Union Middle School, Union Elementary School District, San Jose, CA

"*The Essential Guide to RTI* is just that: It brings together the core principles of RTI, including the academic and behavioral components. While recognizing the uniqueness of each educational context, this text provides sound advice on initiating and sustaining the processes that support RTI as a vehicle for powerful educational change."

—*Allan Lloyd-Jones,* coordinator of education support services/educational psychologist, Prince Alfred College, Adelaide, South Australia

"This book provides a solid understanding of the importance of a schoolwide model of 'problem solving and collaboration' when addressing the needs of children with educational and behavioral challenges. As both a school psychologist and an ADHD specialist, I cannot think of a better resource to have on hand when advocating for a child who is educationally and behaviorally challenged at school."

—*Richard Lougy,* credentialed school psychologist, ADHD specialist, and published author

Jossey-Bass Teacher

Jossey-Bass Teacher provides educators with practical knowledge and tools to create a positive and lifelong impact on student learning. We offer classroom-tested and research-based teaching resources for a variety of grade levels and subject areas. Whether you are an aspiring, new, or veteran teacher, we want to help you make every teaching day your best.

From ready-to-use classroom activities to the latest teaching framework, our value-packed books provide insightful, practical, and comprehensive materials on the topics that matter most to K–12 teachers. We hope to become your trusted source for the best ideas from the most experienced and respected experts in the field.

The Essential Guide to RTI

An Integrated, Evidence-Based Approach

Silvia L. DeRuvo

WestEd.org

JOSSEY-BASS
A Wiley Imprint
www.josseybass.com

Published by Jossey-Bass
A Wiley Imprint
989 Market Street, San Francisco, CA 94103-1741—www.josseybass.com

Jossey-Bass books and products are available through most bookstores. To contact Jossey-Bass directly call our Customer Care Department within the U.S. at 800-956-7739, outside the U.S. at 317-572-3986, or fax 317-572-4002.

Jossey-Bass also publishes its books in a variety of electronic formats. Some content that appears in print may not be available in electronic books.

Library of Congress Cataloging-in-Publication Data
DeRuvo, Silvia L.
    The essential guide to RTI : An integrated, evidence-based approach /
Silvia L. DeRuvo.
        p. cm.
    Includes bibliographical references and index.
    ISBN 978-0-470-54801-1 (pbk.)
    1. Remedial teaching–Handbooks, manuals, etc. 2. Slow learning children–
Education–Handbooks, manuals, etc. 3. Learning disabled children–
Education–Handbooks, manuals, etc.. I. Title.
    LB1029.R4D47 2010
    371.9'043-dc22
                                        2010020675

Printed in the United States of America
FIRST EDITION
PB Printing   10 9 8 7 6 5 4 3 2 1

About This Book

The Essential Guide to RTI was written for visionary administrators, teachers, and school personnel like you, who are ready to take on the challenge of making achievement for *all* children a priority. The book presents a clear explanation of the philosophy of response to intervention (RTI) and how RTI can be the vehicle for bringing about powerful change, with practical strategies that will move your school through the phases of the implementation process.

Changing mindsets and beliefs is a tenuous endeavor, and *The Essential Guide to RTI* provides the tools, research, and practice that will help school RTI leadership teams move through this step-by-step process. From identifying the rationale through the consensus-building process to the important tasks associated with infrastructure building prior to implementation, this book will guide teachers, administrators, and leadership teams through these tasks. It describes evidence-based practices that guide educators to construct an effective RTI framework that includes special education services within the schoolwide intervention structures and that supports the success of English learners and other subgroups in the areas of language arts and math. Teams will learn the process for identifying the "what" of focused instruction in the RTI framework with the development of standards-aligned curriculum maps, and the "how" of RTI through the collaborative data-driven instructional processes and positive behavioral approaches discussed within these pages. Finally, this book provides the inspiration necessary to help educators persist in subsequent years of implementation by offering success stories of real schools that have positively and forever affected the lives of the children within their walls by fulfilling the promise of achievement for *all*.

About WestEd

WestEd, a national nonpartisan, nonprofit research, development, and service agency, works with education and other communities to promote excellence, achieve equity, and improve learning for children, youth, and adults. WestEd has seventeen offices nationwide, from Washington and Boston to Arizona and California. Its corporate headquarters are in San Francisco.

The Author

Silvia L. DeRuvo is a special education resources development specialist with WestEd, a nonprofit agency that works with schools, districts, state agencies, and national policymakers in educational research, products, and program implementation. Utilizing a response to intervention (RTI) framework in the comprehensive school improvement process, she works with schools and districts to improve outcomes for students with disabilities, English learners, and other at-risk populations. Silvia has worked with numerous school districts across the country in the implementation of RTI structures with an emphasis on an integrated approach that includes services for students with disabilities and English learners within the RTI framework.

Prior to her work at WestEd, Silvia was a special educator for two decades and a teacher trainer at California State University, Sacramento. She has been a national speaker for the Bureau of Education and Research on topics pertaining to response to intervention implementation practices. She is author of *Strategies for Teaching Adolescents with ADHD: Effective Classroom Techniques Across the Content Areas,* published by Jossey-Bass; and coauthor of *Teaching Young Children with ADHD: Successful Strategies and Practical Interventions for PreK–3,* and *The School Counselor 's Guide to ADHD: What to Know and What to Do to Help Your Students,* both published by Corwin Press.

Silvia received an MA in communicative disorders from California State University, Fresno, and holds credentials in Multiple Subjects; as a Special Education Specialist: Communications Handicapped; as well as Resource Specialist certification. Silvia lives in northern California with her husband, two grown children, a dog, and six cats.

To my husband for his undying support and admiration, to my children for their ongoing understanding and patience, and to my Maker and Creator, who put this passion within me that I may do whatever I do, heartily, as to the Lord and not to men.

Acknowledgments

My deepest thanks to all the stalwart administrators, teachers, and other school staff members who have embraced the vision of equitable education for all students and have taken the first tentative steps of faith in the RTI implementation process. I applaud your courage.

To the schools and districts that have allowed me to practice the implementation steps in these pages while in their imperfect form, carrying your trust that the hope and promise of RTI would be fulfilled. I hope your students have found that fulfillment.

To Tracy Galongo and Lisa Somerville-Bennett, who took the vision and gave it form at Ray Wiltsey Middle School in your Alternate Service Delivery Model. You have changed the lives not only of students with disabilities but of the teachers who have had the privilege of working with them.

To Erik Burmeister, his leadership team, and his staff, who all took a vision and made it a reality at Union Middle School simply because it is the right thing to do.

To Erika Benadom, who taught me the most comprehensive and effective standards alignment process. Thank you for your exceptional linear thinking skills and your adept ability to figure out the next step, even when I was lost!

To the Jefferson Elementary Staff, who have earned their "Pilot Wings" in this past year for their tireless work in the development of an effective RTI framework. Your flexibility and your true passion for your students did not go unnoticed.

To Blanca Estrada, Yesenia Alvarez, and the Learning Center team at Lennox Middle School 6 for your vision to eliminate labels and create equitable educational opportunities for all students. You are a model of what special education will become.

To my exceptional colleagues at the WestEd Center for Prevention and Early Intervention for your expertise that helped fill these pages and your ongoing support and willingness to be on the cutting, and sometimes bleeding, edge of change.

To my church family at Foothill Bible Church, who regularly hold me up in prayer. Your support has helped me through many long and tiresome days.

To my family, who has sacrificed beyond measure in order to allow me to work out the steps in this book in so many different schools and districts, allowing me to follow the passion that God has put in my heart. To you I am forever grateful.

Contents

Part IV
Appendixes

Introduction: Why RTI Now?

Why another book on response to intervention (RTI)? Why is there such a strong surge of support for this type of research-based instructional framework? Why RTI? Why now?

The answers to these questions are multifaceted. The impetus for response to intervention comes from special education law, but RTI is not only about special education and special education practices. It is also about an equitable educational opportunity for each child, no matter what his or her label, socioeconomic status, or ethnicity. The promise and hope of RTI is the door that allows access to achievement for all students, but do we really need another book on RTI? While I recognize that many books have been written on the subject by numerous experts in the field, this one is different. The focus is on the process that holds the promise of equity and achievement for *all* students, *including* students with disabilities and English learners.

While the RTI process itself can be used to identify those students in need of special education, other resources do not focus on how the framework of RTI *is* the special education service delivery model that allows *all* students the opportunity to learn within a single standards-aligned system. RTI is not only the process to get to special education; RTI is the framework in which special education services are delivered. In this framework, students do not qualify for special education and "go" somewhere else; they continue to benefit from the rigorous research-based instruction and interventions provided *within* the multi-tiered interventions of a school. They no longer need to "go" to special education to receive their specially designed instruction, because it is provided within the RTI triangle.

In a like manner, English learners do not need to be excluded from the rich instruction and intervention provided within a schoolwide framework of intervention. Their label as "English learners" should not preclude them from benefiting from the exceptional research-based instruction and intervention provided within the three tiers of RTI presented in this book.

The inclusion of students with disabilities and English learners within this seamless system of instructional supports is what RTI is truly about. There may be aspects of specific student needs in special education that need a more specific focus than can be provided within the triangle of interventions, but this need alone should not be an excuse to preclude students from the benefit of the framework. Similarly, English learners may need more specific vocabulary development than they may find in the schoolwide hierarchy of supports, but this need alone should not keep them from accessing the programs offered to all other students. This book tells how to develop an inclusionary model of response to intervention that creates a framework to meet the instructional needs of all students, including those identified by former Secretary of Education Rod Paige as "difficult to teach."[1] This book was written for those educators who agree that it is our responsibility to teach each and every child, regardless of labels or learning challenges.

> "The inclusion of students with disabilities and English learners within this seamless system of instructional supports is what RTI is truly about.... This book tells how to develop an inclusionary model of response to intervention that creates a framework to meet the instructional needs of all students, including those identified ... as "difficult to teach.""

I hope this book will help those visionary administrators, teachers, and school personnel who are ready to take on the challenge of making educating *all* children a priority. If you are one of those visionaries, buckle up your boot straps, grab your flak jacket, and get prepared for one of the most meaningful and fulfilling adventures of your educational career.

In this process, you will be creating powerful change at your school sites. You will be changing mindsets and expectations. You will see students achieve at levels never thought possible, and you will see the walls between perceived expectations and true skills come tumbling down. You will be surprised and amazed at what your students can do, you will be pleasantly surprised at how much your colleagues really know, and you will find within yourself the ability to stretch your skills in order to create the equitable, effective learning environments necessary for all students to succeed.

Implementing an RTI framework is a multifaceted undertaking. This book is divided into three sections to help the reader maneuver through the various stages in the RTI journey. Part One investigates the law and practice that have brought about the promise of Achievement for All. This section provides the reader with the "why" of making this paradigm shift. Part Two covers the "what" of RTI as it is described in special education law and the relationship of RTI to students with disabilities. Understanding of the why and what leads to Part Three, which addresses the practical "how," through the step-by-step implementation process.

Part One: Achievement for ALL: The Promise of RTI

In order to make such momentous change, one needs a clear understanding of what RTI is and what it is not. There has been much confusion in the field regarding RTI and whom it "belongs" to. The core principles of RTI must be clearly understood if we are to avoid false hopes and the subsequent frustration when we perceive that our "silver bullet" has failed. Part One clearly defines RTI and its purposes and provides the reader with a common understanding of the law and the structures that create an RTI framework.

Chapter One identifies the core principles and practices associated with RTI frameworks. Although the RTI framework at each school site will differ according to the specific compilation of skills of each staff and at each site, the core principles of RTI must be implemented in order for the process to effectively include students with disabilities and English learners.

The foundation of an effective RTI process is a three-tiered instructional framework that is geared toward meeting the needs of each and every learner. This hierarchy of academic and behavioral supports creates the nucleus of change that takes place at a school site. This change occurs when all students belong to all teachers, and the instructional and behavioral support provided to each child is dependent on data, not on labels, ethnicity, or free or reduced lunch status. Multi-tiered instruction and intervention enables each and every child to get what she needs, when she needs it. Chapter Two covers the research and the practices behind the basics of prevention and intervention found in the typical three-tiered RTI model for both academic and behavioral supports.

> "The foundation of an effective RTI process is a three-tiered instructional framework that is geared toward meeting the needs of each and every learner. This hierarchy of instructional and behavioral supports creates the nucleus of change that takes place at a school site. This change occurs when all students belong to all teachers, and the instructional and behavioral support provided to each child is dependent on data, not on labels, ethnicity, or free or reduced lunch status."

Part Two: Beyond Tier III

While RTI as a framework is not about special education, its origins are in special education law. This has created much of the confusion about what RTI is and whom it really belongs to. Part Two addresses this confusion by defining the eligibility process within an RTI framework and explaining how special education and general education can share the responsibility of educating all students.

Chapter Three looks specifically at how the RTI framework is used to determine eligibility for special education services under the specific learning disability (SLD) category. While some states have adopted specific regulations regarding SLD determination using an RTI model, federal law is discussed here to help schools and districts in states that allow for the use of an RTI framework for making SLD decisions.

Much has been written about the prevention and intervention aspects of an RTI structure; yet a percentage of students move up the pyramid of supports to a point at which they have exhausted the most intensive level of intervention and are evaluated for special education. The question often arose, What now? Where does the child go once he or she has exited the top of the RTI pyramid? Does the child receive a parallel type of instruction labeled "special education"? Does this special education have to exist in a separate setting in order to be considered "special education"? Can a child receive special education services within an RTI framework? Chapter Four looks specifically at the changing face of special education that fits well within an RTI framework. Collaborative models bring all students into the mainstream of instructional supports to make special education no longer a place but a level of support within the RTI structure. In this model, students don't exit the triangle; they move between tiers with collaborative supports and the accommodations and adaptations prescribed within their individualized education plans.

Part Three: Response to Intervention Process Steps

How does a school take on such a huge paradigm shift? How can the instructional leadership of a school that holds the vision of RTI spread that vision to the rest of the staff? How does one even start to move forward with such a challenging endeavor? Part Three provides the step-by-step processes along with the tools that will help schools navigate through the challenges.

Chapter Five addresses the process steps necessary to support the change that is required before initial implementation steps can be taken. It discusses how to begin the process of implementation and how to best develop the action plan necessary for those first important RTI process steps.

The research is very pointedly clear that the foundation of an effective RTI framework is a strong core instructional program. Good "first teaching" has been identified as the undergirding of an effective model, but what does good "first instruction" mean? What constitutes an evidence-based supplemental intervention program? How are intensive interventions implemented to meet the needs of all learners? How can English learners benefit from an RTI framework? Chapter Six addresses the evidence-based instructional practices associated not just with RTI but also with good teaching and positive outcomes.

The *how* of good first teaching is the instruction, but the *what* can often be contentious, especially for those teachers who see themselves as teachers of "content" rather than students. When teachers have the freedom to determine the *what* within the kingdoms of their own classrooms, RTI is not possible. The *what* must be broken down to what the standards describe as a "common curriculum" before teachers can share the learning of all their students. Chapter Seven tackles the difficult task of curriculum alignment and instruction. It provides a framework and process for identifying essential standards and the mapping of these standards so that teaching teams can share the instructional load of student need as well as planning. Within the framework of standards-aligned instruction, this chapter also looks specifically at how to ensure that standards are the focus of instruction, even for special education students, and how this focus will improve academic achievement for each and every student.

Making sure that all students receive the instruction that they need is a tall order. This can only be accomplished when effective data systems are in place. But how can teachers know exactly what the instructional needs of each child are? How can they know who needs more help? How can they know who is at risk? The core component of screening and progress monitoring is tackled in Chapter Eight. Here teachers and leadership teams will find the reasons for ongoing screening and monitoring and learn why this practice is so important. Data-driven instruction is more than just determining who needs what instructional interventions; it also includes reflecting on current teaching practices and adjusting instruction based on whole-class responses. Teachers reflect best when they work within teams to reflect on teaching practices and how best to meet specific instructional goals for a class or grade level.

> "Data-driven instruction is more than just determining who needs what instructional interventions; it also includes reflecting on current teaching practices and adjusting instruction based on whole-class responses. Teachers reflect best when they work within teams to reflect on teaching practices and how best to meet specific instructional goals for a class or grade level."

The multi-tiered interventions addressing behavior begin the same way as they do when addressing academics. A strong "good first" behavioral approach must be built into the foundation of the school practices before interventions can be developed. The prevention piece must be built through a strong positive school climate. This will take a strong commitment to change from the school staff. It will mean removing the negativity inherent in most school "discipline" plans; the entire school staff will need to identify the behaviors they want to see rather than the behaviors that they want to ban. This approach to behavior and classroom management, along with numerous process steps for implementing this lasting and powerful change, is described in Chapter Nine.

Without communication and collaboration, RTI is not possible. This paradigm shift is about educators moving out of isolation into a collaborative environment in which teaching and learning are the shared responsibility of all teachers and all students. Without time and structure for communication, sharing, planning, and problem solving, teachers cannot share the instructional responsibilities of their diverse students. How to collaborate effectively within an RTI structure is the focus of Chapter Ten. There are many levels of collaboration necessary to meet the needs of all students. The chapter discusses not only how those collaborative meetings might be organized across content areas, across student specific teams, and across grade levels; it will also describes ways to ensure that time for collaboration can be identified within the school schedule.

Finally, as schools work toward implementation of an RTI framework, they will find that they need encouragement from those who have gone before them. The Conclusion showcases some of these pioneers to help developing teams recognize their own strengths and see how others have made the hope and dream of an equitable education for all students, and opportunity of achievement for all, become a reality. My hope is that this book will provide you with the tools you need to make this dream a reality at your school site. Thank you for taking the challenge.

Part I

Achievement for All: The Promise of RTI

Core Principles and Practice of RTI

What is response to intervention (RTI)? How can this process be succinctly defined, so that once grasped, it can be effectively implemented? It is difficult to put RTI in a "box" and define it as a specific entity or process. The National Center on RTI uses the following definition:

> Response to intervention integrates assessment and intervention within a multi-level prevention system to maximize student achievement and to reduce behavior problems. With RTI, schools identify students at risk for poor learning outcomes, monitor student progress, provide evidence-based interventions and adjust the intensity and nature of those interventions depending on a student's responsiveness, and identify students with learning disabilities.[1]

This definition of RTI emphasizes the integration of assessment and intervention with a multilevel prevention system to maximize student achievement and reduce behavior problems.[2] The framework of RTI, at its core, is an instructional service delivery model founded on two key premises:

1. All children can learn when provided with appropriate, effective instruction.
2. Most academic difficulties can be prevented with early identification of need followed by immediate intervention.

In order to provide this appropriate, effective instruction, RTI must be built upon a multi-tiered framework of increasingly intensive and focused instruction and intervention for serving the needs of all students, including those with academic and behavioral concerns.[3]

Other definitions include:

A practice of providing high-quality research based instruction and intervention that is matched to student need. Student outcome data based on this instruction are gathered and monitored so that instructional adjustments can occur, or student goals can be adjusted.[4]

A systematic decision-making process designed to allow for early and effective responses to children's learning and behavioral difficulties, provide children with a level of instructional intensity matched to their level of need and then provide a data-based method for evaluation effectiveness of instructional approaches.[5]

RTI is a combination of effective instructional practices based on data that focus on the positive outcome of academic and behavioral achievement for all students. As one expert in the field put it, "In essence RTI is the license to do the right thing."[6] The specific definitions and core components of these effective instructional practices are difficult to nail down, because they differ from building to building with student population and staffing differences. Unfortunately, it is impossible to say, "Follow these steps, and you'll have RTI." There is no recipe for RTI. Thus this entire book is dedicated to working through the possible options and scenarios for putting together an effective RTI framework with systems that align assessment, instruction, and intervention in order to prevent learning problems and maximize student achievement.

The Rationale

Before he or she can begin process steps, the implementer must clearly understand the rationale for the sweeping changes that encompass RTI implementation. Current federal laws have pushed the inequities in the educational system into the spotlight, revealing the inherent and urgent need to change our current systems. Why the urgent need? There are numerous factors, including the structures of public education in the twenty-first century and the implications of No Child Left Behind (NCLB; 2001), the Elementary Secondary Education Act (ESEA; 2002), and the Individuals with Disabilities Education Act (IDEA; 2004).

Many different disconnected silos of educational programs and initiatives have characterized our education system. Each program had its own agenda, its own labels, its own purpose, and, most important, its own funding. Very few individuals within a program wanted to share any of their resources, and they may not have trusted others to do as good a job as they did with their own set of students, whose labels identified them as "mine." As Reynolds put it, "Our education system has grown up through a process of 'disjointed incrementalism.'"[7] This process is illustrated in Figure 1.1.

Each of these silos created its own set of rules about who could enter, who could exit, and what type of instruction the funding and program would support. Many times these programs would be controlled by nonsensical rules about program availability and

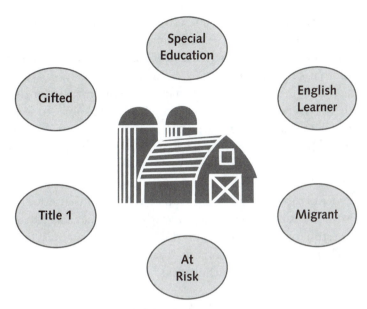

Figure 1.1 Disjointed Incrementalism

use. It seemed at times that the more students identified to fit into the criteria of that particular silo, the better, because then the funding would increase. This often created an incentive to identify students with specific labels, as the more identified, the greater would be the funding stream. Making sure that a child had a label had become profitable to schools and programs. In the United States today, although federal laws limit special education funding so that overidentification is not a financial incentive, many states continue to support such funding models. High numbers of special education students are often not due to disability clusters, but to a bureaucracy that allows the funding stream to course in such a way that the more students identified, the greater the funding. In addition to instructional dollars to support the labeled students, each silo needed funding to support the administration and implementation of often parallel programs.

The traditional silo of special education has had its share of problems, which have now come to light because of ESEA. The practice of segregation, which in the 1970s and 1980s was deemed the *only way* to provide "specially designed academic instruction" for students with disabilities, did not prove to demonstrate positive outcomes for the majority of children. The practice of remedial instruction in a segregated setting created a situation in which students received inequitable educations, all in the name of providing individualized and prescriptive instruction at "their levels." In many states this remedial mode of instruction created an achievement gap that is glaring. It would seem from the data that special education with a focus on segregating students with disabilities in disability-alike groups did not prove effective. In research by Glass on the effectiveness of special education, the findings revealed that, generally, student scores in academic achievement and social skills decreased once students were placed in special education. He summarized his results with the following statement: "Special education placement showed no tangible benefits whatsoever for the pupils. Either someone thinks otherwise or special placements continue to be made for reasons other than to benefit pupils."[8] Keeping special education in its own silo did not pay off in educational achievement.

The unintended effects of such disjointed systems include the overidentification of students for these programs. As mentioned earlier, incentive funding creates a situation in which students with labels mean jobs, and in a struggling economy one cannot discount that such exploitation does exist.

The traditional systems of special education in the twentieth century have focused too much on segregation and labels, which allowed some students to receive substandard educations. The benefits of segregated special education have been questionable at best, with instructional services that have often been unrelated to grade-level standards. The "wait-to-fail" model left students with huge gaps that even the best special educators could not fix. The heavy reliance on special education as the only game in town that could help students receive any small-group or targeted instruction created the perfect storm for the overidentification of students with disabilities and a disproportionate number of minority students. Those who could not qualify and could not get a label were left out to dry. There were no programs or small-group interventions for this population, and one by one they fell through the cracks. Obviously the traditional system was in need of an overhaul.

Shifts in Thinking

ESEA has caused education to shift its focus from what is "yours" and what is "mine" to the academic achievement of *all* "our" students. Prior to the accountability driven by NCLB, states were not required to report student achievement at a federal level. Many states had their own accountability systems, but within these systems, scores for the disadvantaged, ethnically diverse, English learners, and students with disabilities were not disaggregated. The scores of the average-to-high achievers hid the poor outcomes of these groups. NCLB shone a fierce and unfriendly light on the outcomes of these subgroups. It was not too surprising that these subgroups were not faring very well—thus the major shifts in thinking.

The implementation of NCLB, as flawed as it may have been, led education to scrutinize its practices and realize that the archaic structures of the past thirty years needed a complete overhaul. How the needs of students were addressed needed to be changed. Thinking focused more on student learning. With academic achievement the bottom line for all schools and all student groups, the RTI framework across disciplines and grade levels remained congruent with NCLB by promoting the idea that schools have an obligation to ensure that all students participate in strong instructional programs that support multifaceted learning.[9]

Special education law supported the NCLB focus on improved academic achievement for students with disabilities. The current emphasis is on results based on scientifically based instruction in the core curriculum. This is a far cry from the segregated special education silos that had been common in the past three decades. Special education and general education law as well had gone their separate ways in the past, but now for the first time, they send a common message.

While general education and special education law have differed significantly in the past, the language of these two laws now shows common agreement with a focus on achievement and accountability for all students, as the following excerpts show:

From NCLB: "holding schools, local education agencies, and States accountable for improving the academic achievement for *all* students" and "promoting school-wide reform and ensuring the access of all children to effective, scientifically-based instructional strategies" (emphasis added).[10]

From IDEA: "to improve the academic achievement and functional performance of children with disabilities including the use of scientifically based instructional practices, to the maximum extent possible."[11]

Together these two laws present a common message. ESEA emphasizes the academic achievement of all students, while IDEA focuses on improving academic achievement for students with disabilities. These commonalities are presented in Table 1.1.

These two laws work in tandem, describing the need for a cohesive instructional system that is geared toward meeting the needs of all learners, because all learners now are expected to achieve grade-level skills. This standards-aligned accountability has created a need for an educational framework that focuses on a system that offers an equitable opportunity for all students to achieve at high levels.

The Promise of RTI

RTI is the framework that allows students to achieve this goal. The targeted instruction and intervention guarantees that no one child or group of children is allowed to fall through the cracks. This will require momentous change, but it is a need long in coming, and RTI provides the promise to meet the need.

The promise that RTI brings all students is the assurance of early identification of learning and behavior problems through a strong focus on academic and behavioral results generated by targeted instruction that is driven by progress monitoring. All students are included in a single, schoolwide, standards-based accountability system. No different expectations for children of color, no lowered expectations for English learners, no substandard expectations for children with disabilities. The promise of RTI is that all student populations have the opportunity to receive an equitable education in a cohesive system that leads to the acquisition of skills necessary to be able to make postsecondary choices.

Table 1.1 Commonalities of ESEA and IDEA

ESEA (2002)	IDEA (2004)
Ensures *all* students achieve at high levels	Emphasizes results
Requires states to develop standards to define what students should know and do	Access to/Progress in the general education curriculum
Requires accountability through assessment for all students	Standards-based accountability
Requires *all* students to make adequate yearly progress	Educational benefit and procedural guarantees

> The promise that RTI brings all students is the assurance of early identification of learning and behavior problems through a strong focus on academic and behavioral results generated by targeted instruction that is driven by progress monitoring. All students are included in a single, schoolwide, standards-based accountability system. No different expectations for children of color, no lowered expectations for English learners, no substandard expectations for children with disabilities.

What RTI Is

Response to intervention was born of special education law, but only a part of the RTI process is about special education. Providing instruction that is scientifically research based as the part of a special education evaluation is only a very small part of the whole of RTI.

Prevention

The focus on ensuring high-quality, evidence-based instruction in the general education setting is the first line of defense for preventing later learning difficulties.[12] The impetus for research-based instruction and intervention came from the research of Reid Lyon and his colleagues that suggested that reading failure was due not to learning disabilities but to a lack of effective instruction.[13] Much of the early work on RTI models focused on early reading interventions, and from these practices we've learned that effective prevention requires schoolwide screening of all students, especially incoming kindergarteners and all new students who come in during the school year. This screening process allowed teachers to focus and target instruction to the needs identified in this screening. Screening naturally led to targeted instruction that is aligned to the core curriculum or the grade-level standards. The student's progress on learning these standards and on the specific target skill is measured on a regular basis by ongoing progress monitoring.

For example, the schoolwide screening might identify eight first graders who could not segment words into phonemes. Without screening, the classroom teacher may not have noticed this skill weakness and would not be able to provide the targeted instruction needed to teach this skill. Now that screening has identified this weakness, the teacher provides the needed instruction in her classroom, and further reading failure due to this weakness has been prevented. This early instructional intervention occurred without the need for a child study team meeting, further diagnostic assessments by additional personnel, or a waiting-to-fail model of qualification in order to receive small-group instruction. The reading weakness was identified through screening and was targeted in small-group instruction in the core, and reading failure was prevented.

Intervention

Intervention is instruction that is applied to students whose progress is not commensurate with their peers.[14] The intent of intervention is to close achievement and learning gaps as quickly as possible. Although prevention has been the primary focus at the elementary grades, intervention is recognized as drop-out prevention at the secondary level. Intervention might be taken in primary grades, where, for example, two of the eight first graders continue to struggle with phoneme segmentation. These two students may need further intervention, because the first round of instruction did not prove effective. These students do not need to be removed from the core, but they may need additional intervention time to practice the phoneme segmentations skills and close the gap that exists between themselves and their peers. The increase in instructional intensity or time characterizes the intervention part of RTI.

As mentioned, intervention can occur at any grade level, but many times intensive intervention does not begin until fourth grade or beyond. At this grade level, a greater focus on curricular and instructional change is needed to meet the needs of struggling readers. Some states have adopted intensive intervention programs that are considered "the core" for students who fall several grade levels below their peers. While this practice is controversial, because students are often removed from the language arts core class, when these curricular changes are used with fidelity students are able to move back into the core within a two-year period. For students in upper grades who have few reading skills, the trade-offs in learning to read in an intensive intervention program are well worth it. One student remarked that the intensive intervention program was the most important thing that had ever happened to her. Learning to read in an intensive intervention program is the targeted instruction that nonreaders need and that a schoolwide RTI framework can deliver.

Effective intervention across the grade levels includes a hierarchy of instructional support, frequent progress monitoring to measure the effectiveness of the instructional support, and instruction that is data-driven and based on progress-monitoring results. For some students, this intervention can mean an alternate core curriculum or an intensive intervention program. Integral to any intervention is ongoing progress monitoring to determine whether the student is responding to the research-based instruction and intervention.

Specific Learning Disability Determination

Last, RTI focuses on determining eligibility for the specific learning disability category of special education services. The original language reads, "A local education agency may use a process that determines if the child responds to scientific, research-based intervention as part of the evaluation procedures...."[15] In the special education research literature, the process mentioned in this language is generally considered to refer to response to intervention.

The process of determining SLD cannot occur without an effective RTI framework that encompasses prevention and intervention prior to SLD consideration. Only when all children who are suspected of having a learning disability have had research-based instruction and interventions that have been targeted to student needs can the consideration of SLD eligibility be made. The progress-monitoring data from the instruction and intervention become the real-time data that allow the multidisciplinary team to identify patterns of strengths and weaknesses that would point to a specific learning disability. The RTI process cannot be utilized to make SLD decisions unless it is implemented with fidelity, but when it is, it provides rich, valid data that are an integral part of the decision-making process of SLD determination.

What RTI Is *Not*

Recognizing that RTI is not just about special education eligibility is key to truly understanding what RTI is and is not. First and foremost, RTI is not special education or a special education program. It is not "run" by special education or special education teachers. While students may qualify for special education services through an RTI process, RTI is not about special education programs or services. Some states have determined that their Tier III interventions (more about Tier III in Chapter Two) may be special education services, but usually general education students also benefit from the instructional interventions provided at this level. Some states have made the mistake of allowing special education teachers to take on the brunt of instructional intervention, giving the wrong message that special education and RTI are synonymous. These states are rethinking their approaches and are finding that a greater focus on "good first teaching" is where the greatest strength in the RTI framework lies.

Second, RTI is not a system to "track" students. While is it multi-tiered, the movement between tiers is fluid. In the figures in this book, you will always see an arrow going both ways in or near the RTI model. This arrow emphasizes that students don't only move up into more intensive interventions; they also move down, back into the less intensive interventions once the targeted instruction has improved their skills. Students are not tracked; frequent progress monitoring does not allow a student to languish for any period of time in an ineffective intervention. If progress-monitoring data do not show results within four data points, the instruction must be adjusted in order for progress to occur. If a lack of progress persists, despite the most intensive interventions, then a referral for special education is warranted. Within an RTI framework, a lack of achievement is not ignored; a student not making progress is never allowed to stay in any one track for any length of time.

Additionally, since RTI represents such a complex and complete structural change, it is not something that can be purchased out of a box. Each school site has its unique student population and its own unique set of resources, so no out-of-the-box program will provide process steps tailored to each specific site. RTI is a schoolwide change model; no two schools will go through this process in exactly the same manner, nor have the exact same needs. That is why a needs assessment and tailored steps are necessary for RTI implementation. The process steps may be similar, but no "product" will meet the challenges of making the paradigm shift necessary to successfully implement an RTI model.

RTI is not a quick fix or the new flavor-of-the-month kind of change. This process takes time—time for changing thinking, time for assessing current systems, time to determine what to keep and what to change, time to train, and finally time to implement. For the weak-hearted, this is not a task to take on thinking that it is the magic bullet for bringing about quick changes to test scores. Most schools and districts take a year to plan, and slowly, very slowly, begin the implementation process. The Center on Instruction, in their implementation research, identified proceeding with caution with a small vanguard group as one successful way to ensure implementation with fidelity.[16]

It takes time for programs and teachers to let their silos go. This won't happen overnight. It also takes time for those married to their silo mentality to realize that RTI is not another silo to add to the collection but rather is the barn in which all programs can work together in an effective manner that focuses solely on providing students exactly what they need, no matter what their label. See the integrated instruction approach shown in Figure 1.2.

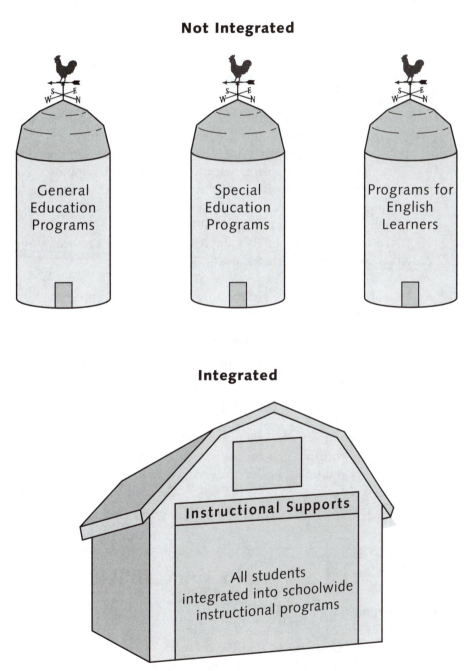

Figure 1.2 An Integrated Instruction Approach

Core Principles of RTI

RTI is based on a singular belief in doing what is best for students, on the core principle that *ALL children CAN learn*. If teachers, administrators, and staff believe that students with disabilities, students who are English learners, and students who live in poverty cannot learn, then RTI will not prove successful, and the self-fulfilling prophecy will have been fulfilled. Coming to common ground on this primary core component can take some time. Sometimes, it will take the few who believe to step forward and move ahead of the others, using data as their proof that they are correct in their beliefs about student ability.

Identifying Core Components

While the list of core components differs among researchers, the most common core components are related to data-based decision making, about universal screening and progress monitoring. Based on this data, research-based instruction and interventions are applied within a multi-tiered instruction and intervention model that is frequently monitored for fidelity of implementation. Professional development is also included, as it is an essential part of providing effective research-based instruction and intervention. In addition, many listings of core components include a problem-solving process or a problem analysis process as part of the RTI structure.

In the ongoing work of RTI implementation, the core components most often recognized as essential are the following:

- Schoolwide commitment to meeting the needs of all students
- Universal screening of all students
- Multi-tiered research-based instruction including "good first" teaching
- Data-based decision making through ongoing progress monitoring to assess the effectiveness of instruction
- Targeted interventions that increase over time

Many different experts have identified the core components of RTI. While each expert's approach may differ in one or two aspects, all contain certain commonalities that focus on multiple tiers of intervention, monitoring of progress, and targeted intervention. The following two examples of core components provide an overlapping view of the necessary elements of an RTI framework.

Core Components of RTI

Universal Screening

Evaluation of all students to systematically identify:
- Those making adequate progress
- Those at some risk of failure if not provided extra assistance
- Those at high risk of failure if not provided specialized supports

Continuous Progress Monitoring

Student progress assessed on regular and frequent basis:
- To identify when inadequate growth trends occur
- To increase instructional support when needed

Continuum of Evidence-Based Instructional Practices and Intervention

A hierarchy of varying intensity levels of instructional support
- Core curriculum for all students
- Modification of the core by increasing instructional time and intensity
- Intensive instruction or curriculum for those not responding to the modification of the core

Data-Based Decision Making and Problem Solving

Instructional decisions based on student performance
- Core curricular performance
- Performance on modifications or adaptations

Implementation Fidelity

Specific procedures for regular documentation of the level of implementation of each feature of the model

Source: L. Fox, J., Carta, P. Strain, G. Dunlap, and M. L. Hemmeter, *Response to Intervention and the Pyramid Model.* Tampa: University of South Florida, Technical Assistance Center on Social Emotional Intervention for Young Children, 2009.

Necessary Elements of an RTU Framework

High-Quality Research-Based Classroom Instruction

All students receive high-quality general education classroom instruction that is research based. All teachers assume an active role in the assessment of classroom curriculum.

Universal Screening

All students are screened with specific criteria to determine who needs further assessment.

Progress Monitoring at All Tiers

Progress on meeting expected standards is monitored and the effectiveness of interventions determined.

Research-Based Interventions at Tiers II and III

Research-based interventions are applied based on student needs.

Fidelity Measures

Systematic assessment of the fidelity of the instruction and intervention is performed.

Source: D. F. Mellard and E. Johnson, *RTI: A Practitioner's Guide to Implementing Response to Intervention.* Thousand Oaks, CA: Corwin, 2008.

RTI Approaches

There are two common RTI approaches: the standards treatment approach and the problem-solving approach. Both look carefully at the fact that some students are struggling and that they need attention. Both focus on schoolwide screening, targeted instruction, and continuous progress monitoring within a multi-tiered model of instruction.

Standard Treatment Approach

Although individualized intervention through problem-solving methods was the norm in early RTI models, the research suggests that a set of evidence-based practices or standard treatments be provided for those students who display predictable difficulties in learning, specifically in reading. These standard approaches are designed to be used in a systematic manner with all participating students and are usually delivered in a small group in a prescriptive manner. This standard treatment approach has a high probability of producing change for large numbers of students.

In the standard treatment approach, all students are screened, and when students fall below a certain cut score, further assessment may determine the need for a standard intervention. This group may include students within a certain score range who receive supplemental or additional instructional time, and others who receive more intensive instruction. The intervention prescribed for the group that falls within each cut score range is monitored for effectiveness through frequent and ongoing progress monitoring, The treatment provided may be a predetermined research-based program, such as an intensive reading or math intervention program. If the response to the treatment is not adequate, an additional treatment may be applied. If there is still a lack of progress, a referral to special education may be made.

Problem-Solving Approach

In the problem-solving approach, screening is of primary importance. Students identified as at risk through screening are brought to the problem-solving team. The team reviews the students' needs that have been identified through screening and develop a plan to meet those needs. In the problem-solving approach, the problem is defined, the problem is analyzed, a plan is developed, and the plan is evaluated for effectiveness. Figure 1.3 shows the problem-solving method that is essential to the problem-solving approach.[17] This customized intervention for individual students has been foundational in the RTI models developed in numerous states.

If after several attempts at problem solving, the student is still not responding to the intervention, a special education referral may also be made.

The approach taken differs from state to state, and many states use an RTI framework that is a combination of both. Lynn and Doug Fuchs, experts on RTI, recommend that schools rely on a combination of approaches, with a standard treatment protocol used for academic difficulties and a problem-solving approach used for obvious behavioral problems and persistent learning problems combined with behavioral problems.[18]

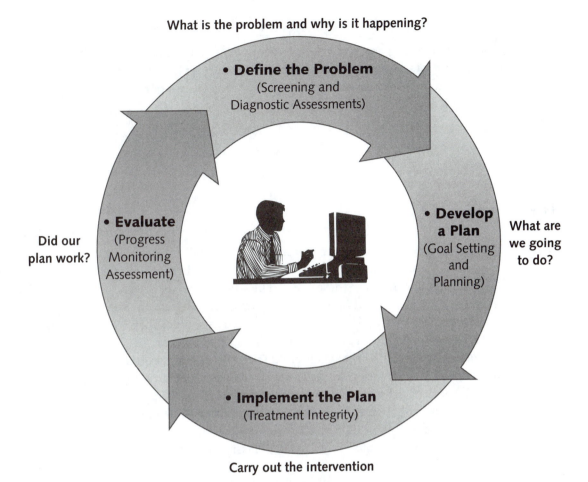

What is the problem and why is it happening?

• **Define the Problem**
(Screening and
Diagnostic Assessments)

• **Evaluate**
(Progress
Monitoring
Assessment)

**Did our
plan work?**

• **Develop
a Plan**
(Goal Setting
and
Planning)

**What are
we going
to do?**

• **Implement the Plan**
(Treatment Integrity)

Carry out the intervention

Figure 1.3 **Problem-Solving Process**

The combined approach focuses on data from screening and further assessment to identify those students who are at risk or in need of intervention. Cut scores are determined, and a standard treatment or intervention is applied. If a student fails to respond to this intervention, then the team takes a problem-solving approach in which individualized interventions are developed and applied. If the student continues with an inadequate response, a referral to special education is made. This combination of approaches provides the special education multidisciplinary team with ample data for making decisions about special education eligibility.

Both of these approaches rely heavily on data for decision making. Some states have identified their RTI models as "data-based decision-making models." Just as RTI cannot occur without screening, RTI cannot continue without progress monitoring and data. Students not making progress in an intervention program do not exit and move up to a more intensive intervention because of a teacher's hunch or a feeling. The data make it very clear just how and where the student is struggling. Data collected over time allow patterns of strengths and weaknesses to emerge that are used to make special education eligibility decisions. Data also play an essential role in identifying the effectiveness of interventions and the time when students should return to the core or to a less intensive intervention.

Benefits of RTI

There are numerous benefits in implementing an RTI framework, and students receive the greatest reward. Screening identifies student needs, and instructional interventions are immediately applied to these needs. The student does not need to wait to qualify for a label that indicates a need for small-group targeted instruction. Students experience less frustration, and instructional holes can be filled as soon as they are recognized. Reading and instructional failures are averted by this simple process.

Parents are satisfied that their child is receiving the help that he or she needs. They do not need to fight for or wait for a special education referral to get their child the help that is warranted. Parents appreciate the instructional supports that their child gets, and a positive collaborative relationship between parents and the school, rather than a combative defensive one, is created.

Meeting the needs of all students in a classroom is an impossible task. Many teachers feel isolated and alone in trying to "get to" all the kids in their classes and provide them with what they need. This leads to early teacher burnout. An RTI approach provides teachers a golden opportunity to share the instructional responsibility of their students. Teachers can utilize peer problem-solving strategies and use teaming across the grade level to share students and specific student needs. Teachers feel supported by each other and find that the collegial support of their grade-level or content area team provides them with the collaborative problem-solving opportunities that they need.

According to a teacher retention study conducted in California in 2007, the number one reason for teachers staying in the teaching profession is collegiality. Teachers commented that when they had at least one other person whom they could talk to and problem-solve with, they could remain in teaching. The number one reason for leaving the field was isolation and a feeling of nowhere to turn.[19] Inherent to the RTI structure is problem solving and collaboration.

Site administrators benefit tremendously from the RTI framework, not just because it guarantees good instruction and instructional practices, but because the collaboration between teachers provides for a positive school climate that is focused on positive academic and behavioral outcomes. When teachers are working together, problem-solving together, looking at data together, and are focused on academic achievement for all students, administrators find that they can focus on instruction rather than on staff management.

RTI frameworks, even when instituted at the site level, provide a positive payoff at the district level. When schools employ an RTI framework and philosophy, they carefully scrutinize all their resources and use them to the most advantageous manner. In the RTI framework, silos are broken down; a more effective and cohesive use of financial and human resources is the result. While RTI in IDEA legislation does not bring with it any financial resources, schools and districts that focus on decision making based on academic achievement for all, within the structure of the barn rather than the silo, ultimately will not need more funding but should be able to implement the best possible programs with existing resources.

Chapter Two will provide further insight into the what of the multi-tiered RTI framework, as the concepts and practices of each tier are clearly defined and identified. Having a clear understanding of the impetus behind the change and the structures that make the change brings you one step closer to implementation.

Wrapping Up the Main Points

How does RTI improve on history? It takes a fragmented system and makes it cohesive. It provides for a fair distribution of resources that are allocated to the point of need. Students get fair treatment, not equal treatment. Students who need more, get more. Students don't need to wait for the correct labels to be applied in order to obtain resources. Students are provided with opportunities for an equitable education in an all-inclusive environment. Students become "ours," and within the RTI framework, each and every one of our students has a chance to experience academic and behavioral achievement.

Multi-Tiered Instruction and Interventions

Implementation of response to intervention (RTI) requires the use of a tiered model of intervention. The IDEA Partnership describes these tiers as levels of instructional intensity with a multi-tiered prevention system.[1] Every definition of RTI includes multiple tiers or a hierarchy of instruction and intervention. The instruction and interventions within these tiers are specifically matched to student need, and progress is monitored with frequency at each level. Data from this progress monitoring determine the next level of instruction or intervention needed. This circle of targeted instruction, monitoring, adjustment, and further instruction is what makes academic improvement within the RTI framework achievable.

This three-tiered model shown in Figure 2.1 is the most common model implemented across the United States. Although in some models the third tier represents special education, in the model discussed here Tier III does not. In this model, Tier I is characterized by general education, Tier II is general education with supplemental support, and Tier III is considered intensive intervention. Since the multi-tiered model originated in the preventative public health model the terms *primary* for Tier I, *secondary* for Tier II, and *tertiary* for Tier III are often used. In some settings they are referred to as *benchmark* for Tier I, *strategic* for Tier II, and *intensive* for Tier III.

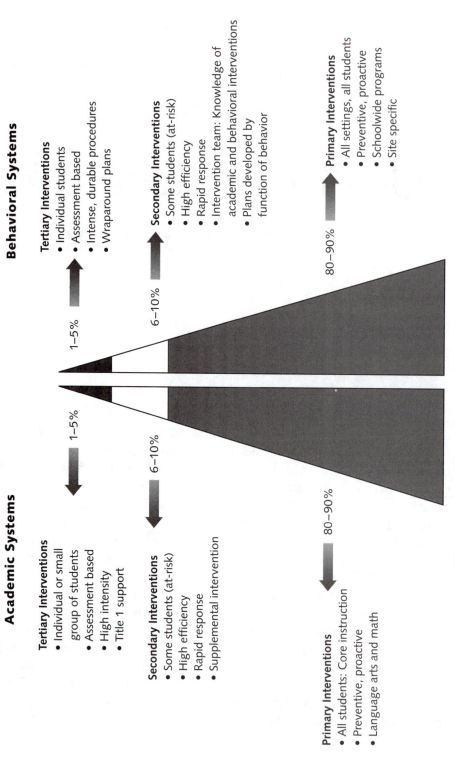

Academic Systems

Tertiary Interventions
- Individual or small group of students
- Assessment based
- High intensity
- Title 1 support

Secondary Interventions
- Some students (at-risk)
- High efficiency
- Rapid response
- Supplemental intervention

Primary Interventions
- All students: Core instruction
- Preventive, proactive
- Language arts and math

1–5%

6–10%

80–90%

Behavioral Systems

Tertiary Interventions
- Individual students
- Assessment based
- Intense, durable procedures
- Wraparound plans

Secondary Interventions
- Some students (at-risk)
- High efficiency
- Rapid response
- Intervention team: Knowledge of academic and behavioral interventions
- Plans developed by function of behavior

Primary Interventions
- All settings, all students
- Preventive, proactive
- Schoolwide programs
- Site specific

1–5%

6–10%

80–90%

Figure 2.1 The Three-Tiered Model of RTI

Flexibility and Fluidity Within Tiers

The circle of targeted instruction matched specifically to student need within the multiple tiers is what makes RTI different from the instructional practices of the past. Previously, teachers were told to "teach to the middle" when they recognized that within their classrooms were students with very high skills and some with very low skills. How was one teacher going to meet all these different needs? One teacher alone could not do it; teacher-training programs helped teachers keep their sanity by suggesting that the top students will enrich themselves and the others will pull the strugglers along. This was a way for teachers to feel less guilty about being unable to meet the needs of all learners! Although in theory, on some planet, high achievers might develop their own enrichment programs, not many to my knowledge ever did. Instead their boredom was often replaced by negative behaviors and lack of instructional engagement. Struggling learners were left to struggle and fell further and further behind.

Then came RTI, a renewed hope for the students who were *not* in the middle. RTI, with its multiple steps of intervention, provided hope for instruction that would meet the needs of all learners, not just those in the middle. As students were grouped at times into homogenous groups, based on data, the high achievers could work together with a teacher to focus on their unique needs of enrichment, and struggling learners could stop the downward spiral of a widening achievement gap.

Many educators shudder at the thought of homogenous grouping. And if you were a "blue bird" rather than the more able "red bird" in your first-grade reading class, I can understand where you are coming from. In the past, homogenous grouping was not based particularly on data, and the group you got assigned to as a first grader was your life sentence. You were "tracked" with this group of students for your entire educational career. Once a blue bird always a blue bird. If you were on a track of lowered expectations, you always received easier, more remedial instruction, with the result that you were without the commensurate skills of your peers.

How are RTI multiple tiers of intervention different from this tracking process of the past? Data make the difference! Frequent progress monitoring identifies whether the instruction within the homogenous group is effective. If no changes are occurring, the instruction needs to change. The goal of homogenous grouping is to allow teachers to provide targeted instruction that is matched to the students' specific needs.

> Data make the difference! Frequent progress monitoring identifies whether the instruction within the homogenous group is effective.

The National Association of State Directors of Special Education (NASDSE) identifies the multi-tier model of interventions as an efficient mechanism of resource allocation.[2] Providing targeted instruction to a small group of second graders who need additional instruction on blending consonants is a much more reasonable use of resources than trying to meet these students' needs on an individual basis. Grouping ten students for targeted instruction is an effective use of resources and makes good instructional sense. The difference from the practices of the past is that these ten students will not always work together, nor will they be tracked together for the rest of their educational careers. These students will receive small-group instruction, will be assessed frequently to see whether this instruction is effective, and will leave this homogenous group as soon as the necessary skills are learned. The decision to exit the group is not based on a sense or a feeling on the part of the teacher that the student "got it" but rather on data that show that the student can now successfully blend consonants at the beginning of a word.

It is this fluidity or flexibility of homogenous grouping that allows students to receive the instruction that they need, be it enrichment or intervention of a specific skill. This concept of targeted instruction to match student need relies heavily on screening and assessment data. It is data that guide the correlation between student need and the level of support provided within the structure of each tier.

Academic Tiers

RTI is defined by multiple tiers of intervention based on student need. Figure 2.2 identifies the approximate number of students usually found in each tier, as well as the differences in the intensity of the intervention provided within each tier. This chapter will further define each tier with an in-depth view of the student and the services provided within each tier.

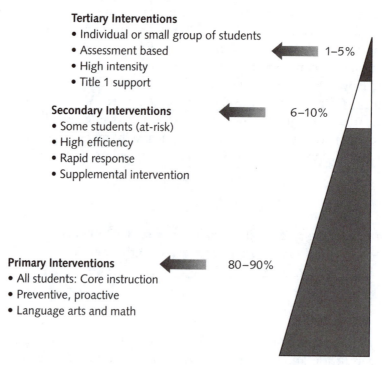

Tertiary Interventions
- Individual or small group of students
- Assessment based
- High intensity
- Title 1 support

1–5%

Secondary Interventions
- Some students (at-risk)
- High efficiency
- Rapid response
- Supplemental intervention

6–10%

Primary Interventions
- All students: Core instruction
- Preventive, proactive
- Language arts and math

80–90%

Figure 2.2 Academic Tiers

Tier I

What is considered Tier I? Although the initial thrust of RTI was focused on intervention, most recently it has been recognized that the "good first teaching" of RTI is the foundational piece that must be in place for the framework to stand.[3] Tier I is defined in some of the literature as the "core" instruction or the "core" curriculum. It is comprised of high-quality evidence-based instruction that occurs in the general education classroom and is implemented by the general education teacher.

> "Tier I is defined in some of the literature as the "core" instruction or the "core" curriculum. It is comprised of high-quality evidence-based instruction that occurs in the general education classroom and is implemented by the general education teacher.... The students who comprise Tier I are often considered *benchmark* students."

Tier I is characterized by instruction provided to all students in the general education classroom. This is high-quality first instruction in which standards-aligned instructional materials are utilized with the support of differentiated instruction. Students in Tier I may be at grade level or one grade level below in reading skill, but this does not preclude them from receiving their instruction in core classes. The differentiation and scaffolding in these classes provided by highly qualified content teachers meets the needs of 75 to 80 percent of all learners.[4] Tier I instruction is supported by effective grade-level and content area teaming and planning supported by screening and regular progress monitoring that allows teachers to target instruction based on student need.

Although core content is the curriculum that is the structured set of learning outcomes based on the standards for a prescribed course of study, many view this core content as the textbooks.[5] Although the textbooks contain the curriculum, they do not define it. If any teachers have attempted to match textbooks and state standards, they have experienced the frustration of finding that although the textbook publisher has identified a particular lesson to "teach" a particular standard, the materials only touch on an "essence" of the standard. For this reason, relying on the textbook alone to ensure that the standards are covered is not good practice. Too many teachers have felt the strain of trying to teach a textbook from cover to cover, thinking that this process alone will ensure that each and every standard will be covered. Unfortunately, they often find out when assessment results are obtained that many of the standards were only brushed upon in the textbook. Teachers need to have the opportunity to identify the standards for their grade levels and content areas and then determine how the text will *support* the instruction of the standards. This standards-aligned good first teaching is part of what constitutes an effective Tier I. (See Chapter Seven for more on the process of identifying essential standards and mapping these for instruction.)

In addition to standards-aligned instruction, Tier I instruction is differentiated to meet a broad range of student need. Within the core instruction, as teachers recognize the need to reteach or provide additional instruction based on informal observations or checks for understanding, they provide targeted instruction when the need arises. In an RTI framework, teachers do not need to do a diagnostic assessment or meet with a child study team in order to provide small-group instruction to the students in their classrooms when need is recognized. In a good Tier I, teachers recognize a need and provide the instruction that is needed to meet that need. This is what good first teaching is about. Small-group instruction within the core is essential to effective differentiated core instruction.

The students who comprise Tier I are often considered *benchmark* students.

Tier I: Benchmark Students

- Achieve at or within one year of grade-level skills
- Benefit from standards-aligned quality instruction
- Utilize core curriculum and ancillary materials
- Benefit from differentiated curriculum

Although benchmark students may be one year below grade level in reading skill, good scaffolded teaching still allows this group of students to benefit from the core curriculum. Typically, benchmark students are able to read the textbook and access the material presented in the text when accompanied by differentiated instruction and instructional scaffolding. Most textbook publishers provide ideas and materials, often referred to as "ancillary materials," that will help this group grasp the concepts and receive the extra practice they may need to be successful in learning the content. Table 2.1 provides an outline of one possible Tier I scenario for language arts instruction for benchmark students.

Table 2.1 Tier 1 Core Instruction for Reading: Benchmark

Focus	Core content area: Reading/Language arts
Program	Evidence-based core curriculum utilizing differentiated teaching strategies
Grouping	Multiple grouping formats to meet student needs
Time	Ninety minutes per day or more
Assessment	Benchmark assessment at beginning, middle, and end of academic year
Interventionist	General education teacher
Setting	General education classroom

Source: www.ode.state.or.us/initiatives/idea/rti.aspx.

Tier II

Tier II is characterized by general education, good first instruction, *and* additional time to provide evidence-based intervention to those students who are at risk for failure or who need additional support and instructional time to maintain progress. When effective programs are evaluated, it is increased instructional time that seems to have the greatest value. Tier II involves supplemental instructional time. Not more of the same, but the opportunity to provide the homogenous targeted instruction mentioned earlier in this chapter. Tier II goes beyond the good first teaching provided by the general education teacher in his own classroom and includes the collaboration between teachers at a grade level in order to group students based on needs. This level of intervention is powerful. Teachers are able to utilize their own expertise to meet the myriad of needs found at a particular grade level. In Tier II instruction, some teachers work with larger, more able groups, and some teachers work with smaller groups that have more specific needs. It is here that the high achievers are able to receive small-group instruction that will allow them to reach even higher levels of achievement, and where the group that struggles most will receive the targeted help that allows them to fill in the holes in their instruction and obtain the missing skills that they need.

> "Tier II is characterized by general education, good first instruction, *and* additional time to provide evidence-based intervention to those students who are at risk for failure or who need additional support and instructional time to maintain progress. . . . The group needing the most targeted intervention at Tier II is often referred to as the *strategic* group."

Although some schools provide this supplemental instruction only to those students identified as being at risk or needing additional small-group instruction, many schools have found that having all students move to a homogenous group during this additional instructional time makes more logistic sense. Some schools call this "universal access time," some call it "flex time," and others call it "walk and read" because all students move to another room or space to read. Although this leveled instructional time may be called any number of things, it is characterized by targeted leveled instruction for a specific period of time on a regular basis.

The Tier II groups are determined by data, and the movement between tiers is determined by frequent progress-monitoring data taken from the instructional and interventions. The group needing the most targeted intervention at Tier II is often referred to as the *strategic* group.

This group is usually identified as those who may be one and two years below grade level in their skills, primarily in reading. The additional targeted instructional time is focused on providing this group with the specific skills that will address their skill deficits and accelerate them to the benchmark group. Frequent progress monitoring determines the effectiveness of the intervention instruction. Data from this progress monitoring determine who needs to continue in this small-group supplemental intervention, who is failing to respond and needs more intensive instruction, and who can move back into the larger group during the supplemental instruction time.

Tier II: Strategic Students

- Achieve one to two years below grade level in reading skills
- Utilize core curriculum with instructional scaffolding
- Receive standard protocol interventions matched to need
- Benefit from increased instructional time to target specific skill deficits
- Receive small-group interventions in general education or other settings

Although some may view Tier II as a stepping stone to Tier III and more targeted intensive intervention, the goal is to bring the student back into the benchmark group. The bulk of this Tier II instruction is provided by the general education grade-level or content area team, but the team can include additional instructional experts such as Title I teachers, reading specialists, intervention specialists, special education teachers, and others trained to provide small-group additional instruction. Since this group of students needs smaller group instruction, having these additional resources available during supplemental instructional time is essential to making an effective use of this time. The scheduling of these "human" resources is very important in developing an effective Tier II intervention. Table 2.2 provides an outline of one possible Tier II scenario for language arts instruction for strategic students.

Table 2.2 Tier 2 Supplemental Instruction: Strategic

Focus	For students identified with marked reading difficulties and who have not responded to Tier I efforts
Program	Specialized, evidence-based supplemental program
Grouping	Homogenous small-group instruction (1:3 to 1:8)
Time	Minimum of 30 minutes per day in small group in addition to 90 minutes in core program
Assessment	Progress monitoring more often (weekly or biweekly) on target skill to ensure adequate progress
Interventionist	Personnel determined by the school (classroom teacher, special reading teacher, external interventionist)
Setting	Appropriate setting designated by the school; may be within or outside of classroom

Source: www.ode.state.or.us/initiatives/idea/rti.aspx.

Tier III

Tier III is characterized by intensive instructional intervention to high-risk students who have not responded adequately to Tier II instruction. Students who need Tier III intervention are usually at two grade levels below in reading or math skills. This intense level of intervention is intended to increase the student's rate of progress so that he can close his skill gaps. Intensive intervention is provided in small groups or one-on-one with increased intensity of time and specific fidelity of implementation. This instruction is very specifically targeted to skill deficits and is monitored very frequently, often daily, to check the effectiveness of the intervention. This third tier can include longer-term interventions and may in some states or districts include special education services. These intensive interventions are delivered in more substantial blocks of time and may be prescribed specifically based on the recommendations of a problem-solving team or comprised of an evidence-based standard treatment protocol. In either case, the problem-solving team frequently monitors progress, and data are carefully analyzed to recognize responsiveness or a lack of responsiveness to this intensive intervention.

> "Tier III is characterized by intensive instructional intervention to high-risk students who have not responded adequately to Tier II instruction. This intense level of intervention is intended to increase the student's rate of progress so that he can close his skill gaps. Intensive intervention is provided in small groups or one-on-one with increased intensity of time and specific fidelity of implementation. . . . Students in Tier III are often referred to as the *intensive* group."

For some students, this intensive intervention can consist of a standard treatment protocol that is an alternate core program. These core replacement programs are intended to close skill gaps when implemented with fidelity within a two-year period. These research-based programs are intended for the lowest readers. A list of these intervention programs can be found at the Florida Center for Reading Research Web site at www.fcrr.org.

Fidelity of implementation is extremely important at this intensive level, since the prescribed research-based program is intended to accelerate reading skills under the research conditions. Implementers of intensive reading intervention must also provide the same conditions in order to expect the same result. This is often where program failure occurs. When research-based programs are not implemented with fidelity and are diluted either through inadequate time or too large a group size, implementers will often claim that the program and process have failed. Unfortunately, it is not the program that is at fault; rather the onus of blame is on the school for not implementing the program with the research-based conditions for fidelity.

Students in Tier III are often referred to as the *intensive* group.

Intensive Group

- Are usually more than two grade levels below in reading skills
- Receive small-group or individualized specifically targeted intervention
- Use research-based intervention program that may replace the core
- Require additional instructional time based on standard treatment protocol model
- Benefit from small class size and fidelity of implementation
- Receive interventions determined by problem-solving team

The students in this group often lack the skills necessary to access the core curriculum materials. When reading skills are more than two grade levels below, most students cannot read their textbooks. For this reason, it is essential that students are provided an opportunity to access an intensive reading intervention program, even if it costs them the access to their grade-level English language arts instruction. Although removing the student from the standards-aligned core instruction is a very serious and weighty matter, in light of the cross-content struggles that these students have, it is essential that they learn to read. We as educators can give them no greater gift. Table 2.3 provides an outline of a possible Tier III scenario for language arts instruction for intensive students.

Tier III intervention is intended to be temporary. Students should not be in an intensive reading intervention program for more than two years. If the intervention is implemented with fidelity, this group of students should be able to move into the strategic part of the triangle, where they will still need supplemental instruction. However, with the scaffolded support of extra instructional time and a focus on skills development, these students should be able to successfully access the core. The goal of Tier III instruction is not another step in the special education referral process but an opportunity for students to receive the intensive intervention necessary to accelerate them into the core at the strategic level and, over time, to close the skill gaps enough to be able to return to the benchmark group. As shown in Figure 2.3, the arrow in this triangle of interventions indicates that within an RTI multi-tiered framework students should not only move up into more intensive interventions, but also ideally move back down through the tiers to success within the good first instruction of the core.

Behavioral Tiers

While academic interventions are often the primary focus in RTI implementation, the links between academic achievement and behavior are widely supported by research. When schoolwide, proactive, preventive behavior strategies are in place, most students

Table 2.3 Tier III Intensive Intervention

Focus	Students with marked difficulties with reading who have not responded to Tier I and Tier II efforts
Program	Sustained, intensive, evidence-based approved intervention program emphasizing the critical elements of reading
Grouping	Homogenous small-group instruction (1:1 to 1:10)
Time	Minimum of two 30-minute sessions per day in small group in addition to 90 minutes of core instruction (intervention program is core for students two grade levels below)
Assessment	Progress monitoring more often (weekly) on target skills to ensure adequate progress
Interventionist	Personnel determined by the school (classroom teacher, reading teacher, external interventionist, special educators)
Setting	Appropriate setting designated by the school

Source: www.ode.state.or.us/initiatives/idea/rti.aspx.

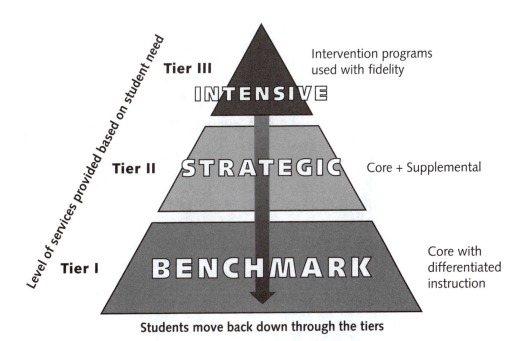

Figure 2.3 Three-Tiered Model

Source: RTI Technical Assistance Document. Sacramento: California Department of Education, 2009.

are successful both behaviorally and academically. The multi-tiered behavior supports in the RTI behavior triangle shown in Figure 2.4 identify the behavioral supports that go beyond the schoolwide model, providing proactive behavior changing structures within the tiers to meet the needs of all students.

Focusing on Behavior

Problem behaviors continue to be the primary reason that individuals in our society are excluded from school.[6] Students arrive in schools today with widely differing understandings of socially acceptable behaviors, creating significant challenges for schools in managing behavior. Many schools have faced these challenges by implementing punitive policies that focus on "getting tough" and "zero tolerance" that end up being insufficient in meeting the myriad of students' behavioral needs. For the most part, schools have not been equipped to meet these needs.

The RTI framework provides the social and behavioral supports that schools need in a systematic fashion that not only improves student behavioral outcomes but academic outcomes as well. The RTI framework that utilizes a School-Side Positive Behavior Supports (SWPBS) establishes a social culture in which both academic and social and behavioral success is more likely. The SWPBS builds a continuum or hierarchy of supports that begins with the whole school and extends to intensive individualized support as needed.

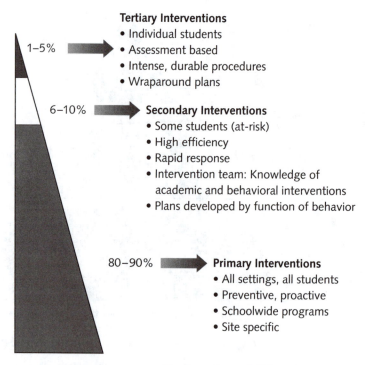

Figure 2.4 Behavioral Tiers

Special education has focused on these intensive individualized supports as part of the individualized education program (IEP) for those students identified with specific behavioral needs. These supports have been provided through behavior intervention plans (BIP) as part of the IEP. The focus has been on specific students and specific behavior change processes that constitute the intensive intervention of the third tier of the behavioral RTI triangle.

The link between RTI and SWPBS is based on effective foundational practices, good Tier I universal screening to identify students for Tier II, and a continuum of services based on student need with a primary focus on prevention and intervention. Schoolwide positive behavior supports provide a comprehensive systematic positive behavior plan across school settings that meets the behavioral need of the majority of students in a preventative model.[7]

The SWPBS processes have been in place for the past ten years with a current implementation of more than nine thousand schools in forty states (www.pbis.org). The premise of SWPBS is that schoolwide positive behavioral expectations will meet the needs of the majority of students, or the benchmark group of students, who traditionally understand the rules and believe that these rules apply to them. This group usually comprises about 80 percent of the student population.

Tier II interventions apply to those students who have been identified through screening or other data measures to need additional or supplemental support. One colleague refers to these students as the "fence sitters." This term applies because students often do not have significant maladaptive behaviors but are influenced by the people and circumstances around them. Their behavior can teeter either way, often determined by who they are with and what they are involved in. This strategic group of students needs something more than the schoolwide plan and usually makes up about 15 percent of the student population. The Tier III students are those who need intensive behavioral interventions and make up approximately 5 percent of the population.

Tier I

The key to success for the 80 percent of the population that comprises the benchmark group is the consistency of the implementation of the schoolwide positive procedures and expectations. When the school has effective foundational behavioral practices, it provides an effective curriculum, unambiguous instruction of adequate intensity, and an appropriate reward and error correction system.[8]

Benchmark students respond to:

- Schoolwide positive behavior supports
- Articulated expectations
- Monitoring of behavioral progress
- Prosocial and proactive discipline

When school staff have made a commitment to enforcing the behavioral plan developed by the school, students are very clear on the expectations of teachers in every class. With continual reinforcement of appropriate behaviors that follow the schoolwide plan, most students do not find it difficult to comply with these common, clearly articulated expectations.

There are those within the benchmark group of students who will struggle with following the schoolwide plan from time to time. Everyone will have bad days. In the old behavioral models, bad behavior culminated in an office visit; in an RTI Tier I model, the frequency of these bad days is monitored by the classroom teacher. The data are collected to determine how frequently these behaviors occur, the context in which they occur, and whether any patterns emerge. The behavior is monitored over time, and when patterns of behavioral difficulty emerge, the answer does not become suspension or some other punitive unsuccessful punishment; a grade-level or problem-solving team determines that a second tier of behavioral intervention is warranted.

Tier II

Tier II interventions focus on this approximately 15 percent of the school population that struggles with behavioral consistency despite the schoolwide positive plan.

For this group of students, a secondary level of behavioral intervention should be made available before moving toward more intensive behavior supports. These secondary interventions in Tier II usually require minimal time to implement and are very similar to implement from student to student. They typically provide extra doses of positive supports.[9] These strategies usually include an increase in daily structure and organizational support, provision of more frequent behavioral prompts, and frequent doses of recognition for appropriate behaviors.

The students that comprise this strategic group are identified either through frequency of behavioral issues or through schoolwide screening. It is data that determine this population, not perceptions about misbehavior or inappropriate attitudes or actions. Universal schoolwide behavioral screening addresses the prevalence of emotional and or behavioral problems among school-age children, which ranges between 9 percent and 13 percent.[10]

Screening provides a reliable and valid approach to identifying those students with a predominance toward externalized and internalized maladaptive behaviors. Recognizing the needs of these students early on allows for preventative measures, reducing the need for intensive services later on.

A variety of Tier II strategic supplemental behavior interventions that support the needs of these strategic students are discussed in depth in Chapter Nine.

As with supplemental academic supports, strategic behavioral supports will need additional time on the part of the student and the school staff. For some students this time will include small-group trainings or counseling time working with other students on social skills or anger management. For some it involves peer or adult mentoring.

Tier III

Students with persistent maladaptive behaviors will fall into that 5 to 10 percent of the population that requires more intensive interventions. This group of intensive students will benefit from small-group or individualized counseling and the development of individualized behavior plans. Although they will still benefit from peer or adult mentoring, they also need frequent careful monitoring throughout the day with ongoing tracking of behavior.

These intensive interventions involve an individualized assessment of current behavior followed by an individualized intervention plan.

According to Fairbanks and her colleagues, most of these function-based interventions include providing more teacher attention, an increase in self-monitoring, and further development of these self-monitoring skills.[11] These students benefit from the direct teaching of social skills, often in small-group trainings, and the support of counselors or other specialists who can work with them to identify strategies that help them change their behavior.

Tier III interventions are developed by a school team of specialists that include a school psychologist and/or school counselor who do the behavioral evaluation, or functional behavior assessment. Through observations of the student over time, the specialist and the team determine what precipitates the behaviors, and from this data, develop a plan to replace the inappropriate or maladaptive behaviors. The school staff works together as a team to implement the behavior support plan or behavior intervention plan. This plan is monitored on a frequent basis; as the student develops new behaviors to replace the old ones, the student learns to self-monitor behaviors and moves back into the strategic group over time. In the strategic group, the student is able to maintain the adult relationships from the mentoring programs but needs less individualized attention as the new behaviors become a permanent part of the student's daily interactions.

Once you have gained a clear understanding of the prevention and intervention process of RTI, the next step is recognizing how RTI can be utilized in the special education eligibility process. Part Two identifies how the process can be implemented and how students with disabilities can further benefit from the RTI structure even after identification.

Wrapping Up the Main Points

Response to intervention is a framework for meeting individual students' needs both academically and behaviorally. The promise of RTI is that students will receive targeted instruction matched to their needs within the multi-tiered hierarchy of academic and behavioral supports provided at a school site. The goal of this hierarchy is not to continue to move students up through the tiers as a special education prereferral process but rather a process in which students can move fluidly among the tiers with the goal of moving into the benchmark group where they can have successful access of the core curriculum, meet the grade-level standards, and develop appropriate behaviors for school success.

Part II

Beyond Tier III

Special Education Consideration

Initially, response to intervention (RTI) was identified in the Individuals with Disabilities Education Act (IDEA; 2004) as a process that determined whether a student responded to scientific, research-based intervention as part of the evaluation procedure for special education eligibility. In the special education research literature, this process is generally referred to as RTI.[1]

Prior to the reauthorization of IDEA in 2004, a severe discrepancy between student intellectual ability and achievement in one or more of the areas of oral expression, listening comprehension, written expression, basic reading skill, reading comprehension, mathematics calculation, and mathematics reasoning was required in order for a student to be identified as having a specific learning disability (SLD). This requirement that a severe discrepancy exist left many students needing to "wait to fail" until they could qualify for special education services. This was an extreme point of frustration to teachers, parents, and special education service providers; very often the student's need for intervention was recognized early on, but because of the limitations of assessment tools and the level of academic skills required at the early grades, it often took until third grade for the discrepancy to become large enough for the student to qualify for special education services and be able to receive some type of intervention.

Understanding Specific Learning Disability Eligibility

This discrepancy, while well known by special educators, was a point of confusion for parents and general educators. A student in special education would need to exhibit an IQ in the normal range—90 to 109—and an achievement standard score 1.5 deviations below the student's IQ to be considered to have a severe discrepancy. This discrepancy between academic achievement and cognitive skills would make the student eligible under the handicapping condition of "specific learning disabled—SLD." This was confusing; initially, when most individuals think of students in special education, they think of students who have some type of subaverage intelligence. They usually think of students with moderate to severe disabilities, but statistically, the largest group of the special education population is the group identified at SLD; nearly 50 percent of the special education population has this label.[2] By mere definition alone, this group does not have cognitive deficits, as the requirement to be identified in this category is "average intelligence."

While the definition of a student with SLD remains unchanged from the previous versions of the law and regulations, the process used to determine whether the student qualifies under this definition has. The current definition is contained in 20 *United States Code (U.S.C.)* Section 1401(30) and Title 34 of the *Code of Federal Regulations* Section 300.8(c)(10)(i)(ii) and states:

> (i) Specific learning disability means a disorder in one or more of the basic psychological processes involved in understanding or in using language, spoken or written, that may manifest itself in the imperfect ability to listen, think, speak, read, write, spell, or to do mathematical calculations, including conditions such as perceptual disabilities, brain injury, minimal brain dysfunction, dyslexia, and developmental aphasia. (ii) Specific learning disability does not include learning problems that are primarily the result of visual, hearing, or motor disabilities, of mental retardation, of emotional disturbance, or of environmental, cultural, or economic disadvantage.[3]

Different processes can be used to determine whether the student meets the definition:

> (A) Notwithstanding section 1406(b), when determining whether a child has a specific learning disability as defined in section 1401, a public educational agency *shall not be required to take into consideration whether a child has a severe discrepancy between achievement and intellectual ability* in oral expression, listening comprehension, written expression, basic reading skill, reading comprehension, mathematical calculation, or mathematical reasoning. (B) In determining whether a child has a specific learning disability, a local educational agency *may use a process that determines if the child responds to scientific, research-based intervention* as a part of the evaluation procedures described in paragraphs (2) and (3) [emphasis added].[4]

Each state is able to adopt its own criteria for determining SLD eligibility, and although the regulations do not specify the exact criteria for determining this eligibility using an RTI process, it is left to each state to develop its own guidance and policies.

The RTI Process and SLD Determination

The question may arise, "Why is this information important when we are trying to implement a schoolwide intervention model to meet the needs of all students? How does SLD eligibility fit into this picture?" This is a very valid question, especially in light of the ongoing discussion about Tier I "good first teaching" and Tier II general education interventions with little mention of special education. The connection lies with those students who have gone through the standards-based, data-based instruction and intervention structure at a school and do *not* respond to the best of the best instructional intervention provided. These students continue to make minimal if any progress despite good differentiated instruction, increased instructional time, research-based instructional practices, and small-group intensive, sometimes one-on-one intervention. These "nonresponders" are the focus of this chapter.

The Process

What does a teaching team do when they recognize that a student is failing? When multiple measures are in place, these students may be identified at various data points. Some may be identified during initial screening as having a large discrepancy between their current achievement and the achievement levels of their peers. This "red flag warning" from the screening usually leads to some further diagnostic assessment—not special education assessment, but assessment to determine the exact skill gaps that exist. At this point in time, the student shows a discrepancy between the average classroom performance and their own current skill. This discrepancy is depicted in Figure 3.1.

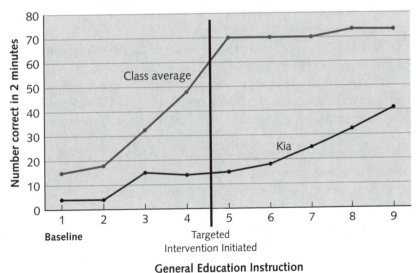

Figure 3.1 Discrepancy 1: Skill Gap

Source: Sharon Schultz. Used with permission.

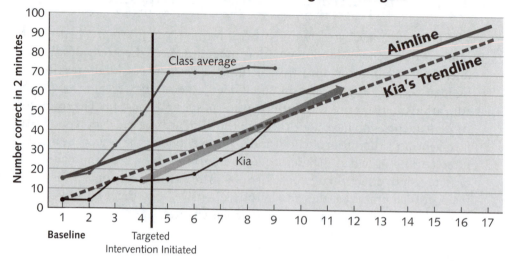

Subtract Positive and Negative Integers

Successful Intervention!!

Figure 3.2 Skill Gap Closed

Source: Sharon Schultz. Used with permission.

The student then receives targeted instruction to close the skill gap. This does not mean special education services and should at this level simply include targeted instruction in the general education classroom, in a Tier I-type intervention. The progress of this student is monitored on a regular basis and compared to the trajectory of progress for his or her general education peers. If the student is making progress that will allow her to meet the trajectory of the class at some point, the intervention is deemed successful (see Figure 3.2).

The student is not in need of any further targeted intervention and this skill gap has been eliminated. No individual skill gap exists.

The second discrepancy is the gap in rate of improvement. In the case described, the skill gap was closed and the intervention was deemed successful. But if this student had not responded to this targeted intervention, an additional intervention would be applied (see Figure 3.3).

This second targeted intervention could include increased instructional time and instruction strategies that support a different learning modality. For the student who does not do well with visual memory and did not learn through the use of flashcards, learning through chants and songs might be a second approach used in the Tier II or supplemental intervention. This second level of intervention will be monitored more frequently for progress, and if the student responds positively, the student's trendline based on the data will at some point meet the class's aimline (see Figure 3.4).

If the student does not respond to this second targeted intervention, his trendline will not be moving toward the aimline. The dual discrepancy of skill gap and gap in

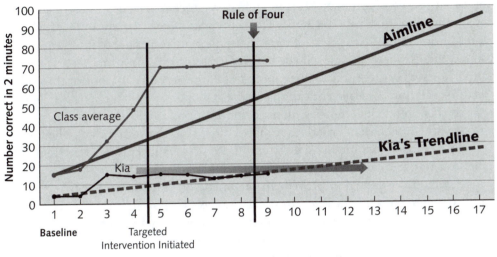

Figure 3.3 Discrepancy 2: Trendline Discrepancy

Source: Sharon Schultz. Used with permission.

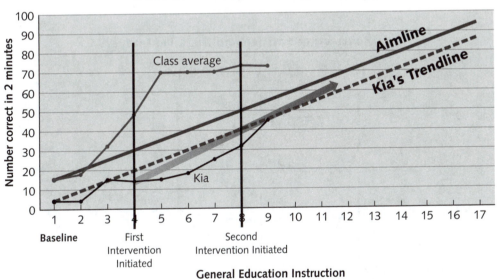

Figure 3.4 Trendline Discrepancy Reduced

Source: Sharon Schultz. Used with permission.

rate of learning persists. It is usually at this point that a student becomes the subject of a more involved problem-solving approach, since it seems that standard protocols are not serving this student's needs. The team would meet to determine which intensive intervention might be the best solution to the ongoing resistance to intervention. In some states, this is where the special education referral begins. In other states and districts, this is the step before special education referral. In this book, we look at this Tier III step as the step prior to special education referral.

At this point, the intensive intervention is applied. This usually constitutes small-group, time-intensive instruction. It may require that the student be pulled out of core classes to receive this intensive instruction. Progress is monitored very frequently, and the student is provided the best instruction possible.

Based on the data, if improvements are made, the dual discrepancy begins to lessen and the intervention continues. In this case, the trendline at some point will meet the aimline. In many of these Tier III interventions, students who have been resistant to intervention in the past will stay in an intensive intervention model for considerable time. Many of the intensive reading intervention programs expect students to take up to two years to make the growth necessary to close the skill gap.

If the student does not respond to this research-based intervention, the team then must decide whether they will apply another intensive research-based intervention or move forward to a referral for special education assessment (see Figure 3.5).

This very thorough process has provided the student with every opportunity to benefit from the general education evidence-based instruction and intervention prior to a referral to special education.

This is the reason a hierarchy of instruction and intervention is necessary to use an RTI process for SLD determination. The data collected during this thorough

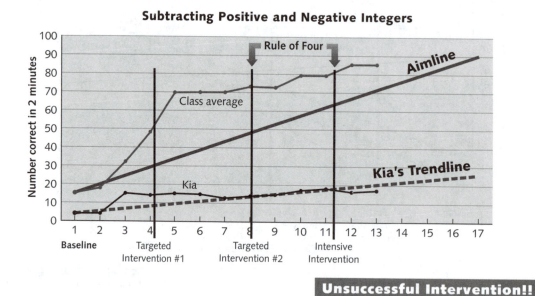

Figure 3.5 Dual Discrepancy Persists

Source: Sharon Schultz. Used with permission.

The Essential Guide to RTI

process are evidence that the student did receive the appropriate instruction and intervention in the schoolwide intervention model. This allows the problem-solving team to make the referral for special education assessment based on the requirements of the law:

> b. To ensure that underachievement in a child suspected of having a specific learning disability *is not due to lack of appropriate instruction* in reading or math, the group must consider, as part of the evaluation described in Sec. 300.304 through 300.306—
>
> 1. Data that demonstrate that prior to, or as a part of, the referral process, the child was provided appropriate instruction in regular education settings, delivered by qualified personnel; and
>
> 2. *Data-based documentation of repeated assessments of achievement* at reasonable intervals, reflecting formal assessment of student progress during instruction, which was provided to the child's parents.[5]

The data from the frequent progress monitoring become the proof that the student received research-based instruction in the general education classroom and subsequent progress-monitored intervention prior to the referral. This stipulation is in place to avoid referrals that are due to "curriculum casualty" in which the student has skills gaps due not to learning disabilities but to poor general education or first instruction.

It is important to note that going through an RTI process alone does not qualify a student for special education under the SLD requirements. A comprehensive evaluation is still necessary, but what comprises this evaluation has changed. Whereas in the past, the evaluation data were based on testing sessions with a teacher and school psychologist, the data that are obtained from a long-term RTI process are much more valid real-time data obtained from the frequent progress monitoring of the student over time. For the special education referral following the RTI process, the following is still required by federal law:

- A variety of data-gathering tools and strategies are used.
- A variety of assessment tools are used, with no single procedure or sole criterion used.
- The data from the RTI process are one component of the information reviewed.

In the past, the process for identifying a student as an individual with a learning disability was very mathematical. The RTI process observes patterns of strengths and weaknesses over time. The determination of which assessments will be used in the multidisciplinary assessment process differs from student to student based upon the patterns observed. No longer is a time-consuming IQ test required for every student suspected of having an SLD; rather, this option is available if the student is suspected of possibly having an intellectual disability rather than SLD. The changes from the old model of multidisciplinary assessment are more in line with a holistic and meaningful approach to evaluation.

Whereas assessments employed in the past were based on national norms, real-time data are often based on curriculum-based measures, progress-monitoring tools, and district and state assessments and are usually in some way aligned to standards. The results of these assessments are much more meaningful to parents and educators because they compare the student to his or her peers and the progress in learning the standards rather than on the placement of a standard score derived from a norm-reference test. When a teacher or parent is told, "He achieved a standard score of 87 on the written language assessment," this statement may hold very little meaning. But, if the parent or teacher is told, "He scored a 2 on a 4-point rubric on the third-grade writing assessment," the parent or teacher has a much better idea of how the student is functioning. Tracking progress or improvement on this score will be easy. If the student scores 3 or better in the future, this makes it very clear that he is improving. Waiting for a standardized assessment for an annual review is quite some time to have to wait to see if the student has improved his standard score from 87. The practice of using curriculum-based measures for special education assessment makes the process much more meaningful for all parties involved.

The Multidisciplinary Team

The composition of the multidisciplinary team will also change in light of RTI. Whereas in the past, this process was a special education process, it now must include general education input as well. The team may include the general education teacher who has provided the Tier I and often the Tier II instruction; the person who has provided the Tier III instruction; an English language specialist if the student is an English learner (EL); the parents; the student; a special education specialist, like the school psychologist, who is qualified to do a diagnostic assessment; a resource teacher; and other related service providers such a speech and language or other specialist.

The Assessment Process

Determining Specific Learning Disability Eligibility Using Response to Instruction and Intervention (RTI²),[6] an SLD guidance document developed by the California Department of Education and a broad technical assistance group, recommends that the assessment team follow several steps to establish whether a student has a specific learning disability.

Determination of Lack of Achievement

Prior to referral, the student has already completed a number of interventions, and the data collected from these interventions will show that the student has not achieved adequately for his or her age or is not able to meet the state-approved grade-level standards when provided with learning experiences and instruction that has been standards aligned and research based. The lack of achievement may be in two or more of the following areas:

1. Oral expression
2. Listening comprehension
3. Written expression
4. Basic reading skill
5. Reading fluency skill
6. Reading comprehension
7. Mathematical calculation
8. Mathematical problem solving

If through the data from the RTI process and additional assessment, the team determines that the student has not achieved adequately in the areas identified, the team then determines whether the student has not made progress within an RTI framework that has included intensive research-based interventions or whether the student exhibits patterns of strengths and weaknesses that are relevant to the identification of SLD.

Eligibility Decisions

The technical assistance group also made the following recommendations around eligibility decisions.

Determination of Lack of Progress Using RTI   The team may determine that a student has not made sufficient progress to meet age or grade-level standards in one or more of the eight identified areas when using an RTI process.

Determination of a Pattern of Strengths and Weaknesses   Additionally, the team may conclude that a student may have an SLD by examining whether he or she exhibits persistent patterns of strengths and weaknesses in performance, achievement, or both, compared to age or grade-level standards.

Determination of the Role of Exclusionary Factors   Once the team has determined that the student has not achieved adequately for his or her grade and has not made progress using an RTI process (dual discrepancy), or the student exhibits a pattern of strengths and weaknesses in performance, achievement, or both, the team *must* determine that these academic deficits are not due to the following exclusions:

- A visual, hearing, or motor disability
- Intellectual disability (mental retardation)
- Emotional disturbance
- Cultural factors
- Environmental or economic disadvantage
- Limited English proficiency

These exclusionary factors are essential in determining that the academic challenges are not due to some concomitant factor such as vision weaknesses, hearing loss, intellectual disability (mental retardation), or limited English proficiency. This is why vision and hearing assessments are a part of this multidisciplinary process. Some specialists may still want to do an IQ test to rule out mild intellectual disability (mental retardation) as one possibility for the academic pattern of weakness.

Determination of Whether a Student Received Appropriate Instruction   The team must also ensure that underachievement of the student being assessed is not due to a lack of appropriate instruction in reading or math. The team must provide the documentation that demonstrates that prior to, or as part of, the referral process, the student was provided with appropriate instruction delivered by qualified personnel in regular education settings. The team will need to provide data-based documentation of frequent progress monitoring at reasonable intervals, reflecting the progress of the student during instruction and intervention.

Observation   In order to document the student's progress in the natural environment, an observation in the general education classroom is also required. Data from previous observations garnered by the problem-solving team may be used, or additional observations may be conducted once the student is being assessed. The purpose of this observation is to determine from an outsider perspective the behaviors of the student and possible causes for the academic discrepancies. It is often in these observations that vision problems may be recognized or attention issues may be identified. This observation is an essential piece of this multidisciplinary assessment.

Determination of Eligibility   Upon completion of the multidisciplinary evaluation, the team, including the general education teacher, parents, student when appropriate, special education specialists, and a site administrator, use the assessment data to determine whether a specific learning disability exists. If the data reveal that the student has had research-based instruction and intervention, and all exclusionary factors have been ruled out, moreover continues to exhibit a lack of progress on grade-level standards with persistent patterns of weakness, the team will create an individualized education program in order to provide specially designed academic instructional services through special education. Services will be prescribed by the team and annual goals developed that will support the student in accessing the grade-level standards. Accommodations or modifications may be recommended to help the student alleviate some of the aspects of the SLD. What will this look like in an RTI framework? How do RTI and special education work together?

A New Framework of Special Education: Beyond Tier III

Although special education has been designed to meet individualized needs in small-group settings, this practice has changed due to a lack of positive outcomes. Some practitioners and researchers believe that students have benefited little if at all academically from special education services.[7] So how has the need for changes in special

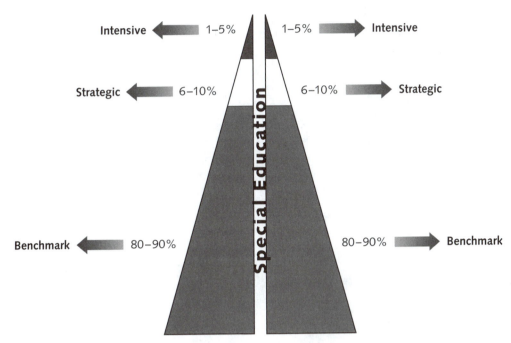

Academic Systems

Behavioral Systems

Intensive ← 1–5% | 1–5% → Intensive

Strategic ← 6–10% | 6–10% → Strategic

Special Education

Benchmark ← 80–90% | 80–90% → Benchmark

Figure 3.6 Success for All Students Framework

Source: Sharen Bertrando, WestEd Center for Prevention and Early Intervention. Used with permission.

education been met within the RTI framework? Initially, RTI was seen as the road to special education, and once identified, *poof*, students "went off" to special education and some kind of magical program that would "fix" all their problems. While this idea still persists in many states today, the promise of RTI is that students with disabilities can be served within the schoolwide framework of support (see Figure 3.6).

Chapter Four investigates the collaborative special education service delivery models inherent to an RTI framework that centers on achievement for all students and the firm belief that all students can learn.

Wrapping Up the Main Points

IDEA 2004 introduced the language that provides states, districts, and schools the option to use the RTI approach when determining the educational needs of students suspected of having specific learning disabilities. The language of the law allows this alternate approach, which does not require the identification of a severe discrepancy between ability and achievement. Using an RTI framework allows educators to meet students at their point of need. The benefit has been far reaching in meeting the instructional needs of at-risk students and creates provisions that guarantee that each and every student has the opportunity to research-based instruction and intervention prior to a special education referral.

Special Education Within the RTI Structure

Why does special education need to change? The answers are numerous and the reasons many. Special education in many forms has been present for more than a hundred years, but special education as we know it today came into being in 1975 with the passage of Public Law 94-142. This sweeping law passed during President Gerald Ford's administration required that all students with a disability be provided a free and appropriate public education or FAPE. The promise of educational equity was made for all students from kindergarten through graduation or age twenty-two.[1]

Although this law has been reauthorized numerous times, the focus of education equity has not changed; the vision on how it is provided has. Initially the concept of segregation of students into similar groups as to provide "specially designed" academic instruction was deemed the ideal. Special education brought with it a Cadillac of service options for all students who qualified under the federal criteria as a "student with a disability." In each case, this best of all services was provided in a separate setting. These classes, with students clustered together with similar disabilities, seemed to be the best way to provide the targeted instruction that met a prescription of instructional goals determined in each child's individualized education plan.

As a former special day class teacher of students with communication handicaps, I found my charge daunting to say the least. The difficulties with clustering students together with similar difficulties were plenty. Each school site would not have enough students with a like disability to create a full class, so students were often bused from their home schools to the school that held their specific "program." Students were denied the opportunity to go to their neighborhood schools and truly be a part of the neighborhoods and communities in which they lived. Parents who had siblings in the home school and in the special education program school were torn between being a part of both. Unfortunately, most parents were not very involved in the school that held the special education program because it was not part of their community.

Additionally, even when students were bused to a common location, there would not be enough students with a similar disability at each grade level to constitute a class, so these segregated classes held multiple grade levels. For several years, I had the only primary special education class in the district and therefore had grades preschool through 3 in one room. The educational needs of these groups were significantly different, and as a teacher, I always felt like someone was being short-changed. Providing an equitable education under these conditions was very challenging. Very few students could be offered their grade-level core curriculum with so many grades and needs in a room, and the hope of equity was quickly vanishing.

As the decade progressed, parents began the push to have their children included in general education classes, since they recognized that clustering students with disabilities together did not provide students an opportunity to learn from age- and grade-level appropriate models. Parents recognized that children learn social skills and appropriate behaviors from each other. These segregated settings did not allow for this kind of learning. So, the initial push for "mainstreaming" was focused primarily on the development of social skills, but surprisingly, parents found that when students were mainstreamed they benefited not just socially but also academically, and the push for inclusion had begun.[2]

The reauthorization of the Individuals with Disabilities Education Act (IDEA; Act 20 *United States Code (U.S.C.)* Sec. 1400) in 1997 and in 2004 continued this push for inclusion with language that required students to have access to the core curriculum, not just specially designed instruction in a segregated setting. The language became even stronger in 2004, stating that the instruction for students with disabilities had to require both access to and progress in the core curriculum with the student achieving skills in order to pass from grade to grade.

This was a far cry from the remediated instruction provided in special education throughout the late 1970s, '80s and '90s. One single teacher alone in a multiple-grade-level class, teaching multiple content standards across all content areas, had an impossible task. Special education could not deliver on the promise of access to and progress in the grade-level core with skills to pass from grade to grade. No educator, no matter how talented, could make this happen.

The need for collaboration between general education and special education became apparent. Unfortunately, nearly two decades of "yours" and "mine" created ownership issues that are still grappled with today. General educators don't often see special education students as their responsibility. Special educators are remiss to "let go" of their special education students, concerned that they will fail in a less restrictive setting. Neither group of teachers held high expectations for these students, assured that if returned to a general education setting, the students would surely drown.

Statistically, special education students were drowning with or without special education segregation. Even with the segregation and prescriptive instruction, these students were not graduating from high school, holding jobs, or living independently.

The high school graduation rate for students with learning disabilities is only 62 percent,[3] with approximately 70 percent of all persons with disabilities in the United States between the ages of 18 and 64 being unemployed or underemployed.[4] The average income for an adult identified as learning disabled is $20,000 a year.[5] The practice of remediated instruction, providing a slower and lower level of instruction for students who struggled with learning, only contributed to achievement gaps that persist today. This practice left students with disabilities even further and further behind. The idea that these students can't learn kept them from receiving the equitable education promised to them by federal law.

Expectations Do Make a Difference

Lowered expectations for students with disabilities have been in part to blame for these dismal outcomes. Johann Wolfgang von Goethe (1749–1842) notes that when a label is slapped on a student, expectations immediately change: "If you see an individual as he is, that is all he will be, but if you see him as he should be or could be, that is what he will become."[6]

If we see these individuals as incapable of learning or incapable of benefiting from the core curriculum, then that is what will happen. How do we go about changing our thinking about special education students?

Some Insight

The following excerpts from IDEA provide an abbreviated definition of the thirteen federal handicapping conditions. If a student exhibits the characteristics defined in one or more categories, they will qualify for special education services. Readers are often surprised how infrequently the term *intellectual disability* is used (or, formerly, *mental retardation*).

How IDEA Defines the Thirteen Disability Categories

1. Autism...
   means a developmental disability significantly affecting verbal and nonverbal communication and social interaction, generally evident before age three, that adversely affects educational performance. Characteristics often associated with autism are engaging in repetitive activities and stereotyped movements, resistance to changes in daily routines or the environment, and unusual responses to sensory experiences. The term autism does not apply if the child's educational performance is adversely affected primarily because the child has emotional disturbance, as defined in #4 below. A child who shows the characteristics of autism after age three could be diagnosed as having autism if the criteria above are satisfied.

2. Deaf-blindness...
   means simultaneous hearing and visual impairments, the combination of which causes such severe communication and other developmental and educational needs that they cannot be

accommodated in special education programs solely for children with deafness or children with blindness.

3. Deafness...

means a hearing impairment so severe that a child is so impaired in processing linguistic information through hearing, with or without amplification, that it adversely affects a child's educational performance.

4. Emotional disturbance...

means a condition exhibiting one or more of the following characteristics over a long period of time and to a marked degree that adversely affects a child's educational performance:

    a. An inability to learn that cannot be explained by intellectual, sensory, or health factors

    b. An inability to build or maintain satisfactory interpersonal relationships with peers and teachers

    c. Inappropriate types of behavior or feelings under normal circumstances

    d. A general pervasive mood of unhappiness or depression

    e. A tendency to develop physical symptoms or fears associated with personal or school problems (the term includes schizophrenia, but the term does not apply to children who are socially maladjusted, unless it is determined that they have an emotional disturbance)

5. Hearing impairment...

means an impairment in hearing, whether permanent or fluctuating, that adversely affects a child's educational performance, but that is not included under the definition of "deafness."

6. Intellectual disability (formerly called mental retardation)...

means significantly sub-average general intellectual functioning—existing at the same time as deficits in adaptive behavior and manifested during the developmental period—that adversely affects a child's educational performance.

7. Multiple disabilities...

means simultaneous impairments (such as intellectual disability-blindness or mental retardation-orthopedic impairment), the combination of which causes such severe educational needs that they cannot be accommodated in a special education program solely for one of the impairments. The term does not include deaf-blindness.

8. Orthopedic impairment...

means a severe orthopedic impairment that adversely affects a child's educational performance. The term includes impairments caused by a congenital anomaly (e.g., clubfoot, absence of some member), impairments caused by disease (e.g., poliomyelitis, bone tuberculosis), and impairments from other causes (e.g., cerebral palsy, amputations, fractures or burns that cause contractures).

9. Other health impairment...

means having limited strength, vitality, or alertness, including a heightened alertness to environmental stimuli, that results in limited alertness with respect to the educational environment. The impairments:

    a. Are due to chronic or acute health problems such as asthma, attention deficit disorder or attention deficit hyperactivity disorder, diabetes, epilepsy, a heart condition, hemophilia, lead poisoning, leukemia, nephritis, rheumatic fever, or sickle cell anemia, and Tourette's Syndrome

    b. Adversely affect a child's educational performance

10. Specific learning disability...

means a disorder in one or more of the basic psychological processes involved in understanding or in using language, spoken or written, that may manifest itself in an imperfect ability to listen, think, speak, read, write, spell, or to compute mathematical calculations. The term includes such conditions as perceptual disabilities, brain injury, minimal brain dysfunction, dyslexia, and developmental aphasia. The term does not include learning problems that are primarily the result of visual, hearing, or motor disabilities; of intellectual disability; of emotional disturbance; or of environmental, cultural, or economic disadvantage.

11. Speech or language impairment...

means a communication disorder, such as stuttering, impaired articulation, or a language or voice impairment, that adversely affects a child's educational performance.

12. Traumatic brain injury...

means an acquired injury to the brain caused by an external physical force resulting in total or partial functional disability or psychosocial impairment, or both. The term applies to open or closed head injuries resulting in impairments in one or more areas, such as cognition; language; memory; attention; reasoning; abstract thinking; judgment; problem-solving; sensory, perceptual, and motor abilities; psychosocial behavior; physical functions; information processing; and speech. The term does not include brain injuries that are congenital or degenerative, or brain injuries incurred by birth trauma.

13. Visual impairment including blindness...

means an impairment in vision that, even with correction, adversely affects a child's educational performance. The term includes both partial sight and blindness.

Reflection

It may be surprising that the term *intellectual disability* was found in only three of the thirteen conditions. Number 6 is the federal definition of intellectual disability formerly referred to as mental retardation. The old term is not commonly used today due to its derogatory nature—the current common term is *intellectual disability*—but the defining characteristics remain the same. The characteristics refer to a global developmental delay across all areas, including gross motor, fine motor, communication, self-help, and adaptive skills, and cognition. This is that small part of the population who, depending on the severity, may struggle significantly with learning and will require alternate assessments and alternate means of instruction. A student with *multiple disabilities* refers to a student who has an intellectual disability combined with another disability such as sensory disability, physical disability, autism, and so on. This student has global delays in addition to another disability.

In the definition for specific learning disability (SLD), intellectual disability is an exclusionary factor or rule out. As discussed in Chapter Three, for a student to qualify as an individual with a specific learning disability, the academic weaknesses cannot be due to mental retardation or an intellectual disability. The student with a specific learning disability does not have delays in communication, self-help, gross motor, fine motor, or adaptive skills. The student with a specific learning disability exhibits average cognitive intelligence and normal development in most other areas, except for learning. By definition alone, this student has average cognitive intelligence.

> "The student with a specific learning disability does not have delays in communication, self-help, gross motor, fine motor, or adaptive skills. The student with a specific learning disability exhibits average cognitive intelligence and normal development in most other areas, except for learning."

Perceptions

Most people, if asked to describe an individual with a disability, would respond in some way to indicate that the individual has subaverage intelligence or an intellectual disability. They may use more derogatory terms such as "retard" or "dumb." They may also describe a person with a physical disability or other sensory disability, but if we look at the statistics, we see that these groups make up a very small part of the special education population.

The entire special education population makes up approximately 10 percent of the general population. Within this global 10 percent of the population with disabilities, there is approximately 10 percent that has intellectual disabilities or subaverage cognitive intelligence. This 1 percent of the total population is definitely not how special education is accurately defined. Figure 4.1 identifies the largest special education subgroup as

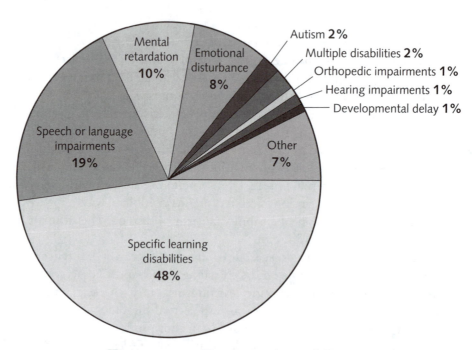

Figure 4.1 Expectations Matter

specific learning disabled, at 48 percent. The other groups combined make up the rest of the population, with only 10 percent being identified as having an intellectual disability. At least 75 percent of students identified with disabilities have average cognitive intelligence.

These data provide a very clear picture that the students sitting in both general education and special education classrooms primarily have average cognitive intelligence. The data drive home the point that these students have the cognitive ability to identify the three main causes of the Civil War in social studies; they can learn to solve for *x* in algebra; they can learn the periodic table in chemistry and the structure of cells in biology; and they can identify figurative language and author's position in language arts. They have the *ability* to learn the core content, but the challenge that educators face today is how to get the content past the students' reading difficulties. If reading printed text is the *only* way that they can learn the content, a frequently used instructional practice, they will not have access to or make progress in the core curriculum. Consequently, instruction both in general and special education must change, and instructional practices that reflect RTI principles and processes must cross over from general education intervention alone to an integral part of the special education service delivery model.

The Challenges of Special Education

We have seen from the research that for some students special education has not been effective. In his monograph entitled *The Road to Nowhere: The Illusion and Broken Promises of Special Education in the Baltimore City and Other Public School Systems*, Kalman Hettleman, a public advocate attorney for families of students with disabilities in Baltimore, commented:

> Despite several years of special education services, many special education students are still reading about three grade levels below their peers. Stigma and frustration cause them to develop emotional and behavior problems that further impede learning. In theory, special education is to be a temporary program for many students. But in practice it has become a one way street.[7]

This is not to say that special education teachers have not put forth heroic efforts to teach their students. From personal experience as a special educator of students with mild to moderate disabilities, I had high expectations for my students, and I expected them to exit special education. I informed them of their disabilities and empowered them to use that knowledge to determine how to compensate. I never let them use their disabilities as an excuse, and although at times they considered me "mean," they knew I cared and that my goal for them was to have options for their postsecondary lives.

But as hard as I worked, juggling the many balls that are special education, I knew I was not able to deliver on the promise to provide each and every one of them an equitable education. I could not provide standards-aligned grade-level instruction for each content area for each grade level in my classroom. I don't think even Houdini could have done it. With the push toward standards, it became very clear that the only way for students in the special education program to receive instruction in the standards at their grade level was to be in their grade-level general education classes.

A New Era of Special Education

The Elementary and Secondary Education Act (ESEA) and IDEA ushered in a new era of special education. The expectation that all students achieve on state-level standardized assessment pushed special education into the main school building. The challenge before educators became, What now? How can grade-level standards-aligned instruction be delivered to each and every student? The answer has taken time to evolve. The underlying theme has been inclusion. If and when students are included in the general education core, they receive the grade-level standards-based instruction prescribed. But if this was true, how could the incongruence between individualized education program (IEP) goals and these standards be resolved? IEP goals drive the instruction in special education. But the practice of writing IEP goals at a student's ability level would no longer suffice if the student was to work on grade-level standards for instruction. This discrepancy created fertile ground for the battle about what special education was and how it should be delivered. The common cry has been, "If the students could learn the grade-level standards, they wouldn't be in special education. They are not at grade level, so why would I worry about writing goals that align to the grade-level standard? That is not special education!" I will agree, that is not what special education was, but the face of special education and how students are served in special education has changed with ESEA, IDEA'04 and the expectation that *all* students will achieve.

Writing IEP goals to grade-level standards is a practice that is spreading across the country because of the accountability required in ESEA and the expectation that students will have access to and make progress in the general education curriculum as described in IDEA'04. When goals are written to grade-level standards, there is a shared responsibility between general education and special education teachers to provide instruction that meets the goal and the standard. One cannot ask a sixth-grade general education teacher to teach to a goal that involves blending consonant-vowel-consonant, single closed-syllable words. This is not part of the sixth-grade English language arts standards that they teach, but if the goal is written that given audio text, the student will identify figurative language, the general education teacher can be expected to teach to that IEP goal. Writing the grade-level goals allows both the general education teacher and the special education teacher to be responsible for the instruction of the student with the disability.

> "Writing IEP goals to grade-level standards is a practice that is spreading across the country because of the accountability required in ESEA and the expectation that students will have access to and make progress in the general education curriculum as described in IDEA'04. When goals are written to grade-level standards, there is a shared responsibility between general education and special education teachers to provide instruction that meets the goal and the standard."

Once goals are written to standards, specially designed instruction within an RTI framework is possible. In this framework, performance goals are consistent for all students, but the difference for students with IEPs is that instructional accommodations provide scaffolds to access the standards. Scaffolds such as audio text, speech-to-text software, keyboarding devices, and the use of research-based instructional practices provide the platform for special education students to make progress in the grade-level curriculum.

An Accelerated Model Within the RTI Framework

The question still arises, "How will that sixth grader with a learning disability who needs to work on decoding get the individualized instruction needed in order to catch up? How will she get the specially designed instruction to meet that need if she is receiving her instruction in general education classes? Where and when does special education happen?"

Once all teachers realize that special education is a service and not a destination, this question becomes easier to answer. Special education is a *service* that is provided to students with disabilities. The services are driven by the IEP and the goals prescribed that will help the student reach grade-level skill and to "progress from grade to grade." Unless otherwise specified in the IEP, these services can be delivered anywhere, by anyone. This opens the door to allow the student access to the schoolwide intervention options that meet their special education goals. The IEP usually does not say who must provide the instruction or exactly where the instruction is delivered. Special education law does not preclude students with disabilities from having their specially designed academic instruction delivered in a general education classroom with a general education teacher. Students in special education can receive the services in their IEPs in a variety of collaborative service delivery models.

Collaborative Models of Special Education Service Delivery

There are many options for special education service delivery. It is important to remember that the *I* in the individualized education program is about *individualized* supports. This means that the level of service provided is determined by the needs of the student, and that any one special educator or special education case manager may have students in any number of collaborative models. No school or program can say, "We only offer a consultative model," or "We only offer a collaborative model." Federal law requires a continuum of services, and in like manner the collaborative models provide instructional support from the least restrictive support to the most restrictive. The level of instructional support depends on the needs of the student; some will be successful in the least restrictive model of consultative support, while others may need more intensive support built into the intensive core instructional model.

The most commonly used collaborative models include:

- Consultative model
- Collaborative model
- Co-teaching or team-teaching model
- Schoolwide intervention model
- Supplemental support model
- Intensive core instruction model

Consultative Model

The consultative model is designed for students who receive their primary instruction in the general education classroom. This student does not receive direct instruction from the special educator and may only have occasional contact with her.[8] In the general education classroom, this student is allowed to use the accommodations and program supports and any modifications that are prescribed in the IEP. The special educator may work with the student initially to teach him or her how to use any assistive devices and how to best use accommodations. The special educator may train the general education teacher on the accommodations and any technology that the student may use. The role of the general educator is to provide differentiated instruction in the core and support the student as needed. While the special educator may not have frequent contact with the student, the special educator may provide regular instructional scaffolds like note-taking guides, graphic organizers, cloze notes, or other adaptations that will allow the student to learn the content. They are also responsible to frequently monitor the student's progress in the class and on the IEP goals.

While the consultative model has been used for quite some time as a way to wean a student off of special education supports, and some states and districts have limitations on how long a student can receive consultative services, this type of support should also be considered an ongoing service for those students who will need accommodations, adaptations, and ongoing monitoring for most of their educational careers. This is crucial for secondary students who change teachers several times a year. Each teacher the student works with must be aware of the student's specific needs and accommodation. The student will need ongoing support, with adaptations to the curriculum and instructional supports for longer than a quarter or trimester. This ongoing consultative model is not a common practice yet, but as more students receive their special education services in the general education classroom from general education teachers, this model will become more common.

Collaborative Teaching Model

In the collaborative teaching model, the student also receives her primary instruction in the general education classroom. The special educator has a similar role in training both the student and the teacher on the effective us of assistive technology and the appropriate implementation of accommodations or other program supports. The special educator provides scaffolded materials and adaptations but may also work directly with the student as needed.[9] This is a more flexible service delivery option because it depends on the curriculum and the specific needs of the student. For example, the special educator and general educator plan together and realize that the test on the periodic table will occur in two weeks. In this case, the special educator will schedule himself to work with the special education student with memory issues for the last ten minutes of class each day for the next two weeks to work on mnemonic devices to help her remember the elements. This extra instruction often happens in the general education classroom, and any students who need additional help are able to access the support of the special educator. The special educator may also support the general education teacher by providing instructional strategies and ideas during their collaborative planning time. The collaborating special educator may provide the instruction to the whole class to model specific strategies or techniques that will meet the needs of the identified students and all her classmates as well.

Co-Teaching or Team Teaching

In a co-teaching or team-teaching model, the general educator and the special educator deliver instruction to a blended group of students in the same classroom.[10] Both teachers provide the instruction, utilizing a variety of co-teaching models. This model provides the best of both worlds in that the instruction is provided by a highly qualified core content teacher *and* a highly qualified special educator with expertise in instructional strategies and differentiated instructional approaches.

While it takes time to develop an effective co-teaching team, co-teaching can take on many forms while teachers learn to work together. The most common co-teaching models include:

- One teaching, one supporting
- Parallel teaching
- Station teaching
- Alternative teaching
- Team teaching[11]

One Teaching, One Supporting

In this model, one teacher maintains the role of managing the classroom while the other leads with the instruction. While one is delivering instruction, the other is walking around and assisting students as needed. This model requires little joint planning time but does not provide the greatest benefit, as both teachers' expertise is not put to use. There is also the concern that if special educators are only allowed the opportunity to monitor, it will undermine their credibility and students will not recognize or respect them as teachers. The constant presence of a "helper" will cause some students to become dependent on another adult in order to do their work. One option for this kind of model is that teachers take turns leading the instruction, and both have the opportunity to provide support so that students will recognize that both adults are teachers.

Parallel Teaching

In parallel teaching, the teachers jointly plan instruction and each teacher teaches half the class. They are teaching the same content but may be providing the direct instruction in slightly different ways. One may be using graphic organizers, while the other may be using a PowerPoint presentation. The content of the instruction is the same; the delivery of instruction may differ. This model works well for test reviews, projects, and drill-and-practice activities.

Station Teaching

When the order of instruction does not matter, the two teachers can divide the instructional content and each take responsibility for planning and teaching part of the lesson. After each teacher has taught his or her part of the lesson, students move from station to station according to schedule. This provides the benefit of small-group instruction and supports the diverse needs of learners; each teacher may use a different style or strategy during his or her instructional session. In this model, students receive the benefit of both teachers' teaching styles. For this model to work successfully, teachers must have time to plan their instruction together, so that the lessons complement each other.

Alternative Teaching

In this model, one of the co-teachers works with a small group while the other teacher instructs the larger group. This model provides small-group instruction to the students who may need reteaching or additional modeling before moving on to independent practice. This option allows for highly intensive instruction to any student with a need in a general education setting. This model is most effective when both teachers take a small group to remove the stigma of the small group always being special education students or students who need help. The general educator, as the content specialist, should use this opportunity to teach the most difficult concepts to those students who are struggling or use this occasion to work with high achievers on extension activities.

Team Teaching

In a true team teaching model, both teachers share in the planning, instructional delivery, assessing, monitoring, and facilitation of group work. They may alternate roles to lead the discussion but are always a part of the discussion by asking clarifying questions, modeling on the board, debating, or role-playing. These co-teaching teams plan together and share each and every responsibility of the class. They share a synergy that invigorates and encourages student participation, and both educators are seen as having equal status. Teachers report that the strategies that they learn from their co-teachers benefit all their students in all their classes. This type of collaborative model is the most effective but also the most difficult to attain.

Schoolwide Intervention Model

This is the model in the RTI framework in which all students, irrespective of their labels, receive targeted instruction based upon their needs. Students with disabilities receive their special education services wherever the data determine is the most appropriate. If the data determine that students are in need of supplemental instruction, they may receive their core in general education and supplemental support in whatever targeted group other students with similar skills receive supplemental support. This may be in a group of students who gets support from the special education teacher, but this group may also receive their instruction from a reading specialist, a general education teacher, or other teacher involved in supplemental instruction. If the data determine the need for intensive intervention, this student will receive his or her specially designed academic instruction in the general education, leveled intensive intervention program. Again, the teacher may be the special educator but does not have to be. In a schoolwide model, all students receive instruction based on need, and whichever teacher provides instruction at the special education student's level of need is providing the specially designed academic instruction prescribed in the IEP, with progress monitored in a collaborative manner by the special educator.

Supplemental Support Model

In this model, students with disabilities receive their core instruction in a general education classroom. It may be a class without special education supports, or it may be a consultative, collaborative, or co-taught class. In addition to this core class, they receive additional supplemental support from the special educator. This allows the student to receive her or his core instruction from a highly qualified core content teacher and then receive additional support from a highly qualified special education specialist. This usually looks like a double-block class in which the core content teacher provides the content instruction in the first period and the special educator teaches the second. This may be referred to a core "plus" class, a shadow class, workshop class, or a strategic class, since it is in addition to the core. The benefit of this model is that the student is given the opportunity to work directly with the special educator to work on prerequisite skills and to allow for the opportunity for reteaching or preteaching of concepts related to the core instruction.

Intensive Special Education Support Model

This model provides the most restrictive setting to meet the needs of students with significant deficits who require small-group, specially designed academic instruction from a highly qualified core-content-competent special educator. In this model, students receive intensive intervention instruction from the special educator in the core content classes. At the elementary level, this may be referred to as the "academic core" program; the students are included in a general education homeroom but receive their language arts and math from a special education teacher in a special education setting. At the secondary setting, these students receive their core instruction from a special education teacher for their math and English requirements. These students are included in the general education classes and electives whenever appropriate to ensure the least restrictive environment.

But What About RTI?

While this chapter has primarily focused on special education and special education services, it is important to conclude with a discussion of how special education fits into the RTI framework. As described in previous chapters, students often move through the tiers receiving "good first" instruction, supplemental instruction, and then intensive intervention before a referral to special education is made. Once a student has exhausted all interventions, has been through the problem-solving team process, is recommended for multidisciplinary assessment, and qualifies for special education services as a student with a specific learning disability, there is no other place that has better services or more powerfully research-based interventions. The best interventions possible are available within the tiers of the RTI framework.

So, then what does special education have to offer that has not already been provided? The answer is not a special education magic wand that will somehow fix the child. Whereas special education used to be the only place where a student could receive small-group targeted instruction, RTI now provides that framework within the general education context. For the student with a learning disability, the schoolwide RTI process, with the collaborative models of special education service delivery options described in this chapter, offers the chance to truly receive an equitable education.

> **Whereas special education used to be the only place where a student could receive small-group targeted instruction, RTI now provides that framework within the general education context. For the student with a learning disability, the schoolwide RTI process, with the collaborative models of special education service delivery options described in this chapter, offers the chance to truly receive an equitable education.**

Armed with an understanding of RTI's role as catalyst for academic and behavioral prevention, intervention, and, for some, special education identification, you are now ready to embark on the implementation of the how process of making the RTI vision a reality. Part Three will detail the baby steps necessary to bring about this immense but rewarding change.

Wrapping Up the Main Points

Specially designed academic instruction prescribed in a student's individualized education program can be provided through collaborative models of special education service delivery. The RTI framework, with a schoolwide commitment to academic achievement for all students and a firm belief that all students can learn, creates a structure that allows all students, including those with IEPs, to benefit from the research-based instruction and interventions provided in the schoolwide intervention model. Most students with disabilities can learn the core content; it is up to the collaboration of professionals and the co-ownership of special education students to create equitable education opportunities for these students so that they too can access and make progress in grade-level content area classes, so that ultimately they will have the same postsecondary choices as their peers.

Part III

Response to Intervention Process Steps

5

Preparing for Implementation

Determining a specific "recipe" for response to intervention (RTI) implementation is impossible. Each building has its own unique human resources and strengths and its unique student needs, but there are certain processes that each school will navigate through to bring them to and through the implementation steps. The order of implementation will be determined by the school and its particular student population, but each school must come to common agreements on the need for RTI implementation before implementation steps can begin. Once a school has grasped the vision for implementation, the infrastructure must be built before the work begins, based on a site needs assessment. These processes are the groundwork for implementing an effective RTI framework. This chapter previews the consensus-building process and will help teams navigate through the infrastructure-building process that will lead to identifying an action plan for moving ahead with the first steps of implementation.

Stages of Implementation

Before the nuts and bolts of the process steps can begin, the rationale for change must be identified. Change does not occur unless there is a reason for change. Without a rationale, the passion behind an effective RTI structure that holds academic achievement for all students in highest esteem is not possible. People cannot be forced to be passionate about this process. It must come from the firm and common belief that all students can learn and that all students have the right to learn.

> **People cannot be forced to be passionate about this process. It must come from the firm and common belief that all students can learn and that all students have the right to learn.**

Unfortunately, one visionary alone cannot create this schoolwide change. The process requires collegiality and the ability to put aside the "way things have been done" to embrace a whole new structure of practice. Change is always hard, and many visionaries have been squelched in the early implementation phase, when their colleagues or other staff members have not shared their enthusiasm. Without support from other staff members, unfortunately the vision is often lost, and because of the supporters' disillusionment the dream dies.

It takes a concerted effort to develop the RTI vision. Only when a staff realizes that the status quo is no longer effective will the impetus for change occur. Fortunately, the Elementary and Secondary Education Act (ESEA) and the accountability measures it requires have brought many schools and districts very abruptly to a place at which they realize that they have no choice but to change. Once the need for change has been realized, the process steps can begin.

The RTI process steps take time. RTI is not a process that can be completed in months or even a year. The process, because it requires a dramatic change in expectations and roles, cannot be considered a quick fix bringing immediate response. According to the research, this process takes years.[1] Schools that have implemented RTI for six to ten years are still making changes and improving their practices each year. Schools and districts that are ready to take on the challenge to implement an RTI framework will recognize that the process typically proceeds through three stages identified by the National Association of State Directors of Special Education:[2]

1. Coming to consensus
2. Building infrastructure
3. Implementation process

The Consensus-Building Stage

The process of coming to consensus takes time and must be carefully planned. It is at this stage that the concepts of RTI are communicated broadly to all implementers, along with the foundational reasons or rationale for implementation. The administration must ensure the site has the time and tools necessary for this process to occur. Some measure of consensus building should have occurred before the administration moves forward to infrastructure building and implementation. Consensus building is essential to the RTI process, and without at least some buy-in from the staff, the implementation process will be extremely difficult at best, with no guarantees for success.

Even in a thorough consensus-building process in which every effort is made to inform, discuss, air concerns, and problem-solve, there will still be some individuals who will neither agree nor provide any support in moving forward with implementation. These few should not keep the building from moving forward. In the implementation study completed by the Center on Instruction, Saro Mohammed, Gregory Roberts, and Katie Tackett recommend that the implementation process begin with a vanguard group that holds the passion, while the outliers can observe and learn from their practice.[3]

The National State Directors of Special Education (NASDSE) *Response to Intervention, Blueprints for Implementation* (2008), identifies certain actions necessary for consensus building, presented in Table 5.1.[4]

Rationale building, based upon a strong foundation of data, is the essential first step. Data are not subjective and are not subject to opinion or conjecture. The data almost always reveal deep gaps for at-risk populations like English learners and students with disabilities. Site-specific data can make a strong statement about the need for change and a strong argument for an RTI framework. Site-specific data should include the following:

1. Which subgroups made Adequate Yearly Progress (AYP) scores?
2. Which subgroups did not make AYP?
3. What gaps exist between the subgroups?
4. If at a high school, did the school meet graduation rate criteria?

Table 5.1 Consensus-Building Process

Action 1 **Provide information and coordinate with district administration**
Establish rationale for building adoption of RTI practices
Determine who will share rationale and how it will be shared
Identify district and site level leadership responsibilities for implementation of RTI
Identify resources necessary to build consensus

Action 2 **Provide information to school staff and others about RTI**
Establish the rationale for building adoption of RTI practices based on data
Determine who will share the rationale and how it will be shared
Determine the resources and other commitments necessary to build consensus

Action 3 **Identify consensus level among staff necessary for implementing RTI**
Identify the level of agreement needed to proceed with RTI

Action 4 **Determine next steps**
Use assessment tools to determine next steps in the consensus-building process

Action 5 **Plan to support change initiative**
Integrate RTI principles and beliefs into the school values, mission, and vision

A graph of this information can send a strong message about the gaps that persist between subgroups. The data should set the groundwork for change. The next step is to develop as a site:

- The belief statements that drive the actions of the school
- The definition of what RTI is and what it would look like at their specific school site

Determining who can strongly, clearly, and carefully articulate the message with the greatest acceptance is critical in the reception of data that will drive the rationale development process. Each and every community is different in this regard. Some communities will listen best to an outside expert, while others will only hear from someone in their own community. Each school and district must thoughtfully consider who would best convey the message so that it is most widely accepted. NASDSE suggests that a cross-stakeholder group comprised of administrators, general education teachers, curriculum experts, administrators, Title I teachers, gifted and talented instructors, teachers of English language learners, and special educators take part in sharing the message.

Once the rationale has been clearly established and the information or content has been communicated, it is essential for the site administration to determine the level of consensus before moving into infrastructure building or action steps. This process is best completed through a survey: this will allow the administration to recognize the level of consensus and to determine the further need for time for further consensus building. The site leadership must determine at which point the implementation process can proceed. If a team is ready to move ahead, then there is enough support to begin the action step process with the specific vanguard group.

Sustaining the change initiative over time takes integrating RTI principles and beliefs into the school values, mission, and vision. This step is integral to ensure that stakeholders do not see RTI as just another "task" to add onto everything else being done around school improvement. Integrating RTI and the common beliefs about *all* students and academic achievement into the schoolwide vision, mission, and goals ensures that everyone involved sees RTI as the framework upon which all decision making, actions, and outcomes rest.

The Infrastructure-Building Stage

Infrastructure building begins with the building of the leadership team. This teaming crosses many levels, as shown in Table 5.2. Highly successful RTI implementation models come with high levels of district support and a top-down initiative that ensures the fiscal and the human resources to support the implementation process. Ideally, teaming occurs across three levels.

District leadership teams have the primary role of defining the rationale, vision, and mission of RTI implementation. It is the leadership of the district-level team that fosters the districtwide consensus or common ground on expectations for student achievement and expectations around the hierarchy of instruction and intervention. Once the district has established a strong rationale and district vision for RTI implementation, school site leadership teams can follow suit in supporting the district vision in their buildings and school sites.

The school site can then begin the work with the benefit of common expectations across sites as to what will comprise the district's RTI framework. The school site

Table 5.2 Three Levels of Teaming

1. District-Level Team

The formation of a district team should include the superintendent, the assistant superintendent (curriculum), the special education director and the assessment coordinator, the school improvement coordinator, and the cross categorical program coordinator, Title I and coordinator for English Learners, and so forth.

2. Site-Level Team

Site-level team should include the principal, the assistant principal, the behavior specialist, general educator teachers, the resource teacher, other special education teachers, inclusion teachers, reading specialists, intervention teachers, Title I teachers, the school psychologist, the speech language specialist, and other categorical teachers.

3. Grade-Level/Content Area Teams

Grade-level/content area teams including all grade-level teachers, Title I, other categorical programs, special educators and ELD teachers, para-professionals, parent volunteers, and so on.

---

leadership team should be made up of people who are respected by their colleagues and whom others will follow. The members of the leadership team should be volunteers from a variety of curricular areas and from across grades and subject areas. If only one area is targeted for implementation, then a strong representation from that subject area should be part of the team.

Each school-level team should include the people and the roles shown in Table 5.3. This leadership team should be an example of teaming that is replicated in the grade-level and content area teams. (Teaming practices are discussed further in Chapter Ten.) This RTI leadership team will need ongoing professional development and coaching to support it as the implementation process moves forward. The opportunities to network with other leadership are essential in order to problem-solve and share resources.

Implementation Process Steps

Once a school staff has developed a vision for RTI implementation and established leadership teams, the implementation process can proceed. The common vision and clear understanding developed in the consensus-building stage allow effective teams to honestly assess current practices and determine their current level of implementation of any of the RTI tiered intervention elements. This needs assessment process is driven by the RTI Tier Aligned Readiness Tool in Appendix B. The current implementation level and identified areas of need will drive the action planning process, and the tool in Appendix C will help teams move to this all-important step.

Needs Assessment and Action Planning

Most schools today are involved in numerous reform processes. Many of these processes cross-walk with RTI implementation processes. The use of an effective needs assessment tool will help a school identify which processes are already fully in place and where gaps exist. Such a tool allows schools to determine exactly which process steps are completed and which need further addressing. The needs assessment will also help the leadership

Table 5.3 School-Level Team Roles

Data mentor	Expertise in collecting, organizing, displaying, analyzing, and interpreting data; should be able to assist others in learning to access and use data
Content specialist	Ensures that implementers are trained in curricular materials Ensures fidelity of implementation occurs Clearly understands and communicates the connection between assessment data and instructional decisions
Facilitator	Supports staff through the change transition—supporting ongoing communication through the process Develops effective teaming across all collaborative teaming processes Facilitates communication within the leadership team and the staff
Staff liaison	Communicates not only with staff on leadership team but gains input from whole staff
Instructional leader or resource allocator	Site principal and other building administrators Supports the change process by emphasizing communication, building culture, gathering input, and creating order by providing routines and procedures for implementation Shares leadership responsibility with others on the leadership team Encourages and supports the development of leadership skills within the leadership team

Source: S. Kurns and D. Tilly, *Response to Intervention: Blueprints for Implementation—School Building Level.* Alexandria, VA.: National Association of State Directors of Special Education, 2008.

teams and teaching teams to determine which process steps have the greatest priority. Many states have developed their own needs assessment tools, many of which can be found at the National RTI Center site at http://state.rti4success.org/index.php.

The Tier Aligned RTI Readiness Tool in Appendix B provides a structure for the school site leadership team's use in determining the current level of implementation. This tool will help schools move ahead toward the courageous step of implementing RTI. The needs assessment process is best done in a facilitated manner, because the tool is less effective when teachers or teams go back to their classrooms to conduct the assessments independently. Since teachers may not be familiar with the tier concepts or curriculum mapping and collaborative processes, it is essential that leadership team members walk them through each section of the needs assessment.

Readiness Element: Teaming

The initial purpose of the readiness tool shown in Table 5.4 is to ensure that the infrastructure needed for effective team development is in place. The responses from each team level will help define the tiers of intervention and also reveal how consistent (or inconsistent) implementation is from site to site and from grade level to grade level.

Readiness Element: Schoolwide Data-Based Decision Making

A school cannot begin to build an RTI framework without data. Even the development of rationale and common goals and mission depend on data. Data systems must

Table 5.4 Readiness Element: Teaming

Readiness Elements	Implementation Level 1 (None)	Implementation Level 2 (Some or Beginning)	Implementation Level 3 (Most or Advanced)	Implementation Level 4 (All or Complete)	Comments
A district-level RTI implementation team has been developed					
A site-level RTI implementation team has been developed					
Grade-level or content area intervention teams have been developed					

be in place before any decisions regarding tiered interventions are made. Ideally the district will have determined which universal screening tools and/or progress-monitoring tools will be used at each grade level. (Data-based decision making is covered in Chapter Eight.) Understanding how to use the data to adjust instruction and determine how to best provide targeted interventions is just as important as effective data-monitoring tools and processes.

Schoolwide Data-Based Decision Making

- School or district has identified universal screening tools for behavior and academics to be utilized for all incoming students.
- School or district has identified progress-monitoring tools, and teachers are trained in how to use the tools.
- Teachers utilize benchmark assessments based on curriculum map.
- School or district has identified entry and exit criteria for tiered interventions based on data.

Once the readiness elements of teaming and data-based decision-making processes are established, teams can then assess the instructional practices and interventions provided at each of the tiers within the RTI structure by continuing to use the Tier Aligned RTI Readiness Tool in Appendix B.

Readiness Element: Tier I

There are numerous elements defining Tier I. Since Tier I is characterized by standards-aligned instruction, the first step in ensuring effective Tier I instruction is the identification of essential standards. The next step is the development of curriculum maps to identify when the standards should be taught and assessments to verify that students are learning the standards prior to statewide assessment. Teachers are involved in collaborative data analysis to ensure that Tier I instruction is effective.

Professional development ensures that all teachers are skilled in the curriculum materials and instructional strategies and practices that support the needs of English learners and students with disabilities through differentiated instructional practices that promote student engagement. Teachers work collaboratively with English language experts and special educators to identify and implement curricular accommodations and adaptations that provide access to the core materials and instruction to these special populations.

Behavioral expectations and practices are also addressed in the development of a schoolwide positive behavior plan that focuses on the development of desired behaviors, rather the suppression of undesirable behaviors. Staffs develop and agree to the schoolwide procedures and routines that support positive social development and appropriate behaviors. Teachers explicitly teach these behaviors and help students become responsible for their own behavior management.

Tier I Elements

- Essential standards for English language arts (ELA) and math have been identified.
- Curriculum maps have been developed that are aligned to the essential standards for the grade level in ELA and math.
- Curriculum maps are used to drive instructional pacing to ensure assessed standards are taught in ELA and math.
- Weekly planning reflects standards-aligned instruction identified by the curriculum map.
- Teachers have regularly scheduled collaboration time to meet as a grade level.
- Teachers use regularly scheduled collaboration time to plan weekly grade-level lessons in ELA and math.
- Teachers utilize data from curriculum-based measures to plan instruction.
- Teachers organize daily instruction to reflect high expectations through the use and display of daily agendas and learning goals and standards.
- All teachers are trained in the curriculum materials and standards for ELA and math at their grade levels.

- Teachers use the core curriculum materials to support the instruction of the grade-level content standards.
- Teachers have a thorough understanding and knowledge of the principles and strategies of differentiated instruction and student engagement.
- Teachers are trained in the appropriate instructional accommodations for students with disabilities and English learners in ELA and math core.
- Teachers have been involved in the development of a schoolwide positive behavior plan.
- Teachers have directly taught positive behavioral expectations to students.

The needs assessment process directed at Tier I will help school sites determine the current level of their core instruction. NASDSE recommends that the action-planning process begin by identifying the strengths and weaknesses of the core or Tier I program. Questions that guide the leadership team through the process of identifying the effectiveness of the core can be found in Appendix A. Further description of the specific actions within these action steps can be found at the NASDSE site in the school building-level Blueprint Document available for free at www.nasdse.org.

When you are determining where to begin in the RTI process, the effective implementation of a good core or benchmark program has the potential to have the greatest academic and behavioral effect on the school. The systematic implementation of an effective core program, both academically and behaviorally, affects *all* students in a building and therefore has the greatest overall impact. Many schools prematurely implement interventions without addressing the core. Improving the core will reduce the number of students in need of intervention in the long run. Making decisions about implementation starting points is difficult; however, it is not advisable to ignore the long-reaching, long-range positive influences of a strong standards-aligned core program in order to rush into the development of intensive interventions.

Readiness Element: Tier II

Tier II elements focus on data-based decision making about the provision of supplemental instruction for those students who are not responding to Tier I instruction. Teachers recognize the benefit of frequent progress monitoring to determine the effectiveness of the supplemental instruction. Data analysis focuses on the response to the instructional intervention and on how the instruction may be adapted or changed to produce a more positive result.

The data analysis also identifies those students with common needs, so that grade-level teams can assemble homogeneous groups in order to provide skills-based targeted instruction. Teachers determine who among the grade-level team provides the skill-based instruction to each group. In their grade-level teams, the teachers plan and implement the intervention, frequently monitoring progress and reviewing data in order to change grouping and instruction as needed. The team members make sure to include students with disabilities and English learners in these supplemental instructional groups and provide excellent skill-based instruction.

As grade-level teams, teachers problem-solve behavioral issues and determine the Tier II or supplemental intervention at the classroom level. They monitor the effectiveness of classroom-level behavioral interventions and may refer a student to schoolwide secondary interventions that provide additional monitoring and support of behavior.

Tier II Elements

- Teachers use ongoing progress-monitoring data and curriculum-based measures to determine student need for supplemental instruction.
- Teachers analyze data as a grade level to determine which students need additional supplemental intervention.
- Teachers use data to determine homogenous groupings for supplemental targeted instruction.
- As a grade level, teachers identify what instructional supplemental interventions will be provided to target students.
- As a grade level, teachers identify which teachers will provide the supplemental instruction in their grade levels.
- The schedule allows for flexible scheduling to allow grade-level teams to provide supplemental instruction.
- As a grade-level team, teachers will determine how to provide supplemental instruction to students within their grade levels.
- Students with disabilities and English learners are included in these supplemental instruction groups.
- Teachers monitor student behavior using data to make decisions about supplemental behavior support.
- Teachers implement supplemental behavior support strategies for students in need of extra support.
- Teachers use data to make decisions about continuing or discontinuing supplemental instructional support.

The grade-level team provides the bulk of Tier II supplemental instruction, but additional human resources are necessary to provide small-group instruction. Tier II instruction may be supported by a reading specialist, a Title I teacher, a special educator, an intervention teacher, a speech and language specialist, and others who support the grade-level team in providing targeted skill-based instruction. Tier II interventions for behavior may involve a school counselor, psychologist, or behavior specialist in the development of a behavior monitoring plan, but it is usually the general education staff that provides the adult mentoring in Tier II behavioral interventions.

Readiness Element: Tier III

Nonresponders are the focus of Tier III interventions. These students have not responded to the targeted skills-based interventions provided in Tier II and have met the entry criteria for intensive intervention. Despite small-group instruction and increased intensity and time, the expected growth has not occurred, the student's subsequent skill development has not met the trajectory of his or her peers, and instead of closing, the skill gap has widened.

Intensive reading and math intervention programs are considered a standard treatment protocol for those students exhibiting skill delays of more than two years. Implementing these evidence-based instructional programs with fidelity usually requires greater investment of time and often smaller group sizes. Not all Tier III interventions are composed of programs, but many programs have been identified that help teams provide the targeted skill-based interventions that will accelerate students' skill development and close the skill gap.

Essential to any intensive intervention program or process is frequent progress monitoring. Whereas Tier I progress monitoring may occur only three times a year, Tier III progress monitoring may occur every day. It is the ongoing data that helps the instructor determine which strategies produce a positive result and how to best adjust instruction to ensure progress. The data generated during an intensive intervention process should also be used to determine when student exit from the intervention is appropriate.

Intensive intervention programs usually differ significantly from the core, therefore requiring program-specific training. Trying to implement a research-based program with fidelity without adequate training leads to less than favorable outcomes. Teachers become frustrated, the students don't make progress, and eventually the program is tossed out as "ineffective," resulting in a waste of money and precious student time! District-level leadership teams need to recognize that professional development for an intensive intervention is an ongoing process, and funding should be set aside for this important aspect of Tier III implementation.

> "Trying to implement a research-based program with fidelity but without adequate training leads to less than favorable outcomes. Teachers become frustrated, the students don't make progress, and eventually the program is tossed out as "ineffective," resulting in a waste of money and precious student time."

Students receiving Tier III behavioral interventions receive individualized attention that focuses on changing and replacing problem behaviors. The behavior intervention plan or behavior support plan is based on the individual student's needs and is developed by a team that includes the psychologist, the school counselor, and all the individuals who work with the student. For the plan to be effective, each and every individual involved with the student must be aware of the plan and how it is implemented. It is the role of all individuals involved to implement the plan and to monitor behavior as recommended by the plan. As counselors and psychologists work with the individual student, they need the behavioral data to determine the effectiveness of the intervention and to provide feedback to the student on his or her progress. Teachers need to understand this important role in the implementation of effective Tier III intensive behavioral interventions.

Tier III Elements

- The school has intensive interventions in place designed to address common and or frequent reading or math problems.
- Decisions on participation in intensive interventions are based on screening and progress-monitoring data.
- Frequent progress monitoring is utilized during the intensive intervention period.
- Entry and exit criteria have been established for students in need of intensive interventions.
- Teachers have been trained with fidelity in the implementation of the intervention program.
- Teachers frequently assess student progress during the intervention period to determine the effectiveness of the intervention.
- Teachers support students by implementing behavior intervention plans.
- Teachers work in collaboration and provide essential data to specialists while implementing intensive behavior supports.

Tier III interventions are often developed first because of the dramatic needs of students who are reading and performing math skills several years below grade level or who have severe behavioral problems. It is difficult to ignore such need while an effective Tier I or good core instructional practice is being developed. While it is a very complex task to develop multiple tiers at one time, some schools have moved ahead in providing intensive intervention in reading to a small group of the neediest students while they build their Tier I instruction.

This practice requires schoolwide screening to identify the students in the lowest 3 to 5 percent based on reading skill. Using existing human resources, such as a reading specialist, Title I teacher, or intervention teacher, the intensive intervention is applied in a triage manner. Some schools will determine which grade level has the most need and provide the intervention at that particular grade level, while others focus only on upper elementary because of the danger of ever-widening skill gaps as students get older. Some schools provide a small number of students with intervention across all grade levels if the schedule of the intervention provider allows it. While this model does not meet the needs of all identified students and should be temporary, those most in need do receive attention while the school builds its base program.

Developing Priorities for Action Planning

Once the different levels of leadership teams have completed the Tier Aligned RTI Readiness Tool, the site can determine what is already being implemented fully and which areas have only partial implementation. From this data they can begin to move forward in developing priorities for action. The action planning tools in Appendix C will help teams in this process. During the action planning phase, different sites will follow different courses, and that is why this book does not purport to provide the reader with a one-size-fits-all recipe or step-by-step directions for implementation. While the tool helps a school identify where they currently are, moving ahead into actual implementation steps requires a much more intensive look at what each implementation step requires.

The action planning steps will reflect the current level of each school's readiness for implementation. The following chapters describe step-by-step processes for the development of each process within the tiers. The implementation process steps listed next will be explicitly detailed to support leadership teams and school sites as they move forward from readiness through implementation.

Implementation Process Steps

    Evidence-based instructional practices (Chapter Six)

        Research-based instructional practices in language arts

        Research-based instructional practices in mathematics

        Research-based instructional practices for English learners

    Standards mapping and curriculum alignment (Chapter Seven)

        Standards and curriculum mapping

        Standards-aligned instructional practices

    Data-driven instruction (Chapter Eight)

        Data tools: screening and progress monitoring

        Data-informed instruction

    Positive behavior supports (Chapter Nine)

        Rethinking discipline and behavior supports

        Creating a positive school climate

    Collaboration (Chapter Ten)

        Collaborative teaming across disciplines

Wrapping Up the Main Points

Building an RTI framework takes time. The first steps in the process are recognizing the need for change, then working forward from that point to build the foundation for the change process. Building effective teams across many levels is the foundation for infrastructure building and sets the stage for needs assessment. After current practices have been thoroughly reviewed, action planning can begin; then, once priorities have been determined, the all-important first steps of RTI implementation can begin. The subsequent chapters and the tools they provide will help dedicated school and leadership teams bring the promise of RTI to fruition.

Evidence–Based Instructional Practices

An overarching goal of a multi-tiered response to intervention (RTI) prevention system is the use of evidence-based instructional practices across all tiers of intervention. While more research has been done on evidence-based practices in English language arts, more and more has been recently accomplished in math.[1] What are evidence-based practices, and why are they such an integral aspect of the RTI process? Evidence-based practices are defined as educational programs, practices, or strategies that have been demonstrated to be effective through scientific research. The importance of evidence-based practices is the premise that intensive early interventions will prevent academic failure. The Individuals with Disabilities Education Act (IDEA) of 2004 encourages the use of scientific, research-based interventions as part of the process to determine eligibility for special education. If schools and districts determine to use an RTI framework to make eligibility decisions, the instructional practice before referral must consist of evidence-based or research-based practices. The focus on instructional practices that are proven to be effective have not only benefited students undergoing a special education referral, but the instructional practices have had far-reaching positive effects on all students.

This chapter highlights evidence-based practices in mathematics, reading, and effective practices focused at English learners and students who struggle with reading and math. While this information only scratches the surface of the research that has been implemented in the past decade, it will, I hope, provide educators with the knowledge needed to identify and implement practices that mirror the ones described in this chapter. A comprehensive document published by the National Association of State Directors of Special Education (NASDSE) titled *Response to Intervention, Research for Practice* is available at no cost at www.nasdse.org.[2]

Evidence–Based Practices: Reading

Teaching all students to read by third grade should be the focus of instruction for all elementary schools. Accomplishing this requires a school-level system to identify at-risk students and a school-level system that will provide the targeted supplementary and intensive interventions that these students need. Evidence-based practices in reading recognize the fact that students come to school with diverse backgrounds. The diversity and the needs of many students may be too great for the classroom teacher to address alone. Some of these students will need three to four times as much instruction as their peers.[3] These students need specific targeted instruction that will accelerate their progress. There are many research-based programs that have been developed to meet this need. They can be found on the Web site of the Florida Center for Reading Research (FCRR; www.fcrr.org/FCRRReports); each program is identified as either a supplemental or comprehensive intervention program.[4]

The FCRR reports describe the components of each program and have identified whether they would serve students best as comprehensive or supplemental programs. They have identified comprehensive programs as those that provide intensive instruction in all five essential components of reading instruction:

1. Phonemic awareness
   - Teaching students to understand the sounds of language and to manipulate them in ways that are associated with improved reading
2. Phonics
   - Teaching students to link the sounds of language to print, to recognized words based on patterns, to decode multisyllabic words, and to generalize rules to new words

3. Fluency
   - Teaching students to read words accurately and with sufficient speed that comprehension is not impaired because of an undue focus on word reading
4. Vocabulary
   - Teaching students to recognize the meaning of words and to build an appreciation of new words and their meaning
5. Comprehension
   - Teaching students to monitor their understanding while reading, linking what they read to previous learning, and actively asking questions and responding while reading

Intervention in all elements is not appropriate for all students at all levels of development. Students who are already reading words do not need intervention that involves phonemic awareness, and students who do not know letters, sounds, and word reading would not require intervention around comprehension.[5] The programs identified are intended for students who are reading one or more years below grade level and are experiencing difficulty with a broad range of skills. The instruction provided through the recommended programs is intended to accelerate student growth in reading. These programs also include frequent assessments and progress monitoring in order to ensure progress in the instructional components.

For those students who are struggling in only a few of the essential components, a supplemental program would be more beneficial. These programs are intended for flexible use as part of differentiated instruction or an intervention that is focused in one or more of the specific areas. Most students can benefit from some additional instruction provided by these supplemental programs.

Evidence-based practices in reading have identified several common factors as effective interventions for students who are at risk for reading difficulties. These interventions should:

- Be offered as soon as the need is recognized in the areas of reading
- Increase the intensity of instruction through increased instructional time and reducing group size
- Provide direct and explicit systematic instruction in the areas identified as in need
- Provide instruction that provides error correction procedures and immediate feedback
- Be guided and adjusted based on data
- Be motivating, engaging, and scaffolded to provide success

Practices: Elementary

Increasing intensity is best provided in small groups, allowing instruction to be targeted with many opportunities to practice and receive feedback. When group sizes are too large, intervention is diluted and the intensity is lost. There are many different options for providing this increase in intensity, as mentioned in Chapter Two. The classroom teacher provides some of this small-group instruction during the regular language arts block. In addition, more intensity can be provided when another trained person supports the classroom teacher to work with some of the most at-risk students. This model can also be supported by grade-level teaming in which one or two teachers take smaller groups while the others have larger groups for this intervention time. Students who need greater intensity will receive additional small-group instruction outside of the language arts block in an even more intensive model. Evidence-based practices support continuity of supplementary instruction and common practices between the core instruction and supplementary interventions. Both teachers should use the same methodology to teach specific reading skills in order to avoid confusion on the part of the student. The instruction in the classroom and the intervention group should be complementary and mutually reinforcing.[6]

> "Increasing intensity is best provided in small groups, allowing instruction to be targeted with many opportunities to practice and receive feedback. When group sizes are too large, intervention is diluted and the intensity is lost."

For those second or third graders who are lagging more than a year behind in a broad range of the basic reading skills, an even more intensive model has proven effective in the research studies. Teachers of these students replace the English language arts block with a comprehensive intervention core program. These comprehensive programs, as mentioned in the FCRR report, are focused on acceleration toward grade-level standards. None of these programs is intended for remediation but rather for the acceleration of reading development.

Staffing these programs is always a concern, since effective reading intervention requires skillful teaching. While ideally the best of the best would be providing the intensive intervention instruction, this is not always possible. Evidence supports the use of trained paraprofessionals or less experienced teachers who have had sufficient professional development and a more scripted or structured program. Many of these programs are available and provide a useful "scaffold" to help less experienced teachers provide powerful instruction.[7] When the use of paraprofessional and less experienced staff is considered into the equation, site administrators will find it easier to identify staff already available in the school who can help with reading instruction.

The implications from the research conducted by the Center on Instruction on effective practices have identified these findings:

- Extensive interventions can be effective when provided by paraprofessionals and less experienced teachers when they receive appropriate training and the interventions are fairly structured.

- Studies that included follow-up assessments showed that gains made from early extensive intervention were maintained over time, at least to second grade.

- All of the effective early interventions examined in the study share the following essential elements:

    - Training in phonological awareness, decoding, and word study

    - Guided and independent reading of progressively more difficult texts

- Writing exercises
- Engaging students in practicing comprehension strategies while reading text
- Other elements related to success include group size (one-to-one, small group), daily or near-daily frequency, and early identification of need.[8]

Recognizing the evidence-based practices that constitute effective early literacy practices and interventions will help school sites and buildings in the development of their own evidence-based practices. The matrix in Appendix D will help the school administrators and leadership teams determine which evidence-based practices are in place and which need further attention.

Practices: Secondary

The Center on Instruction has developed *A Practice Brief on Effective Instruction for Adolescent Struggling Readers* to discuss the specific literacy needs and practices focused on adolescents who may not have had the benefit of evidence-based reading instruction in their elementary years.[9] While there has been much research on early literacy and the prevention of reading failure, little research has been done on meeting the needs of adolescents who struggle with reading. The authors of the brief emphasize the need for effective practices in literacy instruction for adolescents because reading failure at the secondary level has far-reaching and devastating implications. This fact alone requires that any school implementing an RTI framework focus resources on adolescent literacy as a top priority.

The most recent research on effective adolescent literacy practices focuses on the specific needs of students who have experienced reading failure and will need systematic explicit instruction to develop reading skills. The instructional recommendations made by Alison Boardman and her colleagues at the Center on Instruction include literacy instruction organized into five general categories:

1. Word study
2. Fluency
3. Vocabulary
4. Comprehension
5. Motivation[10]

Absent from this list is phonemic awareness and phonics. For most older readers, instruction in advanced word study or decoding of multisyllabic words is a better use of time than instruction in the more foundational reading skills such as decoding single syllable words.[11] Reading intervention programs at the secondary level should include instructional practices that address each of these areas. Supplemental intervention programs may focus on just one or two areas, while comprehensive intervention reading programs should encompass all of the critical areas for adolescent literacy.

Word Study and Fluency

Essential initial literacy skills identified by Boardman and her colleagues are word study and fluency practice.[12]

Word study skills teach students to analyze words by meaning and structure by teaching students to:

- Break words into syllable types
- Read multisyllabic words by breaking them into parts and then putting them back together
- Recognize which words are irregular and cannot be decoded phonetically
- Recognize and know the meaning of common prefixes, suffixes, inflectional endings, and root words to support decoding and comprehension

Fluency and accurate word reading have a positive effect on reading comprehension. Developing fluency skills is essential to achieving reading proficiency. Fluency instruction should include:

- Opportunities for repeated readings of known text
- Opportunities for reading unpracticed passages
- Programs to track student gains in fluency
- Frequent feedback to ensure accuracy
- Appropriate models of fluent reading
- Student monitoring of progress toward fluency goals

Vocabulary

Explicit vocabulary instruction is direct instruction on word meaning to promote the independent acquisition of vocabulary skills. Direct instruction on word meaning can include commonly used approaches:

- Using dictionaries and glossaries
- Using context clues to derive meaning
- Using graphic displays of the relationships among words and concepts such as semantic maps
- Developing "word consciousness," in order to understand the varied use of a word in different aspects of language[13]

Vocabulary instruction can be divided up into three effective research-based practices:[14]

1. Additive vocabulary instruction that focuses on teaching specific words that are broken into three tiers[15]

    - Tier I words: Words students likely know
    - Tier II words: Words that appear frequently in many contexts
    - Tier III words: Words that appear rarely in text and are very context specific

Beck and her colleagues suggest that intervention instruction around vocabulary should focus on Tier II words, as they occur with the most frequency across context and therefore have the most utility.

2. Generative vocabulary instruction teaching word-learning strategies

- Focuses on the relatedness of words and classes of words in which students identify the meaning of new words linked to existing knowledge of specific words or word parts

3. Academic vocabulary instruction addressing the word learning and word learning strategies in specific academic content areas

- Attends to the specific meaning of words in a specific context

These skills must be taught directly and in context. This type of vocabulary instruction can be supported with computer technology and online dictionaries, reference materials, and hyperlinks.[16]

Most comprehensive intervention reading programs identified by the FCRR have all aspects of direct vocabulary instruction practices as part of the program.

Comprehension

Knowing how to apply reading comprehension is essential for adolescent struggling readers. While many readers simply develop these strategies on their own, struggling readers need direct instruction in these evidence-based practices that will develop effective reading comprehension strategies.

Activating Prior Knowledge Activating prior knowledge requires students to connect what they already know to what they are learning. The specific strategies associated with this comprehension strategy are the following:

- Previewing headings and key concepts
- The use of guided notes to enforce connections that are made
- Revisit after reading to review, confirm, or refute predictions

Graphic Organizers Graphic organizers are visual representations that support the identification, organization, and memory of important ideas from the reading. Graphic organizers can be used:

- Before reading to introduce important information
- During reading to represent and discuss connections
- After reading to write summaries, to review, and make connections

Summarizing Summarizing while reading must provide scaffolds that support the demand for consolidating large amount of information into the most important elements. This difficult skill is best taught by:

- Summarizing small amounts of text such as paragraphs
- Frequent practice of summarization rules such as identifying topic sentences, deleting trivial or redundant information, and using graphic organizers to support important points

Self-Monitoring Self-monitoring teaches students to recognize when comprehension breaks down. These comprehension strategies include:

- Teaching students to recognize poor comprehension such as noting confusing words
- Recognizing the need to reread a passage or restate a passage to determine the meaning of confusing words

These evidence-based practices support comprehension skills across all content areas and should be considered as common practice in all classes in a building or school site.

Motivation

Adolescents who have experienced reading failure do not routinely enjoy reading. This lack of motivation further affects their comprehension and limits their ability to develop effective reading strategies. Guthrie and Humenick identified critical components for increasing adolescents' motivation to read.[17]

- Provide content goals for reading
  - Create a question or purpose for reading related to the content
- Support student autonomy
  - Allow students to choose what they read, the activities they are engaged in related to reading, and with whom they work
- Provide interesting texts
  - Choose texts on topics of student interest and background that appear pleasing and readable
- Increase social interactions among students related to reading
  - Allow collaboration by reading together, sharing information, and explaining and presenting knowledge

Creating curiosity around a concept will drive the student to read. Providing students with texts and facilitating interactions around reading will supply the necessary motivation to read.

Secondary Evidence-Based Processes

While intervention at the elementary level can often be provided in a more fluid manner, the rigidity of bell schedules makes the provision of supplementary and intensive interventions a challenge at the secondary level. Building a schedule that allows for both supplemental instructional time and intensive intervention time requires serious thought. Interventions need additional time, and making this time available will not just affect how classes are built but will also affect the number of credits a student will receive on the road to graduation. Providing additional instructional time for intervention always means that there will be a cost to the student in electives or even credits.

There is often much argument about the loss of electives that results from enrollment in an intensive reading intervention or supplemental intervention program. While elective classes are important, they are not as critical to lifelong success as learning to read. With academic achievement as the core of all decision making, educational decision makers will recognize that enrollment in an intensive evidence-based reading program has greater potential for far-reaching academic improvement than does participation in elective classes. While this is a hard line to follow, literacy skills in our world today are nonnegotiable.

> "While elective classes are important, they are not as critical to lifelong success as learning to read. With academic achievement as the core of all decision making, educational decision makers will recognize that enrollment in an intensive evidence-based reading program has greater potential for far-reaching academic improvement than does participation in elective classes."

While elementary students can move between classes or go to intervention for a specific amount of time, intervention at the secondary level almost always requires a second period of either language arts or math. These classes usually only earn elective credit and do not count for grade-level content credit. The structure of these supplemental instruction classes that focus only on one or two skills identified in the evidence-based practices is usually in addition to a core class. This scenario allows the student to earn credit for the core class, but the second class earns elective credit. The purpose of the second class, or "shadow class," is similar to the supplemental intervention provided at the elementary level, providing targeted skills-based instruction. This Tier II class is aligned with the instruction in the core, often allowing an opportunity for preteaching of skills or concepts and/or reteaching as needed.

Intensive intervention classes usually replace the core instruction. These Tier III classes provide instruction, using evidence-based comprehensive reading intervention programs. Intensive intervention programs require additional time and intensity, resulting in classes that take up to two periods of the day. Because these classes do not address the grade-level standards, students cannot receive grade-level credit for the intervention class. Most schools allow these classes to be taken for elective credit. When academic achievement is the bottom line for all students, district and school site decision makers need to determine how to meet the credit requirements of these students. Many districts implement summer school, Saturday school, and mandatory after-school programs in order to recover the lost credits.

Building effective evidence-based literacy practices into a school site can be a daunting task, but the payoff in providing students the gift of literacy is priceless.

Evidence-Based Practices: Mathematics

Recent research has identified several evidence-based practices in mathematics. While the longitudinal research on these strategies is not yet available, some correlations have been identified between early literacy and early math interventions.[18]

Effective research-based practices are still emerging, but from the research that has been completed thus far, certain practices can be identified to have positive effects in all tiers of a multi-tiered intervention model. The greatest challenge is defining specific practices that correspond to each level of intervention. The current research in the field of mathematics is just beginning, with little research done on intensive math intervention programs. Therefore, currently, few replacement core programs have been identified.

In *A Summary of Nine Key Studies: Multi-Tier Interventions and Response to Intervention for Students Struggling in Mathematics*, the authors provide an overview of several evidence-based practices that focused on Tier II interventions.[19] One of the studies, completed by Fuchs, Fuchs, and Hollenbeck, identified the effectiveness of providing the classroom instruction and a tutoring program as a Tier II intervention.[20] Similar to evidence-based practices in language arts, evidence-based practices in math offer increased intensity by including additional direct instruction time and small-group instruction. Tier I in math emphasizes primary prevention, which is comprised of evidence-based instruction to all students. These evidence-based practices include the foundation of mathematics education, which is the ability to problem-solve using mathematical concepts and strategies. In order to problem-solve, students must have both a clear knowledge and understanding of number sense *and* the ability to apply basic skills. Effective core mathematics instruction for all students should include:

- A balanced approach between number sense and problem-solving strategies
- Opportunities to engage in meaningful practice
- Mathematically enriched environments that provide
  - Visible math vocabulary words
  - References and explanations of abstract symbols
  - The use of manipulatives and tools
  - The use of calculators
- Explicit instruction to teach procedural knowledge
- Questioning strategies that require explanations and descriptions
- Progress monitoring
- Problem-solving practice

Evidence-based practices identified by the Center on Instruction for students who have math difficulties and are identified as at risk for math failure focused on the following instructional practices:

- Explicit instruction on a regular basis
- Teaching that includes multiple instructional examples
- Scaffolded instruction that encourages verbalizing decisions and solutions to math problems
- Use of visual representations to represent information in math problems
- Use of multiple strategies to solve problems
- Taking unknown information and applying it to a known skill or strategy
- Peer-assisted learning[21]

These types of strategies benefit all learners and can be implemented as an effective Tier I instructional practice.

Tier II focuses or the supplemental instruction that provides differentiation instruction tailored to students' needs.[22] Some effective supplemental instructional strategies identified in the compilation of evidence-based practices by Rebecca Newman-Gonchar and her colleagues identified primary strategies that support classroom core instruction.[23] These strategies focus both on skills-based practices and problem-solving practices. Strategies identified in a study by Bryant and colleagues included scripted lessons that included modeling, think-alouds, guided practice, pacing, and error correction in tutoring sessions that were fifteen minutes long and lasted eighteen weeks. The outcomes proved statistically significant improvements for second graders.[24] This research makes it clear that supplemental math instruction is not about worksheet packets that focus solely on math facts. Four studies focused on math fluency and used a short intervention applied classwide to solve math facts with modeling, think-alouds, guided practice, pacing, and error correction.

The research shows that supplemental instruction should include fluency-building and skill-building practice as well as problem-solving boosters that focus on concrete representation, visual and pictorial representations, and abstract numeric representations. The Concrete, Representational, Abstract (CRA) instructional strategy builds on each previous part to promote student learning and retention so that the student can gain a greater conceptual knowledge.[25] Five of the nine studies on Tier II interventions focused on strategy instruction processes for solving word problems and using the CRA approach to problem solving:

Concrete. The teacher models instruction with concrete materials. The use of manipulatives is commonly part of this stage.

Representational. The teacher transforms the concrete model to a semi-concrete model that typically includes drawings or some other visual representation.

Abstract. The teacher models math concepts at the symbolic level, using only numbers, notation, and mathematical symbols to represent the numeric concept.

While there is not much national research available on evidence-based mathematics core programs that could be categorized as Tier III, the National Council of Teachers of Mathematics (NCTM) has developed guidelines for identifying or developing intervention programs. They have identified the following necessary components:

- Diagnostic assessments that identify student strengths and weaknesses and fundamental mathematical knowledge
- Instructional activities that are linked to the diagnostic assessment and to the classroom instruction
- Postassessment and ongoing monitoring of progress that address the effectiveness of the program and student progress
- Organizational structure that supports the fidelity of program implementation
- Research that supports the implementation practices

The process steps for developing and evaluation math intervention programs can be found at www.nctm.org/resources/content.

Tier III interventions require greater intensity than supplemental Tier II instruction and are usually characterized by additional time and much smaller groups or intensive one-on-one instruction.

Evidence-Based Practices: English Language Learners in Language Arts

Effective instruction for English language learners (ELLs) provides access to the core curriculum and, at the same time, intentionally develops students' English language proficiency. Special features of high-quality instruction for English learners include explicitly teaching the academic language required to successfully complete assignments while strengthening the student's background knowledge, promoting oral interaction and extended academic talk, and reviewing vocabulary and content concepts to provide repetition of key ideas and their associated language.[26] Evidence-based practices that support the needs of English learners in an RTI framework include effective differentiated instruction in Tier I, using whole-group and small-group formats while utilizing strategies that make the content comprehensible by having clear learning objectives and using a variety of techniques, including visual materials, sufficient opportunity for repetition, and practice of new learning.[27] Tier II interventions include supplemental instruction in addition to the core that supports literacy and/ or English language development. Tier III interventions may include a replacement core that is research based and has been developed to meet the needs of English learners. The RTI framework does not differ significantly for English learners. Decisions about placement should be based on screening, and Tier III problem-solving teams should include an educator who is knowledgeable about second language acquisition and effective practices for English learners. The evidence-based practices identified to meet the needs of English learners focus on early intervention and explicit systematic vocabulary instruction with intentional planning that promotes structured academic talk.[28]

Instructional practices around literacy development for English learners has been clouded by the misperception that English learners' academic difficulties are often related to language acquisition and that giving them more time to acquire language will eventually improve their reading skills. This misperception has kept many English learners from receiving the early intervention they so desperately needed. Research indicates that the five core areas of instruction to promote reading development in native English speakers—phonemic awareness, phonic, fluency, vocabulary, and comprehension—also apply to reading instruction for ELLs.[29] Research-based interventions for English learners identified by the Center on Instruction reflect the need to strengthen and refine current practices in order to meet the needs of ELLs who are experiencing academic difficulties.

David Francis and his colleagues at the Center on Instruction English Learner Strand identified the steps following as recommendations for academic interventions for English learners.[30]

1. **Provide early, explicit, and intensive instruction in phonological aware-ness and phonics in order to build decoding skills.** The research points out that being an ELL does not necessarily result in difficulty in acquiring word-reading skills. Most ELLs develop word-reading skills at the same pace as their peers. With this in mind, ELLs who are struggling with phonological awareness or problems with sound symbol correspondences should be identified for intervention. These students need explicit intensive instruction and/or intervention in phonemic and phonological awareness and phonics. Beginning-level English learners benefit from phonological awareness instruc-tion and activities. Delaying intervention until children have increased proficiency in English is not advised.

Similar to instruction practices within a multi-tiered framework for native speakers, instructional practices for ELLs should include classwide instruction for all learners and their classmates with small-group instruction to focus specifically on targeted skill areas. In addition to the tiers of instructional intervention, English learners need sufficient opportunities to develop English language proficiency. This usually occurs outside of the English language arts core and/or supplemental instruction.

2. **Increase opportunities for ELLs to develop sophisticated vocabulary knowl-edge.** Vocabulary instruction is essential in any evidence-based language arts instruction for both native speakers and English learners. Students need twelve to fourteen exposures to a word and its meaning across multiple contexts in order for the student to gain a deep understanding of the word.[31] Identifying Tier II words and teaching these explicitly are essential evidence-based vocabulary instructional practices for ELLs.

3. **Equip ELLs with strategies and knowledge to comprehend and analyze challenging narrative and expository text.** Comprehension instruction for ELLs and their classmates does not differ from the evidence-based practices described earlier for reading. The practices that promote active reading and engagement with text that fosters comprehension include:

- Teaching students to make predictions while they are reading
- Teaching students to monitor their understanding and ask questions during reading
- Teaching students to summarize what they have read after reading

These evidence-based practices to improve comprehension for both ELLs and native speakers provide support in navigating the text and provide opportunities for structured academic talk. These processes encourage language production and academic language development while working on comprehension skills and increasing exposure to print.[32]

4. **Focus ELLs' reading fluency on vocabulary and increased exposure to print.** Most fluency- and comprehension-related weaknesses are remediated through phonics instruction. The assumption is that improving fluency through phonics instruction will improve comprehension, but increased phonics instruction does not always improve comprehension for English learners. Reading with fluency includes automaticity in word recognition skills and also includes knowledge of word meaning and the ability to hold the information in working memory while constructing meaning from the text. English learners often have strong word recognition skills but are hampered by underdeveloped vocabularies and lack of exposure to print. When they encounter words in the text that they do not understand, reading rate and fluency decrease. This lack of fluency has a

significant impact on comprehension. Focusing on vocabulary and deep word knowledge is more effective in improving comprehension than phonics-based instruction.

5. Provide opportunities for ELLs to engage in structured academic talk. Language development depends heavily on the ability to practice and produce language in academic settings. In research conducted by Arreaga-Mayer and Perdomo-Rivera, English learners spent only 4 percent of the day in oral language engagement, and only 2 percent of the day engaging in "academic talk."[33] English learners learn English by having opportunities to speak English. Teachers must provide opportunities for repeated exposure to the use of words in a structured context and numerous opportunities for feedback.

6. Structure independent reading so that it is purposeful and provides a good reader-text match. Independent reading is a practice that promotes vocabulary development and increased exposure to print and improves fluency and comprehension, but unless it is carefully planned, it can be an ineffective practice for English learners. In order for independent reading to be effective, Francis and his colleagues suggest there must be a careful match between the reader's ability and the text, and there must be explicit goals associated with the reading activity with a connection between the reading activity and the content.[34] Too often the text is too difficult to promote vocabulary or comprehension development and lacks any purpose when not connected to the curriculum.

These evidence-based practices identified by the Center on Instruction apply in Tier I, Tier II, and Tier III interventions for classwide, small-group, and individual instruction.[35] These practices are intended to serve as a starting point for educators who are making decisions about effective instruction and intervention for English learners that will enable ELLs to reach the same academic standards as their native-speaking peers.

Evidence-Based Practices: English Language Learners in Mathematics Instruction

One of the most common misconceptions is that math is a universal language and that numbers and symbols are culture free. However, ELLs struggle significantly with mathematics because of the role that academic language plays in the acquisition of math skills. Effective mathematics instruction for English learners is similar to effective instruction for native speakers. There is no present evidence to suggest that ELLs acquire mathematical knowledge and concepts differently than do English speakers.[36] Although no differences exist between the process of learning math, the practices must focus on bridging the language difficulties of ELLs. When planning evidence-based math strategies that will bridge those language difficulties, David Francis (2006) and his colleagues suggest the following considerations:

- English learners need early, explicit, and intensive instruction and intervention in basic math concepts and skills.
  - Without early intervention, inefficient and or deficient skills are likely to persist over time.

- Research has proven that early explicit instruction can prevent later difficulties for English learners.
  - Similar to practices with native speakers, two complementary instructional formats should be utilized: classwide instruction for all learners and supplemental instruction for students who struggle with specific skills.
- Academic language is as central to math as in other curricular areas, so intentional vocabulary instruction is an integral part of effective math instruction for ELLs.
  - The language of math must be explicitly taught as in other content areas.
  - Instruction should focus on reading, writing, and speaking mathematically.
- English learners need academic language support to understand and solve word problems.
  - Word problems are most frequently used to assess mathematical knowledge on assessments, so sentence frames should be provided as a scaffold.
  - Students need to be taught specific strategies to understand the elements of word problems and the function of the language as it relates to the math questions.[37]

Evidence-based math instructional practices for English learners must recognize the role that academic language plays in the comprehension of math concepts and the acquisition of math knowledge. As a result, math instructional practices both in whole-class instruction and in intervention must be explicit and must intentionally teach the academic vocabulary as well as the process for solving word problems. The ongoing practice of relying on word problems to assess math knowledge requires that ELLs receive instruction that will help them better understand and approach word problems in order to succeed in math.

While these evidence-based instructional practices exemplify how the standards can be best taught, the next chapter will go beyond the how of instruction to the crucial step of identifying which elements in the standards alignment and curriculum mapping process will best ensure targeted instruction.

Wrapping Up the Main Points

An integral component of response to intervention is the implementation of evidence-based instructional practices. While the multi-tiered structures of intervention will look different at each site, decisions about instructional practice and interventions in Tier II and Tier III should be aligned to evidence-based practices in the core content areas. The practices described in this chapter provide the implementing site with the tools needed to recognize their own practices that currently are evidence based and to help them develop and implement further effective practices that take into consideration the needs of elementary and secondary students and English learners. The development of effective practices will require extensive professional development in the evidence-based practices discussed. Research has shown that practices that fail to result in positive outcomes for students must be replaced with the practices that have been proven effective. The practices described provide the knowledge base essential to this crucial instruction.

Standards Mapping and Curriculum Alignment

Effective teachers have a sound knowledge of the standards and the curriculum that they must teach. The identification of these essential learnings helps to create a road map that directly focuses instruction to meet the standards. A focus on standards is essential as teachers constantly grapple with the dilemma of how to effectively spend the currency of education, which is time.[1] In light of this, teachers need to consider how each and every activity associated with a specific lesson is moving students toward meeting the standard. They need to recognize that simply because the lesson is in the textbook is not a sufficient reason to teach it.

Schools that implement a response to intervention (RTI) structure will often find that the Tier Aligned RTI Readiness Tool in Appendix B identifies the need for a commonly paced, standards-aligned curriculum. This is what constitutes the good "first teaching" that is necessary in Tier I and provides the effective structures for accelerating to the standards in Tier II and Tier III. The commonly paced, standards-aligned curriculum no longer allows teachers to have a "private practice" behind their closed doors. The curriculum map or pacing guide, when built collaboratively, can become the greatest impetus for improved instruction and increased academic rigor that has the greatest impact on the majority of students. This practice and process take teachers from simply covering the curriculum to actively being involved in the identification of essential standards and the subsequent targeted instruction that meets these standards.

Welcoming the Standards

While the standards movement has been an integral part of education in some states for more than a decade, many states are still grappling with how to identify appropriate standards that will ensure that students have educational equity across the nation. While the Elementary and Secondary Education Act (ESEA) required all states to identify standards and create assessments that assess those standards, a great disparity still exists from state to state on the rigor and the content of these standards. The National Assessment of Educational Progress (NAEP) is an assessment given to students in fourth and eighth grades across the nation as a means to measure the temperature, so to speak, of the rigor and achievement of students across the nation. This measuring stick has revealed that while many states have a high percentage of students scoring proficient on their state assessments, those same students scored poorly on the NAEP. For some states a huge disparity exists between state-level assessment results and NAEP results.[2] These findings are pushing the surge of support for national academic standards. The National Governors Association Center (NGA Center) for Best Practices and the Council of Chief State School Officers (CCSSO) recently released national standards in the content areas that can be found at www.corestandards.org/Standards/index.htm. While states still have the opportunity to use their own standards for their assessments and federal accountability measures, the move toward national standards seems inevitable.

The equity in education obtained through common standards, even at the statewide level, has had a tremendous impact on students with disabilities and English language learners. Prior to state standards and standardized assessments, the textbook publisher often determined instruction at the classroom level. There was often no continuity between schools or even classrooms. For students with disabilities, who often had no textbooks, the curriculum was determined solely by the teacher and whatever he may have found in a cupboard or made himself. English language learners were often in the same boat, with the curriculum determined by the teacher and differing from classroom to classroom. For migrant students, and other populations that moved frequently, this lack of continuity was devastating.

Although to many educators, the standards movement seemed like the inception of "big brother" telling them what they could and could not teach, over time educators have come to appreciate and embrace the role of state standards in the instructional practices of their classrooms. They have realized that the standards only tell them the "what" to teach but not particularly the "how." Standards allow teachers to plan and collaboratively provide a safe navigational path to ensure that assessed skills are taught. The standards now provide a succinct road map for their instructional practice for the year.

> "Standards allow teachers to plan and collaboratively provide a safe navigational path to ensure that assessed skills are taught. The standards now provide a succinct road map for their instructional practice for the year."

The Process for Standards-Aligned Curriculum Mapping

Curriculum mapping is the process whereby teachers and site administrators step back and look at the big picture in relation to the curriculum that is taught. It must begin with the curriculum—the course of instruction that is aligned to the state standards. The number of standards in any core content area differs from state to state. Some states have identified numerous standards across all grade levels, making creating a map that ensures all standards are taught prior to assessment a daunting task. Finding a process to whittle down the full spectrum of the state standards is integral to the process of developing a map that will effectually allow teachers to teach what is assessed.

Many states have already identified the essential standards for their student population. While not identified as such, these essential standards are often found in state-level assessment blueprints. Each state education agency has on its Web site a section identified as "Standards and Accountability." It is at this site that the process begins. The blueprints identify the number of test questions from the state standards-aligned assessment, often identifying the weight of the standard that is assessed. If states do not have blueprints, they always have test release items that allow educators to see actual tests and to use them to evaluate which standards are assessed.

In states that have numerous standards, this important step allows teachers to focus instructional planning on the important skills that are assessed. It must be made clear at this juncture that this process is not advocating "teaching to the test," only that focusing on assessed standards is a starting point in the development of standards-aligned curriculum maps. There are many standards, such as reading fluency or oral language skill, that cannot be assessed on a state assessment but are equally important to include in the curriculum map. Determining which standards are essential at a grade level or in a content area may be done at the district or site level. The teachers are the most familiar with the curriculum and are best equipped to make considerations on which standards should be emphasized and when they should be taught.

When making decisions on which standards are to be considered essential, teachers will need to look at the standard with several "lenses."[3] These include:

- Frequency and weight of the standard on statewide assessment
- Common standards-aligned instructional practices
- Vertical alignment across grade levels
- English language development considerations

Other buildings and districts will add additional factors or "lenses" when making decisions about essential standards.

Frequency and Weight of the Assessed Standard

Questions to be addressed include:

- Is the standard highly assessed?
- Are there numerous questions linked to this particular standard?
- Has the state itself given this standard a high "weight"?

If the answer is "Yes" to most of these questions, the teacher team should consider it as an option as an essential standard. This determination alone may not be a deciding factor, but the standard under discussion would represent a target. There will be skills that may be given a low weight by the state, but teachers recognize the need for instructional focus on that standard anyway.

Common Standards-Aligned Instructional Practices

If teachers have been teaching common lessons before, they should address the following questions about their teaching practices:

- Have lessons been aligned to the grade-level standards described?
- Have we developed common lessons around these particular standards?
- Have we assessed these common standards before?
- Have we developed effective instructional practices around these standards?

The teacher team should answer these questions as a second consideration or lens in their consideration of essential standards. Many teachers will find that many of them have been providing effective standards-aligned instruction in the past.

Vertical Alignment Across Grade Levels

Third, teachers should consider the grade-level overlap for the standard under consideration and answer the following questions:

- Is the standard addressed in the previous grade level?
- To what extent is the standard or skill addressed in the previous grade level?
- Do the skills identified in the previous grade level provide the foundational skills for the current grade level?
- When is the skill or standard under consideration addressed again?
- Are there gaps between skills in grade levels?

Examining the standard across a vertical slice of previous and future grade levels may help a team identify as essential a standard otherwise not identified when they realize that the current grade level is the only grade level that is assessing that particular skill.

The opportunity to work across grade levels creates a schoolwide accountability that permits the strong foundation for good standards-aligned Tier I instruction. This practice also eliminates the "blame game" as teachers cannot blame the grade level below for "not teaching" a standard when they realize from the blueprints or standards maps that the skill is not even addressed in that grade level's identified standards.

English Language Development Considerations

In addition, teachers of English language learners should determine which standards will positively affect students' English language development. It is only good practice to focus in English language arts on skills that will promote the language skills of English language learners.

Questions the teacher team should consider include:

- Does the identified standard address English language development standards?

- Is there a strong correlation between the English language arts (ELA) standard and the English development standard?

Each school district will use different lenses when making decisions about which standards are deemed essential. Schools with high English language learner populations will find that the weight of standards that support English language development will be regarded in a different manner than a district or school with a low ELL population. This is why it is impossible to establish essential standards that will fit all populations across the state. Each district has its own demographics, and what is deemed essential will depend on the population that the district serves.

Exhibit 7.1 provides an example of how the standards were evaluated through the different lenses in one district.

Pacing the Standards

There is more to pacing the standards than simply putting the essential standards on a calendar. Once the content area or grade-level team has identified the essential standards, the team determines how to pace these standards throughout the school year. This process begins with a cursory look at several questions that begin the planning process:

- What lessons will be necessary to help students master the skills identified in the standard?
- What materials in the curriculum provided will address the standard effectively?
- What are some assignments or projects that will help the students attain the skills needed to master these standards?
- How will we know that students have mastered the standard?
- What types of assessments will be used?
- What adaptations may be necessary to ensure that at-risk students, English language learners, and students with disabilities will also master the standard?

These questions will help guide the discussion and help the team determine the time it may take to teach the essential skills. Exhibit 7.2 is an example of this preliminary discussion with an indication of when the team thought it best to teach the standard.

The next task is to determine which month or when to teach that particular standard. In addition to looking at timelines for instruction, the teaching team will need to look at the scope and sequence chart to ensure that the choices about when to teach a standard or concept falls into correct sequence. For some content areas, the sequence is less important than others. In science and social studies, skills do not always build on each other, so the order of instruction is not always imperative. In language arts, the skills do not always build on each other, but the readability of the text usually becomes more difficult as the year progresses, making teaching out of sequence a little more difficult. In math, since skills usually build on each other, there may be even less flexibility, although when separate concepts such as geometry and algebra are taught as units, it may not be necessary to consider the sequence when making planning decisions.

Exhibit 7.1 Second-Grade ELA Essential Standards Identification

Standard	CST Weight	Grade Level Overlap	Identified in 0809	ELD Taskforce	Lennox Essential Standard
WA 1.1. Recognize and use knowledge of spelling patterns (e.g., diphthongs, special vowel spellings) when reading.	H	✓	✓		✓
WA 1.2. Apply knowledge of basic syllabication rules when reading (e.g., vowel-consonant-vowel = su/per; vowel-consonant/consonant-vowel = sup/per).	H	✓	✓	✓	✓
WA 1.3. Decode two-syllable nonsense words and regular multisyllable words.	H	✓	✓		✓
WA 1.4. Recognize common abbreviations (e.g., Jan., Sun., Mr., St.).	L				
WA 1.5. Identify and correctly use regular plurals (e.g., -s, -es, -ies) and irregular plurals (e.g., fly/flies, wife/wives).	H	✓	✓		✓
WA 1.6. Read aloud fluently and accurately and with appropriate intonation and expression.		✓	✓	✓	✓
WA 1.7. Understand and explain common antonyms and synonyms.	H	✓	✓	✓	✓
WA 1.8. Use knowledge of individual words in unknown compound words to predict their meaning.	H	✓	✓		✓
WA 1.9. Know the meaning of simple prefixes and suffixes (e.g., over-, un-, -ing, -ly).	H	✓	✓	✓	✓
WA 1.10. Identify simple multiple-meaning words.	H	✓	✓	✓	✓
RC 2.1. Use titles, tables of contents, and chapter headings to locate information in expository text.	L		✓		
RC 2.2. State the purpose in reading (i.e., tell what information is sought).					
RC 2.3. Use knowledge of the author's purpose(s) to comprehend informational text.	M	✓			
RC 2.4. Ask clarifying questions about essential textual elements of exposition (e.g., why, what if, how).	M	✓		✓	✓
RC 2.5. Restate facts and details in the text to clarify and organize ideas.	H	✓	✓	✓	✓
RC 2.6. Recognize cause-and-effect relationships in a text.	H	✓	✓	✓	✓
RC 2.7. Interpret information from diagrams, charts, and graphs.	M	✓	✓		✓
RC 2.8. Follow two-step written instructions.	M				
LR 3.1. Compare and contrast plots, settings, and characters presented by different authors.	L		✓	✓	✓
LR 3.2. Generate alternative endings to plots and identify the reason or reasons for, and the impact of, the alternatives.	L				
LR 3.3. Compare and contrast different versions of the same stories that reflect different cultures.	L			✓	
LR 3.4. Identify the use of rhythm, rhyme, and alliteration in poetry.	L				
WC 1.1. Distinguish between complete and incomplete sentences.	M		✓		
WC 1.2. Recognize and use the correct word order in written sentences.		✓			
WC 1.3. Identify and correctly use various parts of speech, including nouns and verbs, in writing and speaking.	M	✓	✓	✓	✓
WC 1.4. Use commas in the greeting and closure of a letter and with dates and items in a series.	M				
WC 1.5. Use quotation marks correctly.	M				
WC 1.6. Capitalize all proper nouns, words at the beginning of sentences and greetings, months and days of the week, and titles and initials of people.	M		✓	✓	✓
WC 1.7. Spell frequently used, irregular words correctly (e.g., was, were, says, said, who, what, why).	M	✓	✓		✓
WC 1.8. Spell basic short-vowel, long-vowel, r-controlled, and consonant-blend patterns correctly.	M	✓	✓		✓
WS 1.1. Group related ideas and maintain a consistent focus.	L				
WS 1.2. Create readable documents with legible handwriting.					
WS 1.3. Understand the purposes of various reference materials (e.g., dictionary, thesaurus, atlas).	L				
WS 1.4. Revise original drafts to improve sequence and provide more descriptive detail.	L				
WA 2.1a. Write brief narratives based on their experiences: a. Move through a logical sequence of events.			✓	✓	✓
WS 2.1b. Write brief narratives based on their experiences: b. Describe the setting, characters, objects, and events in detail.		✓	✓	✓	✓
WS 2.2. Revise original drafts to improve sequence and provide more descriptive detail.		✓			

Source: Erika Benadom, Lennox Elementary School District. Used with permission.

Exhibit 7.2 Sample History/Social Science Grid

Core Content Area: History Social Science
Grade Level: Seventh

Standard Area	Materials	Standard Area	Materials
7.1. Cause and Effect of Expansion of Roman Empire ❑ Contributions of Rome ❑ Establishment of Constantinople **Month: August**	Textbook, video, CD **Assignments** Roman Roads group report **Projects** Poster/map Constantinople **Assessments** Note-taking guide Fill in daily exit slips **Adaptations** Cloze	7.2. Analyze Structures of Islam ❑ Teaching of Muhammad ❑ Significance of Qu'ran ❑ Expansion of Muslim rule **Month: October**	Textbook, trade books, map **Assignments** Mini book: Compare and Contrast **Projects** PowerPoint projects **Assessments** Projects and Compare and Contrast paper **Adaptations** Compare and Contrast Diagrams with paragraphs
Standard Area 7.4. Structure of Sub-Saharan Civilizations ❑ Niger River ❑ Role of trans-Saharan caravans ❑ Growth of Arabic language **Month: September**	**Materials** **Assignments** **Projects** **Assessments** **Adaptations**	**Standard Area** 7.3. Structure of China ❑ Reunification of China and spread of Buddhism ❑ Historic influence of Chinese discoveries **Month: January**	**Materials** Textbook, trade books, map **Assignments** Mini book: Compare and Contrast **Projects** PowerPoint projects **Assessments** Projects and Compare and Contrast paper **Adaptations** Compare and Contrast Diagrams with paragraphs
Standard Area **Month:**	**Materials** **Assignments** **Projects** **Assessments** **Adaptations**	**Standard Area** **Month:**	**Materials** Textbook, trade books, map **Assignments** Mini book: Compare and Contrast **Projects** PowerPoint projects **Assessments** Projects and Compare and Contrast paper **Adaptations** Compare and Contrast Diagrams with paragraphs

Additionally, teachers with experience realize that some of the best teaching times are early fall, when there are not too many breaks in the instructional days, and late winter and early spring, just before testing season. They realize that less rigorous and time-consuming standards can usually addressed in November, December, and February, when continuity in instruction is affected by holidays. Some schools realize that students who live close to Mexico often do not return to the Unites States until after the first week of January, so they adjust their instruction to *not* introduce a heavyweight standard immediately following the winter break. Others realize that snow days, along with February holidays, make this month a better review month.

> " Teachers with experience realize that some of the best teaching times are early fall, when there are not too many breaks in the instructional days, and late winter and early spring, just before testing season. They realize that less rigorous and time-consuming standards can usually addressed in November, December, and February, when continuity in instruction is affected by holidays. "

The form of Exhibit 7.3 is an example of how a team placed the standards on the month-to-month grid, while considering holidays and vacations in their decision-making process.

Exhibit 7.3 Core Content Standards-Driven Pacing Guide

Core Content Area: History/Social Science	
August	**September**
Standards Addressed	**Standards Addressed**
7.1. Cause and Effect of Expansion of Roman Empire	**7.2. Analyze Structures of Islam**
Contributions of Rome; internal weakness: rise and fall	Teaching of Muhammad; connections to Judaism and Christianity
Law, art, architecture, engineering, philosophy	Significance of the Qu'ran and Sunnah; influence in Muslim daily life
Establishment of Constantinople; rise of Constantine	Expansion of Muslim rule, cultural blending within Muslim civilization
Eastern Orthodoxy and Roman Catholic Church; church-state relations	Contributions of Muslim scholars in science, geography, math, philosophy, medicine, art

The Essential Guide to RTI

The team recognized that the first few months of school were the best to address the heavyweight social science standards that would take up to four weeks to cover. They chose to teach a standard with less weight in January, realizing that they only had three weeks to address that particular standard.

Common assessment calendars also play into the development of curriculum maps. In Exhibit 7.4, the grade-level team had determined when the common assessments for particular standards fell and determined from the assessment pacing calendar when direct instruction on specific standards would occur.

Materials alone should not be the determining factor for creating a pacing guide or curriculum map. Most textbook companies provide a pacing guide, but these are created simply based on the number of standards or lessons in the book and the number of weeks in the school year. These pacing guides do not take into consideration the essential standards of each school or district. The pacing guides from the textbook publisher will include all standards and all lessons in the book. The purpose of pacing the essential standards is to remove the lessons that do not deeply address the standards. Textbook companies identify standards addressed in each lesson, but as teachers look at these lessons, they often find that there is only "an essence" of the standard addressed in the lesson. If this is the case, the lesson should be removed. The pacing of the essential standards should allow the removal of lessons that do not adequately address the standards, providing more instructional time for those lessons that are standards aligned. The process of removing lessons can be uncomfortable to some teachers, as they feel assured that the only way that all standards will be addressed is by teaching cover to cover. This liberating process allows teachers to see that many of the time-consuming lessons of the past are truly unnecessary. This process allows for an opportunity to remove some of these lessons from their plate.

Instructional Planning Based on the Curriculum Map

Deep discussions should surround the decisions involved in instructional planning. Once the essential standards have been identified and placed upon the map, the teaching team uses this framework to drive further instructional planning. This process begins with the assessment. From the assessment, the instructional planning should be developed or backward-mapped with the end in mind. If the assessment requires knowledge of the area of trapezoids, the team knows that the assignments, materials, projects, and activities must focus on how knowledge of trapezoids will be assessed. Effective teams look at the test release questions to determine just how the state assessment assesses this type of content. Many teachers are extremely surprised at how differently state assessments, compared to curriculum-based measures, ask questions. While it is important that students know how to perform on curriculum-based measures, they also need to know how to address the same content in a state standardized assessment.

English language arts teachers teach the writing process, but rarely do they have students choose the correct way to write the thesis statement for a paragraph already given. They do not practice recognizing the correct way to punctuate a sentence while using commas around an appositive. This kind of practice is essential to ensure that students who have mastered the standards in the curriculum can reflect this mastery on the state

Exhibit 7.4 Assessment Pacing Guide

Standards: First Grade Weeks of Instruction	1	2	3	4	5	6	7	8	9	10	11	12	13	14	15	16	17	18	19	20	21	22	23	24	25	26	27	28	29	30	31	32	33	34	35	36	37	38
1 WA 1.4. Distinguish initial, medial, and final sounds in single-syllable words.						X										X																						
2 WA 1.5. Distinguish long- and short-vowel sounds in orally stated single-syllable words (e.g., bit/bite).						X										X																						
3 WA 1.6. Create and state a series of rhyming words, including consonant blends.														X		X																						
4 WA 1.7. Add, delete, or change target sounds to change words (e.g., change cow to how, pan to an).														X		X																						
5 WA 1.8. Blend two to four phonemes into recognizable words (e.g., /c/a/t/= cat, /f/l/a/t/= flat).						X										X																						
6 WA 1.9. Segment single-syllable words into their components (e.g., cat =/c/a/t/; splat =/s/p/l/a/t/; rich =/r/i/c/h/).						X										X																						
7 WA 1.10. Generate the sounds from all the letters and letter patterns, including consonant blends and long- and short-vowel patterns (e.g., phonograms), and blend those sounds into recognizable words.																X															X							
8 WA 1.11. Read common, irregular sight words (e.g., the, have, said, come, give, of).										X															X		X											
9 WA 1.12. Use knowledge of vowel digraphs and r-controlled letter-sound associations to read words.																									X								X					
10 WA 1.14. Read inflectional forms (e.g., -s, -ed, -ing) and root words (e.g., look, looked, looking).																									X						X		X					
11 RC 2.2. Respond to who, what, when, where, and how questions.										X										X							X											
12 RC 2.7. Retell the central ideas of simple expository or narrative passages.										X										X							X											
13 LRA 3.1. Identify and describe the elements of plot, setting, and character(s) in a story, as well as the story's beginning, middle, and ending.										X										X							X											
14 WS 1.3. Print legibly and space letters, words, and sentences appropriately.																									X													
15 WC 1.2. Identify and correctly use singular and plural nouns.														X											X								X					
16 WC 1.3. Identify and correctly use contractions (e.g., isn't, aren't, can't, won't) and singular possessive pronouns (e.g., my/mine, his/her, hers, your/s) in writing and speaking.														X																	X		X					
17 WC 1.6. Use knowledge of the basic rules of punctuation and capitalization when writing.														X											X								X					
Each of the nine SBAs at the first-grade level assesses this number of standards:					4				4				5		7				3					6		4				3		5						

Assessment pacing guide identifies when assessment of essential standards occur.

Source: Erika Benadom, Lennox Elementary School District. Used with permission.

standardized assessment. This process is an important part of the instructional planning that takes place for each unit of study with the grade-level or content area team.

Assessing the Essential Standards: Following the Map

Determining how and when assessments will take place is an essential part of this curriculum-mapping process. In order for grade levels to support each other in Tier II instruction, they must be pacing together as closely as possible and must be giving common assessments. Again, determining how and when the standards will be assessed may be a district- or site-level decision. (The process of progress monitoring is covered in depth in Chapter Eight.).

As educators, we know that we cannot assess a standard once and then determine that the student has mastered that particular skill for a lifetime. Frequent revisiting and reteaching of certain target standards is essential for lifelong mastery. Teaching teams need to recognize as they create their maps that certain standards will need to reassessed and retaught. The curriculum map needs to reflect these reteaching periods as well as reassessment periods.

Exhibit 7.5 shows the essential standards of a grade-level team and the timeline for each assessment. The grid allows the team to determine when the initial direct instruction for each standard will occur as well as when reteaching of a previously assessed standard will apply.

The data from the curriculum-based common assessment or progress-monitoring data are then used in the grid shown in Figure 7.1 to help the team determine which instructional practices produced the greatest gain. These data-rich discussions allow teachers to collaboratively share how their instructional strategies supported student success. When weak areas are identified on the common assessments, the grade-level team collaboratively develops instructional plans that will support greater success through the reteaching process.

Fleshing Out the Instructional Plan

The curriculum map alone is not enough to create a common standards-aligned, good first instruction. It is a tool that greatly supports teachers in their instructional pacing and planning, but it must go further than "I am teaching long vowels in November." The curriculum map is one step in the development of standards-aligned instruction. Teachers need to collaboratively develop the instructional plans around the standards identified in the map. The grade-level or content area team must determine how and when the standard will be taught through further unit planning.

From the tools used to make initial decisions about the placement of units within the weeks of each month, the development of an instructional pacing guide can ensue. In Exhibit 7.6, the grade-level team identified the time period for instruction, the focus standard, the weeks of direct instruction and review, as well as test language they would focus on during this instruction. They also determined which materials would support the instruction of the standard and which specific instructional strategies would be used during instruction.

The instructional pacing guide can take on different forms; a number of options for planning are provided in Appendix E. Again, the point of the process is not to create a

Exhibit 7.5 Pacing Calendar for School Year

Week of Instruction

Standards: Fourth Grade	ELA	ELD
1	WA 1.1. Read narrative and expository text aloud with grade-appropriate fluency and accuracy and with appropriate pacing, intonation, and expression.	
2	WA 1.2. Apply knowledge of word origins, derivations, synonyms, antonyms, and idioms to determine the meaning of words and phrases.	EA.8. Recognize some common idioms (e.g., "scared silly") in discussions and reading.
3	WA 1.3. Use knowledge of root words to determine the meaning of unknown words within a passage.	A.2. Apply knowledge of common root words and affixes when they are attached to known vocabulary.
4	WA 1.6. Distinguish and interpret words with multiple meanings.	A.3. Recognize that some words have multiple meanings and apply this knowledge consistently.
5	RC 2.1. Identify structural patterns found in informational text (e.g., compare and contrast, cause and effect, sequential or chronological order, proposition and support) to strengthen comprehension.	A.11. Identify significant structural (organizational) patterns in text, such as compare and contrast, sequential and chronological order, and cause and effect.
6	RC 2.3. Make and confirm predictions about text by using prior knowledge and ideas presented in the text itself, including illustrations, titles, topic sentences, important words, and foreshadowing clues.	
7	RC 2.5. Compare and contrast information on the same topic after reading several passages or articles.	A.11. Identify significant structural (organizational) patterns in text, such as compare and contrast, sequential and chronological order, and cause and effect.
8	RC 2.6. Distinguish between cause and effect and between fact and opinion in expository text.	A.12. Distinguish fact from opinion and inference and cause from effect in text.
9	RC 2.7. Follow multiple-step instructions in a basic technical manual (e.g., how to use computer commands or video games).	I.13. Understand and follow some multiple-step directions for classroom-related activities.
10	LRA 3.2. Identify the main events of the plot, their causes, and the influence of each event on future actions.	
11	LRA 3.3. Use knowledge of the situation and setting and of a character's traits and motivations to determine the causes for that character's actions.	
12	LRA 3.1. Define figurative language (e.g., simile, metaphor, hyperbole, personification) and identify its use in literary works.	EA.17 Identify and describe figurative language (e.g., similes, metaphors, and personification).
13	WS 1.2. Create multiple-paragraph compositions: (a) Provide an introductory paragraph; (b) Establish and support a central idea with a topic sentence at or near the beginning of the first paragraph; (c) Include supporting paragraphs with simple facts, details, and explanations; (d) Conclude with a paragraph that summarizes the points; (e) Use correct indention.	ELD Essential Writing Standards to be identified in 09–10.
14	WS 1.10. Edit and revise selected drafts to improve coherence and progression by adding, deleting, consolidating, and rearranging text.	
15	WC 11. Use simple and compound sentences in writing and speaking.	

Calendar months shown: August–Agosto 2009, September–Septiembre 2009, October–Octubre 2009, November–Noviembre 2009, December–Diciembre 2009, January–Enero 2010, February–Febrero 2010, March–Marzo 2010, April–Abril 2010.

Source: Erika Benadom, Lennox Elementary School District. Used with permission.

2nd Grade Progress Monitoring — Watkins

Standard	WK 6	WK 12	WK 17	WK 24	WK 29
WA 1.1: Recognize and use knowledge and spelling patterns (e.g., diphthongs, special vowel spellings) when reading.			65%		
WA 1.2: Apply knowledge of basic syllabication rules when reading (e.g., vowel-consonant-vowel = su/per; vowel-consonant/consonant-vowel = supe/per).	82%		84%		
WA 1.3: Decode two-syllable nonsense words and regular multi-syllable words.			72%		
WA 1.5: Identify and correctly use regular plurals (e.g., -s, -es, -ies) and irregular plurals (e.g., fly/flies, wife/wives).		74%	70%		
WA 1.6: Read aloud fluently and accurately with appropriate intonation and expression.					
WA 1.7: Understand and explain common antonyms and synonyms.	52%				
WA 1.8: Use knowledge of individual words in unknown compound words to predict their meaning.	15%		48%		
WA 1.9: Know the meaning of simple prefixes and suffixes (e.g., over-, -ing, -ly).			65%		
WA 1.10: Identify simple multiple-meaning words.			68%		
RC 2.4: Ask clarifying questions about essential textual elements of exposition (e.g., why, what if, how).					
RC 2.5: Restate facts and details in the text to clarify and organize ideas.		67%			
RC 2.6: Recognize cause-and-effect relationshiops in a text.					
LRA 3.1: Compare and contrast plots, settings, and characters presented by different authors.					
WC 1.1: Distinguish between complete and incomplete sentences.	65%				
WC 1.3: Identify and correctly use various parts of speech, including nouns and verbs, in writing and speaking.		76%			
WC 1.4: Use commas in the greeting and closure of a letter and with dates and items in a series.					
WC 1.5: Use quotation marks correctly.					
WC 1.6: Capitalize all proper nouns, words at the beginning of sentences and greetings, months and days of the week, and titles and initials of people.		72%			
WC 1.7: Spell frequently used, irregular words correctly (e.g., was, were, says, said, who, what, why).	74%	70%			
WC 1.8: Spell basic short-vowel, long-vowel, r-controlled, and consonant-blend patterns correctly.		69%	72%		

Figure 7.1 Second-Grade Progress Monitoring Data Form

Source: Erika Benadom, Lennox School District. Used with permission.

Exhibit 7.6 Instructional Pacing Guide

Time Period	Standards	Weeks of Direct Instruction (D)/Review (R)	CST Testing Language	Materials	Instructional Strategies
Aug. 24–Oct. 2 (6 weeks):	• WA 1.2. Identify and interpret figurative language and words with multiple meanings.	D: 2, 3, 4, 5	• Meaning of. . . . • Which word can best be used to replace . . . . • Underlined phrase suggests	• Dictionary • Novels • Poems • Measuring Up pp. 9–23 • Measuring Up ELL pp. 4, 6, 12 • Spectrum p. 8 • Holt Voc. Dev. pp. 46, 188, 202, 207, 233, 322	• Bubble Maps • Cloze Method • PRS Clickers • Fan-N-Pick
	• WA 1.4. Monitor expository text for unknown words or words with novel meanings by using word, sentence, and paragraph clues to determine meaning.	D: 4, 5	• Meaning of. . . .	• SS Materials • Magazines • Holt Voc. Dev. pp. 16, 41, 110, 166, 307, 372	• Cloze Method • Rally Coach • Showdown
	• LRA 3.2. Analyze the effect of the qualities of the character (e.g., courage or cowardice, ambition or laziness) on the plot and the resolution of the conflict.	D: 3, 4	• No test release questions	• Holt "Eleven," "The Bracelet," "Ta-Na-E-Ka" • Measuring Up pp. 110–119 • Measuring Up ELL p. 32 • Spectrum pp. 22–32	• Flow Maps • Multi-Flow Maps • Bubble Map w/ Text Support • Fan-N-Pick • Showdown

Source: Lennox Middle School 6.

product that looks a certain way but rather that discussion and intentional instructional planning occur around the essential standards. The purpose of unit planning is not to add another burden to teachers but to streamline planning so that, collaboratively, teachers can work smarter and not harder on instruction that is pointedly standards aligned.

The curriculum map doesn't tell us the exact time that a standard will be taught; it gives the order in which the standards should be taught. We as educators recognize that some lessons will take longer than originally planned or that some concepts will need reteaching. Extra time should be built into the pacing process to allow for these detours.

The Collaborative Planning Process

Curriculum planning around the standards emphasizes the standard and not particularly the textbook or materials. This significantly changes the way teachers teach and allows access to the curriculum to students who struggle with reading, for example, or English learners and students with disabilities. Textbook-focused instruction creates roadblocks to the content by requiring students to gain the content primarily through reading of the text. The collaborative planning process that includes special education teachers and instructors of English learners allows this process to encompass student needs proactively rather than reactively.

The Curriculum Planning Process

The team proactively identified adaptations to the instruction, assignments, and assessments that would support the needs of diverse learners in a proactive manner.

The process involved guided discussion around the following topics:

Standard Area(s)

This is the standard identified from the essential standard.

Date and Month

The date and month are determined by several factors, including the common assessment calendar, the school calendar, the scope and sequence of the particular standard within the continuum of skills, the breadth of the standard and what it entails.

Timeline

The timeline is determined by many factors. The breadth of the standard, the lessons involved, and whether it is being taught the first time or is a review of a previously taught standard will determine the timeline.

Essential Learning Topics

The essential learning topics break the standard down into its skill areas. Each standard may address several skill areas. These subskills comprise the essential learning topics.

Content Vocabulary

The content vocabulary words are the words specific to the unit of study. These words are important to know and understand and must be directly taught, but they are not particularly high-use words, and therefore an inordinate amount of time is not needed to ensure that students can use these words in a variety of contexts.

Academic Vocabulary

Academic vocabulary words are related to the content and are usually high-utility words whose meanings cross content areas and may be found in a variety of contexts. These words, sometimes referred to as "Tier II words," have a high frequency and are found across a variety of domains.[4] These words have a powerful impact on verbal functioning and are essential to the development of academic language for English learners. These are the words that require greater direct instruction.

The instructional planning process is enhanced when strategy specialists are part of the planning discussion. When strategy experts such as special educators, English language development specialists, or intervention teachers are part of the instructional unit planning process around one standard, the instructional plane will be developed with these special needs in mind. The instructional planning process includes:

Materials

- When planning teams realize that textbooks are not the best way to access the content, they frequently identify electronic and visual media to enhance the content instruction. Materials should always include visual media such as maps, pictures, PowerPoint presentations, visuals on SmartBoards, videos from YouTube and TeacherTube, and other online resources.

Assignments

- The development of assignments should take into consideration the needs of students who may not have strong writing skills. Both English learners and students with disabilities struggle with "showing what they know" through writing. Providing opportunities for cooperative projects, visuals such as maps, posters, oral reports, and other multimedia options allows these students to display their skills in nontext formats.

Projects

- Projects are an ideal opportunity for students to work collaboratively on a common assignment and allow students to create products that do not always focus on writing as the result.

Assessments

- Assessment should occur in every class every day. This is how students show that they have met the objective for the day. Unfortunately, many teachers recognize assessment only as a test that is given at the end of the week. The ongoing assessment, such as exit slips, answers on white boards, and warm-up questions, allow learners to immediately show what they know and allow the teacher to recognize if reteaching is necessary. These formative, ongoing assessments or checks for understanding are an essential part of an effective classroom.

- Summative assessments do not need to be tests either. If the summative assessment is based on the standard of understanding the significance of the Roman roads, the assessment does not have to be a test. The summative assessment can constitute an oral report, a poster presentation, or a visual display such as a PowerPoint presentation or other visual media. A culminating project can serve as a summative assessment rather than a test.

Strategies

- Common strategy instruction across a grade level is critical. As students work with different teachers within the instructional tiers, common instructional strategies allow them to adapt more quickly to new teachers and their instructional practices. As teachers implement different strategies and monitor their effectiveness, they can determine which strategies worked best for the entire class and for particular students in helping them learn the standard.

Adaptations

- The special educator and the English language development instructor are assets to any planning team. They bring with them the expertise on instructional adaptations that will meet the learning needs of students with disabilities as well as those who are learning English. These adaptations are a critical aspect of the instructional practices that allow all students "access to and progress in the core curriculum" as stated in special education law. The adaptations that support English learners include those that promote oral and written language development, which include sentence frames and structured talk activities.[5]

Exhibit 7.7 provides an example of an instructional unit plan that includes all the components described.

For truly effective use of the curriculum map, teaching teams that include specialists meet regularly to plan weekly or bi-weekly lessons based on the unit plans developed in the mapping process. This practice allows the special educators and English language development specialists to align any supplemental instruction in their programs to coincide with the instruction aligned to the standards. It allows any supplemental instruction to be cohesive in nature and to support both the standard on the map and the instructional goals of the special program. This also supports the proactive scaffolding of instruction in the core classes as the specialists are aware of the upcoming lessons and can provide materials, suggestions, and instructional strategies that will support the differentiation needed by these populations. The data review process involved in determining when reteach is necessary, when done collaboratively, will be richer for the presence of the strategy specialists like the special educators or Title I teachers.

Exhibit 7.7 Instructional Unit Plan

Standard Area 7.1: Cause and Effect of Expansion of Roman Empire

Month: September
Timeline: Four weeks

Essential Learning Topics

- Contributions of Rome
  - Law, art, architecture, engineering, philosophy
- Establishment of Constantinople
  - Eastern Orthodoxy and Roman Catholic Church
  - Church-state relations

Content Vocabulary

Ancient world
Archaeologist
Artifact
Civilizations
Trade routes
Commodities

Academic Vocabulary

Commerce
Commodity
Crossroads
Autonomy

Materials

Textbook, CD, DVD, Internet map resources, Graphic organizers

Assignments

Roman roads group report
Trade routes maps
Compare and Contrast paper

Projects

Poster or map of Constantinople
Booklet group work

Assessments

Formative: Note-taking guide, fill-ins
Exit slips
Warm-up questions

Summative

Oral, poster, or written: Contributions of Rome
Booklet: Law, architecture, engineering, or philosophy
Compare and Contrast (four paragraphs): Eastern Orthodoxy and Roman Catholic Church

Strategies

Note taking and summarizing, Venn diagram

Adaptations

Cloze notes
Venn diagram provided
Read Please downloaded on one computer
Text on CD
Sentence frames for reports

> For truly effective use of the curriculum map, teaching teams that include specialists meet regularly to plan weekly or bi-weekly lessons based on the unit plans developed in the mapping process. This practice allows the special educators and English language development specialists to align any supplemental instruction in their programs to coincide with the instruction aligned to the standards. It allows any supplemental instruction to be cohesive in nature and support both the standard on the map and the instructional goals of the special program.

When these specialists have the full-year curriculum map for the entire year for all the students that they work with, they can plan and pull from their arsenal of tools to support the instruction within the core. Special educators can share their wealth of knowledge and their resources by providing general education colleagues with tools that not only provide scaffolds for the special education student but for many of the general education students as well. (This regularly scheduled collaboration time for instruction planning is discussed in greater depth in Chapter Ten.) It is critical that school teams recognize that curriculum mapping is not just a general education function and is most efficient and effective on the outcomes for student achievement when other experts are involved.

While the curriculum map and essential standards create the road map for instruction, the effectiveness of this targeted instruction cannot be measured without data. The next chapter takes an in-depth look at the role of data to drive the instruction that makes RTI such an effective process.

Wrapping Up the Main Points

Key points to remember when developing curriculum maps are that it is best to have teachers involved in the development of the curriculum map and pacing plan. It provides the perfect opportunity to truly recognize which standards are assessed to determine which are truly essential. The process has been defined as "empowering" by many school teams that have undergone the identification of essential standards process and the collaborative development of the curriculum map. Teachers no longer need be at the mercy of textbook publishers; when the standards define the curriculum and the instruction is planned collaboratively, the instruction becomes meaningful and purposeful. The curriculum map then becomes the effective framework and roadmap that ensures that assessed standards are taught in a focused and thoughtful manner.

Data-Driven Instruction

Data-driven decision making is a foundational change in current educational practice. It is doubtful that many school leaders are making "ignorance-based" decisions[1] about their schools, since the Elementary and Secondary Education Act (ESEA) has made "data" the catchphrase of education today. But despite how frequently these words roll off the tongue of both policymakers and teachers, they are very weighty and incredibly important words in the implementation of a response to intervention (RTI) framework. It is data that make the response to intervention process such a catalyst of change. Without data to reveal a response or lack of response, current practice would be no different than the past. It is the data that allow us as educators and decision makers to realize whether our efforts have been in vain or have been effective. The data tell us point blank if what we are doing is working or not! Without data, we would be doing the same things we've always done, yet expecting a different result. It is data that have made the RTI framework such an effective catalyst for change.

Data Overload

What does it mean to use data to drive instruction? How are data best used to inform teachers for instructional practices? What data are best used to inform instruction at the student level? What data are used to determine the best instructional interventions options, and how do we use data to identify those students who need help? How as a school do we use data to identify students with behavioral needs? How much data do I need? What are these data saying? Figure 8.1 reflects the confusion that exists around data today.

The need for data in an RTI framework has been established, but the questions persist on what data are needed and how to best use this data. A proliferation of data

Figure 8.1 Organizing the Data

exists, but without guidance on how to best use it, Frederick Hess warns educators that they can quickly move from the "old stupid" of being resistant to performance measures to the "new stupid" of using this proliferation of data in half-baked ways.[2] Schools must be careful to ensure that they are not relying on a few simple data points to make sweeping changes in educational practices and structures. This chapter is intended to help leadership teams and data coaches identify the different levels of data in order to make informed decisions that promote academic achievement within an RTI framework.

It's Not Just About Grouping

Using data to determine specific student needs is one of the many purposes of data within the RTI framework. At its simplest level, data can be used to group students with common skill deficits into homogenous groups. While data within an RTI framework have numerous purposes, this question almost always rises to the forefront of discussion: "Well, aren't you using data to track kids?" This valid question should be addressed up front, since many resistors to data-driven instruction try to use it to disparage the use of data in instructional practice. The answer is unequivocally "No!" It is because of data-based decision making that the former practice of "tracking" no longer exists. Due to ongoing progress monitoring data, a student's progress is tracked, allowing educators to know when an instructional approach or an intervention is effective. Instead of tracking students, the data now allow us to track progress. The data allow us to know when instructional practices are working and when they are not. The data clearly signal when a child is ready to move out of this homogenous group because they are no longer in need of instruction on a particular skill. This is how data have changed remediation. That is how students no longer carry a tracking label of "Blue Birds" or "Red Birds" for their entire educational careers. This label used to be a life sentence, but now with data, the tracking label can be frequently changed!

Effective Data-Based Decision Making: The Process

Many books have been written on effective data-based decision-making processes. This book will not purport to have found the most effective model or program. Rather, this chapter outlines the essentials of an effective program defines the different types of data (Table 8.1), and then provides an overview of the different types of progress-monitoring tools available to schools and districts. This is not an exhaustive list, but it provides RTI leadership teams and data coaches with a place to start in determining what the data-based decision-making process should look like at their school site.

Table 8.1 The Assessment Glossary

Universal Screening	Universal screeners are assessments used to target students who struggle to learn when provided a scientific, evidence-based general education.[3] Universal screening is typically conducted three times per school year, in the fall, winter, and spring. Universal screening measures consist of brief assessments focused on target skills (e.g., phonological awareness).[4]
Progress Monitoring	Progress monitoring involves individual, classwide, or schoolwide assessment that is used to demonstrate student/class rate of improvement in curriculum and to identify whose growth is inadequate. Progress monitoring aids teachers in determining when instructional adjustments may be necessary. This type of assessment can be used to sample skills in the yearlong curriculum or monitor progress on a specific skill. The schedule of assessment may vary depending on the students' needs and can occur as frequently as twice weekly to once monthly.[5]
Benchmark Assessments	Benchmark assessments are a means of assessing student progress toward reaching success on the standards. The purpose of benchmark assessments is to use the data derived from the assessment to adjust instruction to meet the standard.[6]
Formative Assessments	Formative assessments are ongoing assessments or checks for understanding that occur during the learning. These are usually interactive and are used primarily to form or alter the ongoing instructional process.[7]
Summative Assessments	Summative assessments occur at the end of the learning, such as unit tests or projects.[8]
Curriculum-Based Assessments	Curriculum-based assessments are assessments that mirror instructional materials and procedures related to the curriculum, resulting in an ongoing process of monitoring progress in the curriculum and guiding adjustments in instruction.[9]
Standards-Based Assessments	Standards-based assessments consist of assessments that have been developed to measure the achievement of individual students in attaining the standards that have been established by the district or state.[10]

The Continuum of Data Points

Understanding the different types of assessments is not enough to become a data-based decision maker. School teams must also understand the purposes of the different tests as they develop their own data-based decision-making models. Following are the primary data points, along with their frequency:

- State assessment data (annually)
- Periodic state assessment data (quarterly)
- Local education agency (LEA) data (quarterly)
- School site-level data: common assessments (quarterly or more frequently)
- School site screening data (annually at the start of school year)
- Ongoing progress monitoring:
    - Quarterly for students at the benchmark level
    - Monthly or more frequently for students at the strategic level
    - Weekly or more frequently for students at the intensive level
- Curriculum-based measures (ongoing)
- Behavioral data (ongoing)
- Attendance data (ongoing)
- Language proficiency assessments (annually)

State-Level Data

ESEA has required that each and every student in grades 3 through 11 be annually assessed in language arts and math, as well as in other content areas in specific grade spans. These data provide each child at least one data point to be considered when making instructional decisions. State assessment data are the first points that should be taken into consideration when determining instructional placement within a multi-tiered instructional model; these data points alone are *not* enough information on which to make educational decisions. This state assessment data are starting points, but they do not provide enough information to inform instruction.

According to Frederick Hess, state-level data are too coarse to offer more than a snapshot of a student and school performance.[11] Darryl Mellard also identifies the issue of the timeliness of state test data.[12] He refers to state assessments reports as an autopsy of last year's practice. Since the group of students has moved on to the next grade level and a new set of standards, the results can do very little to change the instruction that could affect the outcome. For this reason, some states have instituted quarterly state assessments that are voluntary, along with the shift by many districts to implement standards-aligned quarterly assessments. These ongoing assessments on progress toward standards proficiency and the subsequent data allow teachers to change and adjust instruction based on the data before the state accountability assessment occurs.

District or Local Education Agency Data

As the weight of accountability increases at the district or local education agency level, these entities have developed additional tools that monitor student progress. These periodically given standards-aligned benchmark assessments compare students to other students within the district and provide an additional data point for educational decision making. These benchmark assessments are one more progress-monitoring data point that teachers can use for instructional decision making.

School Site-Level Data

Although districts or LEAs have developed district-level benchmark assessments, many schools have developed common assessments that allow teachers at the classroom level to determine how well students are learning the standards that have already been taught. As mentioned in Chapter Seven, these common assessments are the foundation of the curriculum map. This level of data is invaluable to the classroom instructor in determining how best to move forward with the instruction of the next standard. It provides insight into the needs of particular students, but, more important, it provides an opportunity to recognize when reteaching or more practice is necessary. A class doing poorly on a common assessment does not indicate that the instruction should halt until the content is mastered, but it informs the teaching team that different instructional strategies will need to be employed and that additional time for reteaching will be needed. These assessments may occur quarterly or more frequently, depending on the unit of instruction and the standards within that unit. Common assessments should minimally occur on a quarterly basis.

> "Many schools have developed common assessments that allow teachers at the classroom level to determine how well students are learning the standards that have already been taught. These common assessments are the foundation of the curriculum map."

While the purpose of common assessments is to inform instruction, the data from these assessments provide insight into the needs of particular students. In my experience, students who struggle with a common assessment on a particular standard or skill when their peers do not creates a red flag to the teaching team that this student may be in need of additional intervention. This data point alone is not enough to determine an intervention placement, but it is another good source of data when decision about intervention may be made after further assessment.

Screening Data

Much has been written about screening practices and all the variables that should go into the screening process. Some of the best information on screening tools can be found at the National Response to Intervention Center at www.rti4success.org.

There has been much confusion on exactly what screening is intended to do. Some of the controversy on screening and screening tools has focused on the fact that screeners are not always standards aligned and are skills focused. Those who want their screening tools to also measure student progress on particular standards will find that these tools will usually not meet that need. The purpose of screening tools is to identify the risk pool based on certain skills that are highly predictive of reading and math failure. The purpose of screening is not to diagnose but rather to identify those in need of further assessment and/or subsequent intervention and to determine whether additional investigation is warranted.

If a screening "red flags" a student as at risk, then further diagnostic assessments are conducted to determine the student's specific strengths and weaknesses and to further guide instruction. This screening and further diagnostic data are additional data points that should be used to determine which level of intervention the student will need.

Screenings are given periodically and may be similar to a type of measure that is used for ongoing progress monitoring throughout the year, although screening and progress monitoring do not have the same purpose. Screening tools that are frequently used can be administered quickly and are based on research that offers reliability for predicting reading and math failure. The screeners allow teachers to identify students who are struggling early on, so that preventative instruction can be applied. The true benefit of screening is to identify these at-risk students at an early age and prevent reading and math failure.

> "Screening and progress monitoring do not have the same purpose. Screening tools that are frequently used can be administered quickly and are based on research that offers reliability for predicting reading and math failure. The screeners allow teachers to identify students who are struggling early on, so that preventative instruction can be applied."

The timing of screenings can vary, but most schools do schoolwide screening three times a year to determine which students need additional diagnostic assessment and subsequently more intensive intervention. Some schools use the last progress-monitoring data, often given in late spring, as screening data for the fall of the following year. A beginning of school year screening of all students is best practice. All new incoming students must be screened upon entering school. Again, this alleviates the problems of having to wait until the student fails before realizing that additional instructional support was needed.

Progress Monitoring

Progress monitoring and benchmarking are often confused, since periodic checks provided by benchmark assessments could be considered a type of progress monitoring. The way to clarify the difference is to determine what information the data are providing.

Progress-monitoring data produce information about student academic levels and corresponding rates of improvement and thus are sensitive to student improvement. Benchmark assessments, as described earlier, are given quarterly and show a student or a group of students' progress on a specific standard rather than on a specific skill.

Progress monitoring is a data-based instructional decision-making tool. Effective progress monitoring involves the process of gathering baseline information, setting instructional goals, providing targeted instruction, and monitoring the student's progress toward these goals. The data from the student progress-monitoring assessments inform the teacher to adjust the goal upward or to modify instruction as needed.[13] Step-by-step processes for the development of progress-monitoring probes and the progress-monitoring process can be found in the IRIS Center's RTI Web modules on classroom assessment at www.iriscenter.com.

> " Progress monitoring is a data-based instructional decision-making tool. Effective progress monitoring involves the process of gathering baseline information, setting instructional goals, providing targeted instruction, and monitoring the student's progress toward these goals. The data from the student progress-monitoring assessments inform the teacher to adjust the goal upward or to modify instruction as needed. "

The level of intervention usually determines the frequency of the progress monitoring. Students who are in intensive intervention programs may have their progress monitored on a daily or weekly basis, while students in a strategic or less intensive intervention may only be monitored monthly. All students at the benchmark level may only take the progress-monitoring assessment three times a year to ensure that they have not developed any skills gaps while the year has progressed.

As mentioned previously, district-level benchmark assessments and grade-level common assessments, while not intended as screening tools, often produce data that help teams determine which students should be considered at risk and are in need of further evaluation to determine appropriate instructional interventions.

Ongoing Curriculum-Based Measures

When grade-level and content area teams collaborate around data in an effective manner, they use their curriculum-based measures; the unit tests, projects, assignments, and other formative assessment data to inform their instruction at the classroom and student levels. It is often these ongoing formative assessments that allow for the patterns of strengths and weaknesses to emerge in those students who may have disabilities. It is also an opportunity for teachers to collaborate around effective practices that help their students with disabilities and English learners to be more successful. While curriculum-based measures are not always considered scientifically "sound," they can serve as indicators of general reading and math skills. They won't measure all the skills, but they can provide snapshots of skills in a periodic manner. Curriculum-based measures allow teachers and teaching teams to determine progress on skills and standards within regular instructional practice.

Behavioral Data

There is usually concern when the subject of screening and progress monitoring of behavior is broached. How can a school staff screen all students for behavior? The Systematic Screening for Behavior Disorders (SSBD) has been in use since 1994, but many schools are reluctant to screen for behavior because of concerns about "stigmatizing" students and about the resources available to support identified youth.[14]

While some schools have used screening tools effectively for some time, most use data from their behavior monitoring system to identify students at risk for developing more serious behavior issues. It is the data monitoring that identifies the frequency of infraction that becomes that red flag that the student needs further support. The behavior data system that monitors classroom behaviors and school behaviors can be utilized as the screener. Unfortunately, this type of screening practice usually only identifies externalizing behaviors.

The frequency and type of behavioral issues determined from the data help the team determine which Tier II interventions would best provide the support the student needs. Once in a Tier II intervention, ongoing progress monitoring will occur on a regular basis. Students in a Check-In, Check-Out program have their behaviors monitored each period of the day, with a report to a responsible adult at the end of each school day. Students in Tier III behavioral interventions are monitored even more frequently, often in incremental periods of minutes throughout the school day, with checks in that occur frequently during each school day. The data from this ongoing progress monitoring are then used to help the student to identify patterns of behavioral difficulties and identify ways to avoid them. (Types of behavioral intervention are discussed in Chapter Nine.)

Attendance Data

When looking at all the variables in determining the best possible instruction or intervention for a student, it is essential to remember attendance data. This data point is often not brought up until the student is involved in the problem-solving process in Tier III, but it should be considered early on when making decisions about placement in intervention programs. Attendance data may reveal that a student who moves frequently or is a child of a migrant farm-working family may only have had partial years of school enrollment. This alone can explain why an achievement gap exists. The decisions about the intervention applied should be affected by the students' transiency and attendance. If it is known that the student routinely leaves the country for several months to allow the parents to work elsewhere, a more intensive intervention should be applied, even if the child may not have the cut scores that warrant that particular intensity. Also, low attendance must be taken into consideration when making decisions about specific learning disability eligibility. Low attendance must be a consideration when making decisions about a lack of achievement when compared to peers when the peers have had average attendance. A team cannot say that the lack of skills is due to a learning disability when it may in fact be a lack of instruction based on poor attendance. For this reason, the team must take attendance records into consideration when making decisions about the intensity of intervention and special education eligibility.

Language Proficiency Assessments

Language proficiency assessments must also be taken into consideration when making judgments about intervention instruction and placement. Students who are early English learners (ELs) may struggle with screening tools that depend too heavily on academic language or highly verbal instruction. When screening and progress-monitoring tools are considered, language proficiency must be part of the equation. Poor scores on these screening tools should not automatically qualify them for the most intensive intervention. The research on screening and intervention for English learners supports early screening and intervention even when language proficiency is at a beginning level (as discussed in Chapter Six). Language proficiency scores alone should not determine the level or intensity of instructional intervention. Language proficiency is a very important data point when making decisions about instruction and intervention; English language development and reading and math skills must be considered when determining appropriate instruction and intervention for ELs.

The Whole Picture

When making placement and instructional decisions around data, it is clear that no one data point alone can be reliably used for this purpose. A myriad of possibilities for data-based decision making is available for making these instructional decisions. School- or district-level RTI leadership teams and data coaches will need to work with staff and teaching teams to determine how the data can be used to inform instruction and target instruction to best meet the needs of students.

As the pendulum swings back and forth, many schools and districts now have numerous data points in place but don't know how to use them to make instructional decisions. Some have computerized programs that score the screening and progress monitoring tools but do not use the data to drive, change, or adjust instruction. We can see why some might cry, "Data, data everywhere. Too much to let us think!"[15] Having data is only half the equation. Knowing what to do with it and developing an action plan is the next step.

Action Planning for an RTI Framework

Once teams have become familiar with the data points available to them, they need to determine exactly which ones provide them with the information that they need. Classroom instructional-level data look different from data that are used to determine intervention. The data used to make intervention decisions must include a combination of data points for a standard treatment approach for intervention within the RTI framework. A more involved data process will be required once a student has moved into a problem-solving process.

Standard Treatment Approach

For schools that use a standard treatment approach for Tier II or Tier III interventions, the universal screening of all students becomes the first data point. The team needs to determine which screening tool will be used and who will do the screening. Will it be the classroom teacher, the intervention teacher, other school staff, or will a screening team be hired to complete the process? Many districts hire retired teachers and others from the community to do the initial screening and three progress-monitoring sweeps during the school year, reducing assessment time for classroom teachers and ultimately increasing instructional time.

Placement

Once the screenings have been completed, the schoolwide leadership team, in conjunction with the data coach, must determine the cut scores for the identification for further diagnostic assessment and placement in strategic and intensive intervention. These are often difficult decisions to make, as they are dependent on the number of staff resources available to meet the needs of students who fall below the cut score. As mentioned in Chapter Five, some schools may have the resources to provide strategic and/or intensive intervention to each child identified with a need, but other schools may have to choose only the bottom 3 to 5 percent as eligible to receive the most intensive intervention even when data show that many more than this are reading at more than two grade levels below. With the correct fidelity to these intervention programs, including the small group size recommended, students will exit these programs, allowing other students to access them in a timely manner.

Determining who receives large-group or benchmark instruction, small-group supplemental instruction, and even smaller intensive interventions is a whole-school process and should be communicated to all staff, students, and parents. A flow chart of the schoolwide RTI process is essential to helping parents and all partners involved understand the process. Students should be made aware that their intervention groups are not a result of their being in trouble or doing something wrong. Students must have a clear understanding of the purposes of their goals in the intervention program.

Exit Decisions

Once data-based decisions have been made about placement, decisions about exit must also be considered. Essential to exit decisions are effective student monitoring forms and practices. The staff needs to understand what the data are telling them and how to access the data. Parents need to understand their child's progress, and teachers need to determine the effectiveness of their instruction based on the data. The next step in the action plan is determining what type of data system to use to track screening and progress data.

The National Association of State Directors of Special Education has identified key features of an effective integrated data system that includes assessments as well as reporting systems.[16] They identify effective systems as those that assess skills embodied in the state standards and are sensitive to incremental growth over time. The assessments within these systems can be administered in short periods of time and can be administered repeatedly using multiple forms. These systems must have the ability to quickly and easily summarize these data in teacher- and parent-friendly displays. The information that these systems provide allows teachers to make comparisons across students, monitor individual student progress over time, and have direct relevance to the development of instructional strategies that address areas of need.

Progress-Monitoring and Screening Tools

There are numerous progress-monitoring and screening tools available for purchase or at no cost that include the characteristics described by NASDSE. The most commonly used tool for screening and progress monitoring for reading is the Dynamic Inventory of Basic Early Literacy Skills or DIBELS. This tool is popular because it is research based, is quick and easy to administer, and can be downloaded free from the University of Oregon Web site at http://dibels.uoregon.edu. This popular tool is also available for purchase from Sopris West Publishing and includes a variety of options, including software that allows scoring on typical handheld electronic devices such as PDAs and iPhones.

Other reading screening tools identified as evidence based at the National Center on RTI site are the following:

- Aimsweb
- DIBELS
- Discovery Education Predictive Assessment
- Istation Indicators of Progress
- PALS
- Predictive Assessment of Reading
- Scholastic
- STAR
- STEEP

Progress Monitoring Tools in Mathematics identified by the National Center on RTI include:

- Aimsweb
- DIBELS
- Curriculum Based Measures in Reading (CBM-R)
- Class Math

- Scholastic
- STAR
- STEEP
- Yearly Progress Pro

Curriculum-based measures can be used to screen students and monitor their progress. Grade-level teams can make these tools themselves. The IRIS Center has several online training modules that support teachers in the development of curriculum-based measures. These Web modules can be accessed at http://iriscenter.com. The Intervention Central Web site also contains numerous progress-monitoring tools that teams can download at no cost. These can be accessed at www.interventioncentral.net.

Some of the tools available at these sites include reading comprehension screeners and progress monitoring assessments using the maze fluency process. Maze fluency screening is a quick and effective process for measuring reading comprehension. The maze process allows the assessor to quickly recognize comprehension skills by having the student insert the correct word from word choices in the blank space in the passage. Students struggling with comprehension of the passage find it difficult to choose the correct word.

Exhibit 8.1 is an example of a maze fluency screener. Numerous passage fluency tools are available at the National Progress Monitoring site. These include letter sound fluency assessments (Exhibit 8.2), phoneme segmentation fluency (Exhibit 8.3), word identification fluency (Exhibit 8.4), and passage fluency (Exhibit 8.5).

Exhibit 8.1 Maze Fluency Assessment

SUMMER CAMP

Stuart had nice parents. They did not embarrass him in [glad/ front/ yellow] of his friends. His father did [not/ ant/ soft] yell at him during his baseball [center/ games/ lines], and his mother never kissed him [in/ tot/ put] front of his friends. He generally [liked/ flow/ jeep] his parents, except for the fact [shoe/ went/ that] they were sending him to summer [bus/ dump/ camp] this year.

Stuart did not want [to/ wit/ cow] go to summer camp. The thought [and/ be/ of] it made him picture himself hot [coat/ rest/ and] thirsty, hiking up a dusty trail. [Bit/ He/ Go] knew that summer camp food had [of/ to/ my] be bad news, too. Besides, summer [camp/ free/ dog] was for people with nothing else [fad/ to/ sew] do. He had plenty of things planned [for/ much/ very] his summer at home.

"Summer camp [will/ yes/ belt] be good for you," said Mother. "[Feel/ And/ Lot] I don't want to hear another [catch/ phone/ word] about it!" Stuart moped around the [beat/ opens/ house] until it was time to go. Mother [had/ with/ boy] packed his trunk full of clothes, [and/ sort/ time] she and Dad took Stuart to [real/ glob/ the] bus station. Stuart tried hard not [to/ sun/ we] cry when he hugged them goodbye. [Yet/ He/ Sat] ran onto the bus and buried [beam/ his/ neat] head in his hands. After a [while/ tall/ hate], he looked out the window.

Exhibit 8.2 Letter Sound Fluency Assessment

Score Sheet

Student's Name _____ ; Examiner's Initials _____

Teacher's Name _____ ; Date of Testing _____

School _____

Letter Sound Fluency Test

If child does not say anything after three seconds: do not say anything; point to next letter. If names incorrect letter: keep going. Draw a diagonal slash through any letters the student does *not* say the sound for or says the sound incorrectly. Circle the last item that child attempts. Stop at one minute. If finished before one minute: record time.

g l d i w n b t f f k a p m j v x h o z y c e q s u

_____ number of letters sounded correctly (in _____ seconds)

_____ adjusted score (if completed test in less than one minute)

Exhibit 8.3 Phoneme Segmentation Fluency

Short Form Directions

Make sure you have reviewed the long form of the directions in the Administration and Scoring Guide and have them available. Say these specific directions to the student:

Phoneme Segmentation Fluency

I am going to say a word. After I say it, you tell me all the sounds in the word. So, if I say, "sam," you would say/s//a//m/. Let's try one. (one second pause) Tell me the sounds in "mop."

CORRECT RESPONSE	INCORRECT RESPONSE
If student says, /m//o//p, you say,	If student gives any other response, you say,
Very good. The sounds in "mop" are/m//o//p/.	*The sounds in "mop" are/m//o/ /p/. Your turn. Tell me the sounds in "mop."*

OK. Here is your first word.

Exhibit 8.4 Word Identification Fluency

Student's Name _____;   Examiner's Initials _____

Student's Teacher _____;   Date _____

Score 1 for correct response, 0 for incorrect response.

that ____	school ____	brought ____
for ____	say ____	line ____
by ____	land ____	probably ____
her ____	enough ____	close ____
up ____	live ____	table ____
them ____	against ____	strong ____
has ____	city ____	past ____
than ____	knew ____	friends ____
now ____	state ____	rest ____
water ____	wanted ____	having ____
must ____	four ____	full ____
me ____	toward ____	instead ____
come ____	move ____	case ____
still ____	power ____	worked ____
found ____	feel ____	alone ____
here ____	given ____	street ____
large ____	eat ____	Total score = ____

Exhibit 8.5 Passage Fluency

It was raining outside, and there was nothing for Norman to do.	12
"I have the most boring life," he moaned, as he plopped down on the couch. Just	28
as he switched on the television, the power went out. Watching a blank television	42
was not something Norman wanted to do. He looked around at the four dismal	57
walls that kept him out of the rain.	64
"Now what am I going to do?"	71
"You could tidy up your room," his mom suggested, "or organize your closet.	84
Your closet is a disaster, Norman. I'm actually frightened of what you might find	99
in there. You haven't cleaned it in a decade."	107
There was nothing Norman could say after his mom had made up her mind. He was going . . .	122

Source: www.studentprogress.org.

Intervention Central also has examples of writing probes that teaching teams can use that provide a story starter or stem and provide rubrics for assessing total words written, correct word sequences, and words correctly spelled. The IRIS Center classroom assessment online training modules provide teachers with the step-by-step process on developing and monitoring spelling probes based on the grade-level spelling words. This training information is invaluable to teams that are in the process of developing their own progress-monitoring resources.

Initially most of the progress-monitoring tools focused on early literacy and reading skills, but more and more are now focusing on mathematics. ProEd, Aimsweb, and the others named previously mentioned now have screening and progress-monitoring tools that not only focus on math facts but also concepts and applications and pre-algebra readiness skills. Likewise, the IRIS module on classroom assessment can be accessed to help teachers develop their own math screening tools. Figure 8.2 and Exhibit 8.6 provide examples of some of the math screening tools available at the Intervention Central site or from the National Center on Student Progress Monitoring at www.studentprogress.org.

Behavioral progress monitoring forms can also be accessed at Intervention Central at no cost. The program on this site allows the teacher and student to identify the target behaviors and individualize the online form to include the student's personal information and behavioral goals for monitoring. Figure 8.3 is one example of the behavior monitoring tools available. The National Center on Student Progress Monitoring also provides some simple forms for teachers to use to collect frequency data on target behaviors. (Additional behavioral progress-monitoring forms are discussed in Chapter Nine.)

Sheet #2

Password: **AIR**

Name: _____   Date: _____

A	B	C	D	E
$8\overline{)24}$	$\begin{array}{r} 52852 \\ + \ 84708 \end{array}$	$\begin{array}{r} 8 \\ \times \ 0 \end{array}$	$4\overline{)72}$	$\begin{array}{r} 8285 \\ 4304 \\ + \quad 90 \end{array}$
F	**G**	**H**	**I**	**J**
$6\overline{)30}$	$\begin{array}{r} 35 \\ \times \ 74 \end{array}$	$\begin{array}{r} 4 \\ \times \ 5 \end{array}$	$\begin{array}{r} 7 \\ \times \ 9 \end{array}$	$\frac{2}{3} - \frac{1}{3} =$
K	**L**	**M**	**N**	**O**
$\begin{array}{r} 32 \\ \times \ 23 \end{array}$	$\begin{array}{r} 8 \\ \times \ 6 \end{array}$	$5\overline{)65}$	$6\overline{)30}$	$3\frac{4}{7} - 1 =$
P	**Q**	**R**	**S**	**T**
$\begin{array}{r} 107 \\ \times \quad 3 \end{array}$	$2\overline{)9}$	$\begin{array}{r} 416 \\ - \quad 44 \end{array}$	$\frac{5}{11} + \frac{3}{11} =$	$\begin{array}{r} 6 \\ \times \ 2 \end{array}$
U	**V**	**W**	**X**	**Y**
$4\frac{1}{2} + 6 =$	$\begin{array}{r} 1504 \\ - \ 1441 \end{array}$	$9\overline{)81}$	$\begin{array}{r} 130 \\ \times \quad 7 \end{array}$	$5\overline{)10}$

Figure 8.2 Curriculum-Based Measures: Math Computation

The Graph: An Essential Piece of Progress Monitoring

One cannot underestimate the power of the graph in communicating progress! Without graphic displays, the decision-making process is difficult. Looking at rows of numbers that represent scores can be effective but time consuming and does not provide the level of impact of a graph. In *The Nuts and Bolts of Progress Monitoring*, Hauerwas and Matthes

Exhibit 8.6 Curriculum-Based Measures: Concepts and Applications

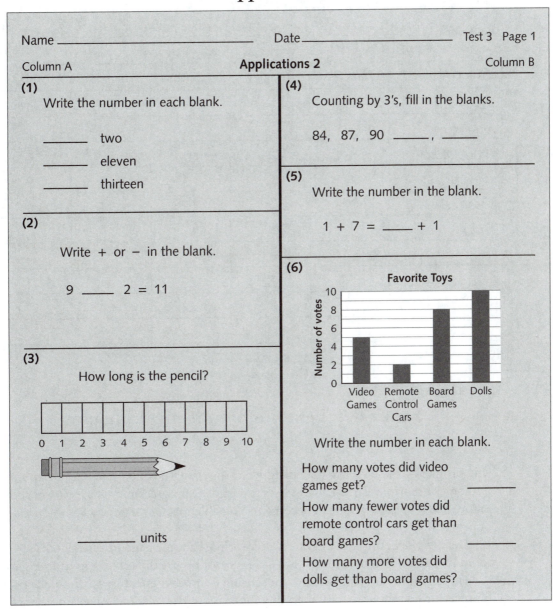

Name _____   Date _____   Test 3 Page 1

Column A   **Applications 2**   Column B

(1)

Write the number in each blank.

_____ two

_____ eleven

_____ thirteen

(2)

Write + or − in the blank.

9 _____ 2 = 11

(3)

How long is the pencil?

0 1 2 3 4 5 6 7 8 9 10

_____ units

(4)

Counting by 3's, fill in the blanks.

84, 87, 90 _____, _____

(5)

Write the number in the blank.

1 + 7 = _____ + 1

(6)

Favorite Toys

Number of votes

Video Games   Remote Control Cars   Board Games   Dolls

Write the number in each blank.

How many votes did video games get?   _____

How many fewer votes did remote control cars get than board games?   _____

How many more votes did dolls get than board games?   _____

provide numerous options for graphing.[17] They realize that schools and districts have different budgets, but they make it clear that no matter what the budget constraints may be, graphing is essential to the effective use of data.

For schools that have no budget for data systems, hand graphing is always an option. This is an effective option because it is something that students can do independently. Since they are plotting the data points, they can readily recognize when they are making improvements and when they are not. For upper-elementary and secondary students, a graph going in the wrong direction becomes the perfect teachable moment to discuss

Frequency Data Sheet

Student: _Mark S._ Week: _10/2—10/6_

Behavior: _Calling out without raising hand during small &_
large group instruction

Time/Activity	Monday	Tuesday	Wednsday	Thursday	Friday
Reading	||	|||	✕	✕	
Math	⑤|	⑤	||	||||	||
Social Studies		|||	✕			
Writing					|||	✕
Science	✕	✕					
Other	✕	✕	✕		|| group project
total =	9	12	3	8	5
					= 37

Figure 8.3 Behavior Monitoring Example

why progress was not being made and what the student thinks they can do to improve outcomes next time. Chris Lagares uses the student progress-monitoring form shown in Figure 8.4 to help his students become responsible for their learning based on graphing of progress.[18]

Deborah Pickering shares some simple forms that can be used at the school level, class-room level, or individual student level to monitor progress.[19] They appear in Figure 8.5.

Having students create rubrics for scoring is another effective way to make progress monitoring less about the numbers and more about the learning. An example appears as Figure 8.6.

How to develop graphs to monitor progress is also discussed at length in the IRIS Web module on classroom assessment. The process includes:

- Establishing a baseline that represents the median score
- Setting up the graph
- Setting the goal based on standards or other common measures
- Determining the aimline
- Measuring student progress

- Plotting student performance
- Connecting data points
- Analyzing performance based on the data points

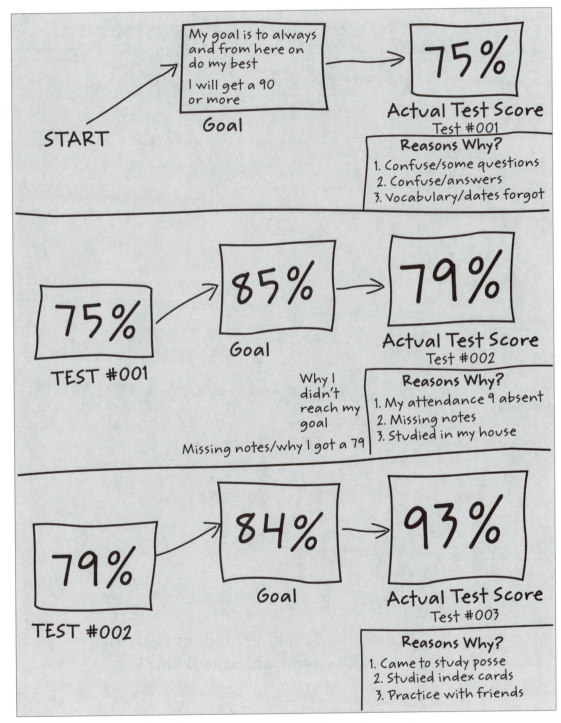

Figure 8.4 Student Self-Reflection on Progress

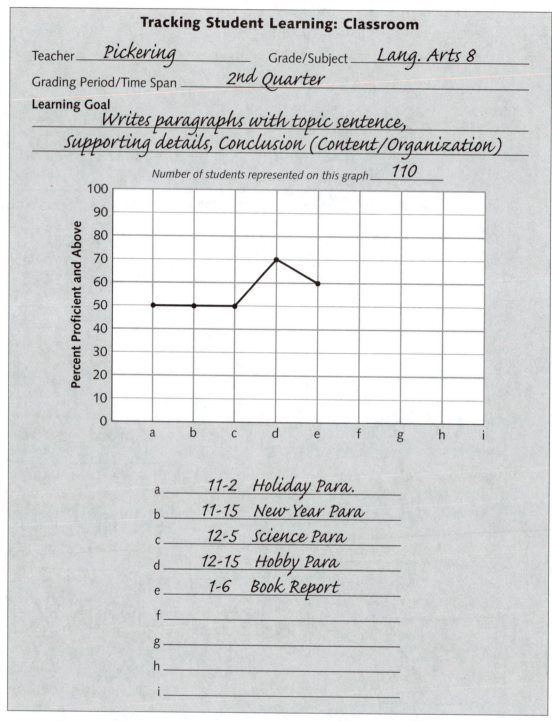

Tracking Student Learning: Classroom

Teacher _Pickering_   Grade/Subject _Lang. Arts 8_

Grading Period/Time Span _2nd Quarter_

Learning Goal

Writes paragraphs with topic sentence,
Supporting details, Conclusion (Content/Organization)

Number of students represented on this graph _110_

a _11-2   Holiday Para._

b _11-15   New Year Para_

c _12-5   Science Para_

d _12-15   Hobby Para_

e _1-6   Book Report_

f _____

g _____

h _____

i _____

Figure 8.5 Tracking Student Learning:
Classroom and School Level

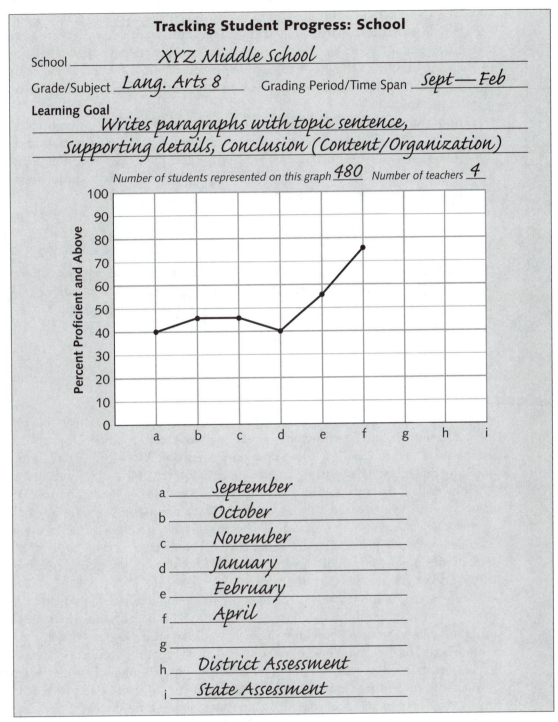

Tracking Student Progress: School

School _____ XYZ Middle School _____

Grade/Subject _Lang. Arts 8_   Grading Period/Time Span _Sept—Feb_

Learning Goal
_____ Writes paragraphs with topic sentence, _____
_____ Supporting details, Conclusion (Content/Organization) _____

Number of students represented on this graph _480_   Number of teachers _4_

a _____ September _____
b _____ October _____
c _____ November _____
d _____ January _____
e _____ February _____
f _____ April _____
g _____
h _____ District Assessment _____
i _____ State Assessment _____

Figure 8.5 (Continued)

The analysis of student performance will provide teachers with a two-pronged approach. One analysis, at the classroom level, will help teachers and teaching teams to determine how to adjust instruction. Analysis at the individual level will reveal whether the instruction and intervention being applied will allow the student's individual trendline to meet the aimline at some future point. If after four different assessments, the student's trendline is not improving, a reevaluation of the instruction and intervention is warranted.

The advantages of hand graphs are that it is free and easy to do and requires no technology. Another benefit is that students can do their own graphing, and it can be done immediately. There is no lag time, waiting for data to be delivered from the system. The downside is that it can be time consuming and involves paper that does not allow for long-term storage or electronic access.

> "The advantages of hand graphing are that it is free and easy to do and requires no technology. Another benefit is that students can do their own graphing, and it can be done immediately. There is no lag time, waiting for data to be delivered from the system."

If the drawbacks of hand graphing are too great, and there still is no funding for a data system, the free programs available online include Chart Dog, available at Intervention Central, and for those who have Microsoft Works, its Excel feature has graphing capability. The benefits include automatic electronic storage and easy usage. The downside is that these two programs require technology and time to enter the data. Students may not be able to enter the data themselves, leaving all the work to the teacher. A graphing program at Create a Graph is fairly simple to use and is intended for student use. The downside is that the storage of the data is only for a limited time, so ongoing updating of progress is difficult. This program can be found at http://nces.ed.gov/nceskids/createAgraph.

Web-based graphing systems are becoming more popular, but schools and districts have to provide the funding for these programs. The benefits are that Web-based programs can be accessed from anywhere. This allows students, teachers, and parents remote access to the data. These have built-in storage capability, and there are a variety of ways that the data can be configured to represent school-level results, class-level results, and individual student results that can focus on rate of improvement over time in relation to the goal. Based on the data, a trendline is drawn automatically and data points are plotted, either based on a teacher's manual input of data or on electronic transfer of data. An example of one of the Aimsweb graphs is found in Figure 8.7.

The major drawback of Web-based systems is the cost. The cost of such a system includes not only the per pupil cost but also the cost for the technology to support the assessments and data processing. With these programs, students are usually not as involved in doing their own data entry, making the data less reflective. The use of these programs also requires training and ongoing coaching for school personnel to ensure that the data are being used effectively.

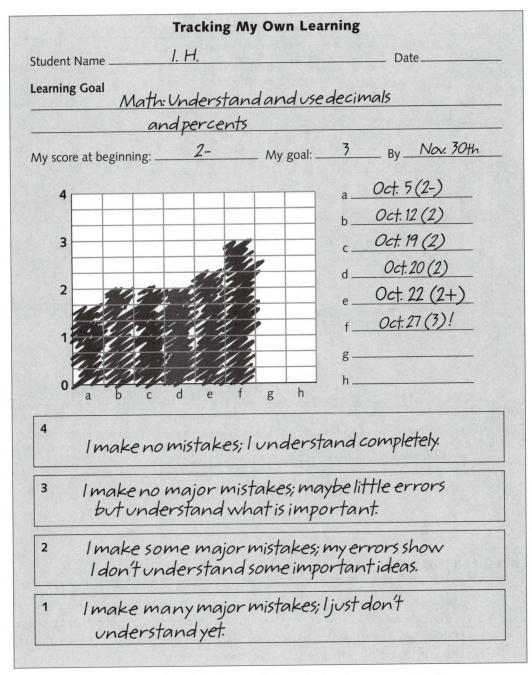

Tracking My Own Learning

Student Name _____ I. H. _____ Date _____

Learning Goal _Math: Understand and use decimals_
and percents

My score at beginning: _2-_   My goal: _3_ By _Nov. 30th_

a _Oct. 5 (2-)_
b _Oct. 12 (2)_
c _Oct. 19 (2)_
d _Oct. 20 (2)_
e _Oct. 22 (2+)_
f _Oct. 27 (3)!_
g _____
h _____

4	I make no mistakes; I understand completely.
3	I make no major mistakes; maybe little errors but understand what is important.
2	I make some major mistakes; my errors show I don't understand some important ideas.
1	I make many major mistakes; I just don't understand yet.

Figure 8.6 Tracking Student Learning: Student Level

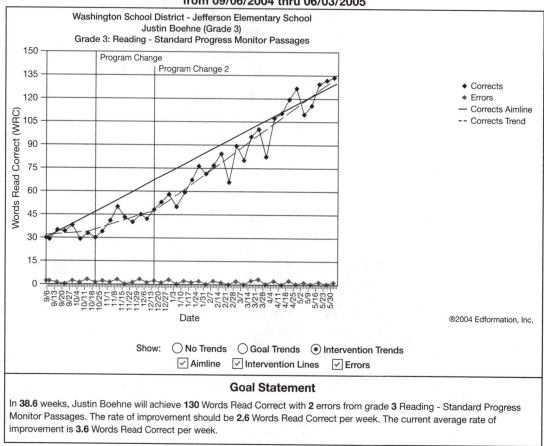

Figure 8.7 Aimsweb Graph

Data Capacity

Data can be overwhelming. It is not enough to have high-quality data; the capacity to manage and use the data is equally as important. Building data capacity means establishing data teams, designating data coaches, creating structured time in the school calendar for collaborative data analysis, building staff skills in data analysis and assessment literacy, and displaying data in formats that can be easily understood.[20] Using a data coach as a facilitator is the most effective strategy to ensure that data are used and that school staff learn how to make connections between data and their instruction.

Learning how to use data is an acquired skill. Teachers may need sensitive coaching and facilitation to guide data discussions so that they do not see this process as an evaluation of their teaching but rather a collaborative process that improves student achievement. It is facilitated problem solving that helps teachers recognize this bridge between data and instructional decision making.[21] The data use process needs to emphasize problem solving and not passing judgment. Discussions around instruction and instructional practices related to data allow teachers to focus on student performance and work with the common goal of helping students improve their skills and outcomes. When coaches are able to help teachers engage in these sometimes difficult yet essential discussions, instructional practices and academic achievement become truly data-driven.

Data play an integral role in the academic improvements determined by the RTI framework. The next chapter demonstrates the vital role of data in the development of schoolwide positive behavior supports.

Wrapping Up the Main Points

Data-driven decision making is here to stay. The past decade has brought educators to a place where they embrace data as an indispensable tool for school improvement.[22] Data have helped schools and teachers identify the priority areas of instructional improvement. Without data there would be no RTI structure, and instruction and instructional practices would be no different than they were during the past century. It is the effective use of data that has led teachers away from a "gut feeling" that what they were doing was working to a stark black-and-white reality that what they are doing instructionally is or is not working. There is no more guesswork involved. The data become the measuring stick that determines whether students are on track for learning the assessed standards and can efficiently and effectively identify those students who are at risk for instructional failure. While the term "data-driven" decision making may seem like another passing buzzword, no one can underestimate the power that data have in bringing about educational change.

9

Positive Behavior Supports

Ineffective responses to behavior remain prevalent in schools today. "Get tough" and "zero tolerance" policies have not proven effective, with the research data indicating that removal through suspension and expulsion has negative effects on student outcomes and the learning climate.[1] While practices such as clamping down on target behaviors and increasing monitoring may create a false sense of security, these actions in fact trigger and reinforce antisocial behavior and further break down the student-adult relationship by putting all the blame on the student. These practices presume that all students are inherently "bad" and will learn appropriate behavior through contingent aversive consequences. These usually include removal from class, which is hard to justify in a day when opportunity to learn is an issue and closing the achievement gap is the goal.

But how does a school keep itself safe and create a learning environment in which all students can learn? Schoolwide positive behavior supports (SWPBS) are an alternative that has been proven to improve overall school climate. It is based on the assumption that when educators across the school actively teach, expect, and acknowledge appropriate behaviors, the proportion of students with serious behavior problems diminishes and the school's overall climate improves.[2] SWPBS builds a continuum of supports that begins with the whole school and extends to intensive wraparound support for individual students and their families. The structure of SWPBS is built on a hierarchy of primary, secondary, and tertiary interventions as shown in Figure 9.1.

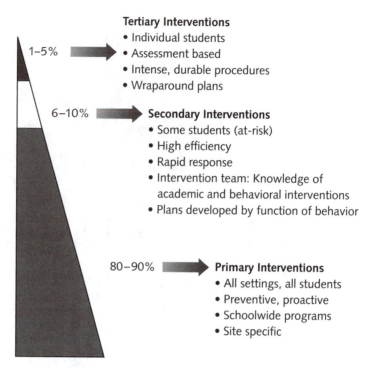

Tertiary Interventions
- Individual students
- Assessment based
- Intense, durable procedures
- Wraparound plans

1–5%

6–10%

Secondary Interventions
- Some students (at-risk)
- High efficiency
- Rapid response
- Intervention team: Knowledge of academic and behavioral interventions
- Plans developed by function of behavior

80–90%

Primary Interventions
- All settings, all students
- Preventive, proactive
- Schoolwide programs
- Site specific

Figure 9.1 Behavioral Supports

> Schoolwide positive behavior supports (SWPBS) are an alternative that has been proven to improve overall school climate. It is based on the assumption that when educators across the school actively teach, expect, and acknowledge appropriate behaviors, the proportion of students with serious behavior problems diminishes and the school's overall climate improves.

In building schoolwide positive behavior supports, school teams establish common approaches and purposes for the behavioral expectations that they collaboratively develop. Within this structure they define exactly what they expect behaviorally from students using positive language. They determine when and how they will directly teach these behavioral expectations, what they will do to reinforce them, and what they will do to deter inappropriate behaviors. They also implement a schoolwide system to monitor and evaluate the current system. The monitoring is essential to determine whether the system developed is an effective one and is producing the positive behavior development that was intended.

Implementing the Behavior Side of the RTI Triangle

The difficulty faced when beginning the RTI implementation process, as mentioned in Chapter Five, is determining how to prioritize implementation steps. It is difficult to give priority to the development of a unified behavior program when so many other important steps need attention. But the implementation of SWPBS provides a foundation for establishing the social behavioral supports needed for a school to have an effective learning environment that provides the behavioral structures for effective academic instruction and intervention. Predictable, consistent, positive, safe learning environments address many of the other implementation processes. When common expectations reach across a school, students receiving intervention from multiple individuals will find common procedures and behavioral norms wherever they go. Positive safe learning environments are the foundation for effective classroom instruction across the tiers. While it may seem like an area that can be later addressed, it is one that the RTI team should consider as an early implementation step.

Prioritizing the implementation process for schoolwide positive behavior supports is a proactive move; the process takes a year of planning prior to implementation. This somewhat time-consuming process is as necessary as the consensus building discussed in Chapter Five. The collaborative process to develop an individual school-"owned" SWPBS involves numerous steps and everyone involved in the building. The payoff is well worth it when schools begin to see decreases in inappropriate behavior, the decrease of discipline referrals, and an improvement in academic performance as teachers are able to teach academics rather than deal with behavior.

Schoolwide positive behavior supports are aligned with the RTI structure. As shown in Table 9.1, the Tier I, or primary, intervention is focused on the needs of all students and the development of a schoolwide structure that teaches all students the common expectations for positive behaviors. The secondary, or Tier II, interventions focus more

Table 9.1 Multi-Tiered Behavioral Interventions

Primary: Tier I	Secondary: Tier II	Tertiary: Tier III
Schoolwide positive behavior supports Articulated expectations Social skills instruction Prosocial and proactive discipline strategies	Strategic supplemental behavior programs Check-in and check-out Small-group training Social skills Anger management Peer and adult mentoring program	Small-group and individualized counseling therapy Individualized behavior plan Frequent, daily mentoring
Universal screening of academic and behavioral performance Continuous progress monitoring	Process and guidelines for fading, continuing, and changing intervention Focused continuous progress monitoring of responsiveness to intervention(s)	Guidelines for fading, continuing, changing intervention Focused continuous progress monitoring of responsiveness to interventions Pattern of inadequate responses may indicate need for referral

on specific student need by providing additional or supplemental intervention, and the tertiary, or Tier III, interventions focus on intensive comprehensive supports for particular students.

Tier I: Primary Interventions

Prevention of behavioral problems is the focus of the Tier I hierarchy of behavior supports. The focus of Tier I includes defining and systematically teaching the core behavioral expectations, such as school rules and procedures, that create a safe learning environment. A general rule framework supports the wide implementation of appropriate and positive behaviors. Teachers define these broad rules and directly teach lessons throughout the year on the behaviors related to these rules. Consistent systems of reinforcement are developed and implemented, ensuring that there is enforcement, monitoring, and positive reinforcement of appropriate behaviors. When schools are consistent with stated expectations and the rules are applied fairly, students develop a respect for the rules and believe and trust in the system to work. The implementation of feedback and recognition supports the long-term development of prosocial behaviors in settings that include all students. In most cases, 80 percent of the school population fits into this tier; these are the students who do believe that the rules pertain to them.

> **When schools are consistent with stated expectations and the rules are applied fairly, students develop a respect for the rules and believe and trust in the system to work.**

The development of an effective Tier I process as described by Brandi Simonsen, George Sugai, and Madeline Negron includes these four critical elements:

- Identify measurable outcomes.
- Invest in systems that will ensure that practices are implemented with fidelity and sustained over time.
- Implement relevant, evidence-based practices.
- Collect and use data to guide decisions.[3]

Identify Meaningful Outcomes

Before beginning the SWPBS implementation planning process, schools need to define what they plan to achieve through implementation. The need to use data to determine their starting point in regard to academics and behavior. They will want to look at office referrals, suspension and expulsion rates, academic achievement on state and district assessments, and other areas that may be identified as needs. From these data they must develop observable, measurable, specific, and achievable annual outcomes.[4]

Establish and Invest in Schoolwide Systems

The establishment of schoolwide systems begins with the establishment of the schoolwide leadership team. This team is integral to the implementation process; the individuals on this team should be positive people who have social influence across the school and represent a cross-section of the school, including the following:

- School administrator
- Select group of teachers
- Representative from special services
- Member of support staff
- Family member

The team then must identify a team coach from their membership. This person is responsible for ensuring that the team meets regularly and develops and follows the data-based action plan. This person "positively" reminds team members of their responsibilities and adheres to the training procedures. Ideally this person has a strong social influence on the building as a whole.

An essential part of the infrastructure or systems process is consensus building around data in order to obtain buy-in from at least 80 percent of the faculty or staff. Whereas academic interventions can begin with a vanguard group at a certain grade level, schoolwide positive behavior supports cannot be implemented without a minimum 80 percent of the staff supporting the initiative. Since it is the school staff's responsibility to implement and enforce, any lower level of support will not produce the desired behaviors.

A very important part of the "systems" process is the procurement of an effective data system that allows for quick and easy input of behavior data and can provide visual displays for output that are easily accessible and easy to use for decision making.

Once these systems are in place, the team must obtain training in the practical classroom and schoolwide implementation of the positive behavior supports process. These trainings occur throughout the country, and training materials can be obtained at http://pbis.org. Following each training event, the leadership team provides training and planning support to the faculty staff. This systems process usually takes a year. Teams typically spend a year developing the infrastructure for schoolwide implementations by training and working on the development of schoolwide agreements, with full implementation occurring in the following year.

Select and Implement Evidence-Based Practices

Once the leadership team has been trained and all the systems pieces are in place, the team is ready to select and implement practices. While the team does much of the work on this process, they are always soliciting input from the staff and incorporating their feedback into the processes.

The first step is to identify three to five positively stated schoolwide expectations. These expectations should encompass the majority of desired behaviors. Rules such as *Be Safe, Be Responsible, Be Respectful* encompass most behaviors that do not need to be identified individually. These positively stated rules can be applied across many settings and include any number of behaviors. For example, "No running" fits under *Be Safe*, "No name calling" fits under *Be Respectful*, and "Clean up trash" fits under *Be Responsible*.

Table 9.2 Respect

	Hallways	Classrooms	Cafeteria	Bathrooms	Library/Media
R e s p e c t	• Use polite language • Keep hallways clean	• Use polite language • Do your own work • Do your best work at all times • Keep work areas clean	• Use polite language • Keep table and floor clean of rubbish and place rubbish in cans • Leave area as you found it	• Use polite language • Keep area clean • Throw paper towels in rubbish cans • Flush appropriately • Keep water in sink	• Use polite language • Keep work area clean • Leave area as you found it or better

> Rules such as *Be Safe, Be Responsible, Be Respectful* encompass most behaviors that do not need to be identified individually. These positively stated rules can be applied across many settings and include any number of behaviors.

The team then specifically defines these common expectations in the context of all settings. Being responsible in the cafeteria may be defined as "Respond to quiet signal immediately," and being respectful may be defined as "Use polite language." Teams often create a matrix of these definitions, and they are explicitly taught to the students. Table 9.2 identifies the target behaviors in a positive manner in different settings.

To ensure uniformity, the SWPBS team develops lesson plans to teach each expectation within each setting or routine. These lesson plans follow a specific pattern to ensure consistency across the school, and are scripted to ensure consistency. Exhibit 9.1 presents a lesson plan format.

Exhibit 9.1 Lesson Plan Format

State the rule and routine.

- Provide students with a definition or description of what it looks like to follow the rule within the routine.
- Model the expected behavior.
- Engage students in activities that allow them to practice the expectation in the natural setting. (Teach cafeteria behavior in the cafeteria.)
- Assess to ensure students have acquired and are fluent with the expected behavior.

Following the teaching of explicit instruction on the desired behaviors, the team develops a plan to increase active supervision in classroom and nonclassroom settings. This allows for specific praise and error correction to help reinforce the new behaviors. Key people like administrators need to be part of the increased supervision process. Students should feel like they are being watched and that any person on the staff, not just their own teachers, will praise appropriate behaviors and provide error correction when needed.

The team then needs to help the staff to develop a continuum of strategies to acknowledge expectation-following behaviors. These strategies need to be specific enough to ensure the use of consistent contingent praise by telling students exactly what they did well when the behavior was observed. Specific common practices for acknowledging specific behaviors need to be developed. Using phrases like, "Good job" is not an effective way to reinforce a specific behavior. The student needs to know exactly what behavior that he or she was doing was appropriate. This will increase the likelihood that it will happen again. "I appreciate that you walked in the hall today," ensures that the student knows exactly what she did right. In addition, many schools add layers of overt reinforcers like raffle tickets or points that can be used to purchase more tangible reinforcers.

The school also must collaboratively develop common strategies to discourage inappropriate behaviors. Consistent responses to different levels of behavior must be established for schoolwide consistency. Responses to minor inappropriate behaviors should receive only brief error correction that identifies the inappropriate behavior and describes the appropriate replacement behavior. "I saw you running, and instead I'd like to see you walk." If necessary, the second response should be the reteaching of the desired behavior.

The team should develop a staff reinforcement system that recognizes staff for their efforts. Specific social recognitions should be applied when teachers have completed teaching behavior lesson plans and have distributed a certain number of positive behavior tickets. Some schools add more tangible reinforcers, such as preferred parking places and lunch coupons, as contingent reinforcers. Teachers are more likely to repeat behaviors when they are reinforced too!

Last, the team needs to determine the best way to roll out the plan for the primary tier intervention once it has been developed. This second-year process needs to specify how expectations will be introduced, where posters will be displayed, when and where lessons will be taught, and how the reinforcement system will be implemented.

Collect and Use Data to Make Decisions

While establishing and maintaining the primary tier, the SWPBS must actively collect and use data on a regular basis. In the planning year, the school should identify or purchase a data system so that the team can use the data effectively.

In order to monitor the effectiveness and the implementation of the schoolwide system, the team must use and review data every time they meet. This data should be reviewed monthly around the following data points:

- Overall rates of office referrals
- Percentage of students receiving more than one office referral for major offenses and potential supports for these students

- Typical locations where problems occur
- Times of the day where problems are occurring
- Nature or type of behaviors

This type of data provides the framework for developing or modifying the interventions that are in place and making adjustments to circumvent some of the problem areas that promote problem behaviors.

Additionally, this data must be shared with the staff so that they can participate in data-based decision making around modified interventions or changes to the program. The data should also be used to celebrate successes! When the data reveal progress toward a goal, the team and administration need to ensure that the staff and students share in a celebration for the improvement. These successes should also be shared with families and the school community. Parents and parent groups should be a part of the celebration process to reinforce their role in the behavior process.[5]

Schoolwide and Classroomwide Systems in Tier I

- Identify a common purpose and approach to discipline.
- Define a clear set of positive expectations and behaviors.
- Implement procedures for teaching expected behavior.
- Differentiate supports from a continuum of procedures for encouraging expected behavior.
- Differentiate supports from a continuum of procedures for discouraging inappropriate behavior.
- Implement procedures for ongoing monitoring and evaluation.

Tier II: Secondary Group Interventions

Even with an effective primary tier intervention in place, a group of students—approximately 11 percent, 26 percent, and 29 percent of elementary, middle, and high school students respectively—will require additional behavior support to experience success.[6] This second tier of intervention is designed to support a targeted group of students who have not responded to the primary interventions but whose behaviors do not pose a risk to themselves or others.

These students are primarily involved in relatively low-level disruptive behaviors such as blurting out, irregular work completion, tardiness, and off-task behaviors. The goal of intervention for this group is to prevent these behaviors from becoming chronic. The development of these targeted interventions is based on data that is related to these low-level disruptive behaviors. These secondary practices focus on intensifying the supports provided in the primary tier. These might include increasing classroom structure, providing more intensive social skills instruction, provision of more frequent behavioral prompts, and the delivery of more frequent reinforcements. These types of interventions usually require minimal time to implement and can be implemented from student to student, resulting in a reduction of problem behavior.[7]

The evidence-based secondary interventions most often implemented include the Check-In, Check-Out (CICO), an individualized version of CICO known as Check & Connect for students who need more personalized intervention than the generic CICO, and small-group social skills instruction for students with social skill deficits. Progress in these programs is monitored regularly for effectiveness, and feedback is an essential part of the behavior change process. Most of these Tier II evidence-based practices share some of the following key features:

- Instruction on targeted skills
- Self-monitoring strategies
- Acknowledgments for appropriate behavior
- Regular performance feedback concerning target behaviors
- Peer tutoring[8]

One of the most common secondary interventions is the Check-In, Check-Out process also known as the behavior education program.[9] This intervention is targeted at students who are regularly involved in relatively low-level disruptive behaviors and need additional support. The CICO incorporates several core principles of positive behavior support, including:

- Clearly defined expectations
- Instruction on appropriate social skills
- Increased positive reinforcement for following expectations
- Contingent consequences for problem behavior
- Increased positive contact with an adult at school
- Improved opportunities for self-management
- Increased home-school collaboration[10]

The CICO process allows students to forge a one-on-one relationship with at least one adult a day. The procedure involves the student "checking in" with this adult at the beginning of each school day. During this check-in, expectations for behavior are reviewed, self-management strategies are developed, and the daily monitoring sheet is provided. At regular time intervals, usually at the beginning or end of the period, the student gets feedback on the target behavior. At the end of the day, the student "checks out" with this same adult by reviewing the point sheet and determining whether behavioral goals were met. The data are charted and the adult provides acknowledgment, encouragement, and a sense of caring. This same information is sent to parents at home.[11] Exhibit 9.2 is an example of a Check-In, Check-Out monitoring form.

The daily data are compiled into weekly charts so that the student is able to analyze his or her behavior to identify improvements and strengths and determine whether there are any patterns related to behavioral difficulties. This ongoing monitoring and data analysis helps students develop self-management skills and take greater responsibility for their own behavior. Over time, the behavior moves from a teacher-managed system to a

Exhibit 9.2 Check-In, Check-Out Daily Progress Report

Check-In, Check-Out Daily Progress Report

Student's Name_____   Date_____

Teachers: Please use the following rubric to reflect student's progress on the following goals:

Mostly (5)   *Sometimes (3)*   *Never (1)*

Goals	*1*			*2*			*3*			*4*			*5*			*6*		
On Time	5	3	1	5	3	1	5	3	1	5	3	1	5	3	1	5	3	1
Prepared for Class	5	3	1	5	3	1	5	3	1	5	3	1	5	3	1	5	3	1
Followed Directions	5	3	1	5	3	1	5	3	1	5	3	1	5	3	1	5	3	1
Completed Tasks	5	3	1	5	3	1	5	3	1	5	3	1	5	3	1	5	3	1
Respectful to Others	5	3	1	5	3	1	5	3	1	5	3	1	5	3	1	5	3	1
TOTAL POINTS																		
TEACHER'S INITIALS																		

Daily Goal: (30/150)   Daily Score: (30/150)

Student Signature_____
Provide brief comments or observations

Period 1 _____

Period 2 _____

Period 3 _____

Period 4 _____

Period 5 _____

Period 6 _____

Parent/Guardian Signature _____

Parent/Guardian Comments _____

student-managed system in which the student is able to monitor behavior independently. This intervention can be implemented by a school staff member and has a high success rate of behavior and academic improvement.

For students who do not respond to the CICO intervention and need a more intensive intervention, Check & Connect (http://ici.umn.edu/checkandconnect) is a personalized model of sustained intervention that involves a mentor or monitor who continues to monitor specific behaviors for an extended period of time. This person is an advocate and a service provider who focuses his or her effort in keeping the student engaged in school and learning. Check & Connect is structured to maximize personal contact and opportunities to build trusting relationships that will help the student stay in school. In this long-term intervention, student levels of engagement (such as attendance, grades, suspensions) are checked regularly and used to guide the monitors' efforts to increase and maintain students' connection with school.

There are many effective social skills program available. Social skills groups should be facilitated and run by school professionals such as counselors, school psychologists, and others trained in the effective use of the specific programs.

Tier III: Tertiary Individual Interventions

Tertiary tier interventions are designed to support individual students who require additional support to benefit from the primary and secondary intervention or whose behaviors are serious enough to require more immediate intensive support.[12] These students make up 3 to 5 percent of the population who require this highly individualized attention. These interventions involve an individualized assessment followed by an individualized intervention plan, which is an important foundation for tertiary tier support.

According to Fairbanks and her colleagues, most of these function-based interventions include providing more teacher attention, an increase in self-monitoring and further development of these skills, the direct teaching of social skills, breaking tasks down into smaller parts to reduce task duration, and scheduled breaks to get to work with adults or peers.[13] Also effective in these plans is interspersing instruction between preferred activities.

Students whose behavior problems are not reduced by secondary interventions or who engage in dangerous or severe behavior will need the development of a function-based behavior support plan (BSP).[14] Prior to the development of the behavior support plan, the function or purpose of the behavior is determined through the process of a functional behavior assessment (FBA). This process includes observations that help identify the settings, events, and antecedents or conditions that trigger the behavior and the consequences of the behavior. Part of the FBA process is to determine why the consequence or the outcome of the specific behavior is rewarding enough to the student to cause him or her to repeat it. Once the purpose of the behavior is identified, replacement behaviors can be developed that will allow the student to obtain the same type of reward with a more appropriate behavior. The FBA may identify that acting-out behavior is associated with a need for attention. The behavior support plan identifies a replacement behavior for the acting out that will allow the student to receive the attention that he or she needs in a more positive manner. Teachers and staff work with the student to minimize events that lead to the behavior, provide reinforcement for the new target behavior, and eliminate or reduce the reinforcement for the problem behavior. An individualized behavior support team develops and supports the implementation of the behavior support plan.[15]

For approximately 1 to 2 percent of the students with the highest levels of needs, the wraparound process is the most comprehensive intervention within the schoolwide positive behavior support system in the RTI continuum.[16] Wraparound includes specific engagement techniques to ensure that the design of the supports and interventions includes the perspectives and voice of the family, the student, and the teacher. This approach is strengthened by the development of constructive relationships and support networks among the student, family, and other key adults, such as social workers, counselors, therapists, psychologists, doctors, and teachers. One of the core principles of the wraparound process is the participation of the family and the student in the development and planning of the interventions. This most intensive of behavior supports is usually facilitated and monitored by a school social worker, school psychologist, counselor, or other clinical staff.

Individual Student Systems

- Support behavioral competence at school and district levels
- Tailor function-based behavior support planning
- Use team and data-based decision making
- Utilize comprehensive person-centered planning and wraparound processes
- Deliver secondary social skills and self-management instruction
- Implement individualized instructional and curricular accommodations

Meeting the behavioral needs of all students requires that teachers work collaboratively to problem-solve and provide consistency in behavioral expectations. Finding the time and processes to make this collaboration effective does not happen automatically. It takes intentional planning and professional development to support effective collaborative processes. The next chapter will discuss how to make collaboration an effective and efficient process to support both academic and behavioral success.

Wrapping Up the Main Points

Currently, nearly six thousand schools in the United States have implemented schoolwide positive behavior supports. These schools are reporting reductions in problem behaviors, improved perceptions of safety, and positive academic outcomes. These studies have shown up to 50 percent reductions in office referrals, with evidence showing that SWPBS can change the trajectory of students who are on a path toward destructive outcomes as well as prevent the onset of negative behaviors in typically developing peers.[17] The implementation of SWPBS provides a system of prevention across all the tiers that supports the development of an RTI framework both behaviorally and academically. Effective implementation of SWPBS will ultimately prevent new cases of problem behaviors, reduce current cases of problem behaviors, and minimize the complications, intensity, and severity of behaviors for students with significant behavioral needs. Schoolwide positive behavior supports are a catalyst for change that not only will improve the school climate and improve academic achievement but ultimately will provide our students with the foundational social skills needed to be successful adults.

10

Collaboration: The Key to Success

The death knell to any school restructuring project is a lack of effective collaboration time. When teachers are expected to collaborate on the fly, the hope of equity for all students is squelched. Regularly scheduled collaboration time is as essential to effective RTI implementation as data-based decision making and the hierarchy of instructional and behavior supports. When educators are not afforded collaboration time to analyze data, data have no purpose. Without collaboration time to set goals and plan instruction and intervention, effective targeted instruction cannot take place. Integral to an effective RTI structure and improved student achievement is effective, regularly scheduled collaboration time.

Key to any RTI framework is the development of effective teaming. This process develops within the team an expanded circle of support and allows teachers to use their collective expertise to problem-solve, analyze data, set goals, plan instruction, and develop curricular adaptations. Without collaborative teaming, teachers and programs can go back to their silo mentality. Collaboration is essential for a common vision for *all* students to emerge. Only through collaboration can inclusive instruction occur, allowing teachers to capitalize on their diversity and varied expertise. Through this combined knowledge and skill, the needs of all students can be addressed and a joint ownership emerges.

But what exactly is collaboration? There are many misconceptions in the field today, and not everything that people do together in schools is really collaboration. These examples exemplify the confusion that exists!

> "We collaborate on everything; we talk all the time!"
>
> "Collaborate, co-teach, isn't it all the same thing?"
>
> "We collaborate every month when we have a faculty meeting."
>
> "Collaboration? Isn't that the same as cooperative learning?"
>
> "We really have good collaboration at my school. Most special education students are in general education classes all day."
>
> "We collaborate with parents. I just sent home a list of supplies that the children should bring."[1]

As you can see from these statements, the concept of collaboration can be quite misunderstood. Marilyn Friend and Lynn Cook, in their book, *Collaboration for School Professionals*, define it as "a style for direct interaction between at least two co-equal parties voluntarily engaged in shared decision making as they work toward a common goal."[2]

They identify collaboration as a style, as an approach for interaction with different parties. This is different from a directive style or an accommodative or facilitative style; a collaborative style defines how the communication occurs during shared interactions when people are engaged in a specific task, process, or activity. For interactions to be considered collaborative, they should have the following characteristics:

- Voluntary participation
- Parity among participants
- Mutual goals
- Shared responsibility for participation and decision making
- Shared resources
- Shared accountability for outcomes[3]

Collaborative processes are effective when the individuals involved value a collaborative style of interaction. This is why some people struggle with the concept of collaborative processes. Those who hold on to a silo mentality will find that this process goes against their frame of reference when making decisions. Additionally, effective collaboration involves high levels of trust between parties as well as a sense of community. Individuals who have taught in "private practice" for some time will find that developing the trust that is required for collaboration takes time and that the development of sense of community is a process that cannot be forced.

Rick DuFour and colleagues describe the challenges teachers face when initiating collaborative conversations.

> Collaborative conversations call on team members to make public what has been traditionally private—goals, strategies, materials, pacing, questions, concerns, and results. These discussions give every teacher someone to turn to and talk to, they are explicitly structured to improve the classroom practice of teachers—individually and collectively.[4]

Many schools have been required to create a master schedule that includes regularly scheduled collaboration periods. While this is a step in the right direction, without accountability and training, this time can quickly become filled with administrivia and lose its purpose. In developing effective collaborative models, it is important to recognize the *what*, the *why*, and the *how* of collaborative teaming. There are several purposes of collaborative interactions, and unless collaborative teams recognize this, they will not use their time effectively to meet each of the specific needs. Collaborative teams are complex and have different purposes for different needs. Recognizing this is an essential step to making these teams most effective.

The What of Collaborative Teaming

It is clear that *collaboration* can be misconstrued. This is partly true because there are so many different collaborative roles and so many different collaborative purposes. Let's look first at the different types of collaborative teams. Each school site is built on different personnel structures, depending on the school's size and the grade levels that it serves. Small rural schools will have the most difficult time with collaborative teaming; one individual may be the only person teaching at a grade level or even a combination of grade levels. A rural secondary schoolteacher also may find that he or she is the only teacher providing instruction in a particular subject area, so collaboration in a content area is difficult. For this reason, a variety of collaborative structural options must be available at each school site.

Grade-Level Teaming

The most common collaborative structure is the grade-level team. Most schools in the twenty-first century have moved to grade-level teaming. This is the process through which teachers from different grade levels work together to plan instruction and help each other in the development and preparation of lesson planning materials. This is usually the first step in realizing that leaving "private practice" means working smarter, not harder. It does not make sense for each of the five second-grade teachers to develop five different instructional lessons and prepare materials for each of these separate lessons. This type of practice is counterproductive. Grade-level teaming allows for teachers to plan the same instruction based on state standards and the common curriculum map as they prepare their students for the common assessments.

Grade-level teaming, as logical as it sounds, is not always easy to implement. There is the factor of personality and the silo mentality that favors private practice. When teachers hold onto the "My classroom is my kingdom" and "My students are my students, and no one else can teach them as well as I can" beliefs, grade-level teaming becomes just a process that teachers will "do" because it is required, but they will not participate in a collaborative style. Breaking down these kinds of walls is very difficult. Sometimes teachers refuse to join in grade-level collaboration, and no amount of persuasion will change their minds. It is best practice at this point to let the "nonvolunteers" continue in their private practice as much as possible and allow the others to move on effectively. When the stick-in-the-muds see that the others are working more efficiently through teaming and that their academic outcomes are improved, they will eventually come around. As an expert on collaboration stated, "It usually takes about nine months to make them believers."[5] Since the definition of collaboration requires voluntary interaction, it is not possible to force grade-level members to collaborate effectively.

The power of grade-level teaming becomes even stronger when data discussions become part of the regularly scheduled collaborative planning time. This takes the team beyond functional to highly effective. These teams look at data regularly, not simply to "admire" the problem, but to determine what to do about students who have done poorly and how to use the strengths of those teachers whose students have done well. It takes a great level of trust to develop for this to occur, but when it does, the discussions are powerful! Collaborative data discussions allow teachers the opportunity to learn from each other and to expand their arsenals of effective strategies. As teams stand back and peruse how their classes have done on common assessments, they are able to see which classes have done better than others. This is not intended to be evaluative but to determine instructionally what the teacher did to get better results. This kind of problem solving is one of the ways that collaborative teaming is the most effective.

One step beyond sharing data at the classroom level is sharing data at the student level. In this scenario, all second graders who took the common assessment are aligned based on score. The teachers determine who in their grade level has the skills to work with the group that requires instruction in a particular skill area, who will work with the strategic groups, who will work with the benchmark groups, and who will work with the advanced groups. At this point, all second graders *belong to all the second-grade teachers*. Ownership of all students, including students with disabilities, at-risk students, and English learners, occurs. All teachers at this grade level, including reading specialists, special educators, and Title I and Title III teachers, become responsible for the instruction and intervention of this group of second graders.

While this makes perfect sense in an RTI framework that is focused on targeted instruction, the logistics of providing this targeted instruction is not always that easy. Again, it takes a level of trust and ownership to realize that some teachers will be working with fewer students and some will be working with more. Some will be providing instruction that comes essentially from the core curriculum and that others will need to supplement the core with other materials. The teachers working with the advanced students will need to develop advanced lessons. All of these things can become roadblocks with a team that does not recognize joint "ownership" of all students.

Another logistical issue related to collaborative instruction is the scheduling of language arts and math time. Many teachers still feel that they should be able to determine their own daily schedules around the schoolwide bell schedule at the elementary level. In the past, when private practice was the norm, this type of scheduling did not really matter, but in a collaborative model, when teams share students for at least part of the instructional time, they will need common schedules to be able to share students. In order for a specialist to be used most efficiently across grade levels, the English language arts schedule will need to be staggered over the day, so that the support staff can rotate through each grade level. This will mean that some students will get language arts instruction in the afternoon. For some teachers, this is not a big deal, but for others who have always taught reading at 9:10 a.m., this is a huge shift in practice.

Changing instructional practice is difficult. It cannot be forced. The research from the implementation practices of schools across the nation from the Center on Instruction suggests that schools start with a vanguard group who are totally bought into collaborative practices and support them as richly as possible.[6] The data and practice of this vanguard group will be enough to convince the others to join.

Grade-level teaming is the foundation for collaboration at the elementary level.

Content Area Teaming

At the secondary level, the content area team plays a similar role to the grade-level team at the elementary level. Most schools require content areas or departments to meet on a regular basis, but much of this time is wasted on administrivia. Department meetings should not be about who is buying the nacho cheese for the snack shack or who is covering the dance for their department; they should be focused on instruction and instructional planning! Collaborative department meetings should involve the planning of lessons, assessments, and instruction based on the curriculum and the common assessments. The working smarter, not harder, idea should prevail. No one teacher within a department should be doing his or her own thing when instruction is aligned to the standards and the common core curriculum.

Department meetings are not the most effective of collaborative teams. Within the math department, you will have different grade levels or different content areas, like algebra, geometry, algebra II, calculus, and so on. The teams that teach these content areas make up the effective collaborative team. They can share instructional planning, assessment data, and strategies used to improve student outcomes. These teams need the time to analyze data so that they can recognize when they need to adjust their instructional planning and which students may need more attention or targeted instruction. Sharing students or homogenous grouping, often seen on the elementary grade-level team, is unusual at the secondary level, but some schools that are on block schedules have brought their instruction "outside of the box" and have students move between classes in order to get targeted skill-based instruction for at least some of the block of instructional time. Having students move between bells may seem like an unlikely solution, but for teachers who understand the power of focused and targeted instruction, it is a risk they are willing to take.

When teachers recognize the shared ownership of all students, both Tier I and Tier II instruction can be provided primarily by the grade-level, core content teachers. Tier II with shadow class intervention is supported by specialists like the Title I teacher, the special educators, and other interventionists. This level of intervention is not considered intensive. It takes a high level of collaboration to provide this type of effective tiered instruction; schoolwide frameworks that support this take greater responsibility for student learning, since the student is not "sent" off to intervention but rather receives it from the grade-level or content-specific team.

These common content area teams are often called professional learning communities or PLCs, and together they work toward the development of goals for their instruction and their students' progress.

Student-Level Teaming

The collaborative teams discussed thus far are focused primarily on data and classroom instruction based on this data. Highly effective teams also look at data to make decisions about homogenous strategic intervention groupings, but the teams discussed so far have not been focused on specific student needs. The highly effective collaborative team will recognize that there is a need for collaboration time that focuses specifically at the student level. This is not a collaborative meeting to whine about particular kids and their problems but to use the problem-solving expertise of the grade-level and content-area team to develop strategies that will support the needs of a particular student. These teams are often composed of cross-curricular groups that make up a small learning community or SLC.

The SLC process, sometimes referred to as a "school within a school," is a structure that is more common at the secondary level. The purpose is to subdivide large school populations into smaller autonomous groups of students and teachers in order to create a more personalized learning environment where a team of teachers shares common students. This allows the teachers to collaborate and problem-solve together across the content areas around the needs of a student that they share. This unified approach allows the teachers who together provide the spectrum of content to a particular student to strategize together on common strategies and interventions that they will focus on all their classes. This common group of teachers can support the student in a stronger, more united way simply because they all are aware of particular needs and together can best determine how to meet them.

In schools where teaching teams in small learning communities take the time to problem-solve at the student level, students usually respond to the knowledge that teachers are communicating with each other about them. When they realize that their behavior and progress are a concern to a number of teachers, they often respond in a positive manner. For many adolescents who feel lost in a world of thousands of teenagers, the knowledge that an entire team of teachers has a concern or is working together to help them be successful is motivating. Students also respond when they realize that teachers are talking to one another, and they cannot pull off things in one class without it getting to the other teachers on the team. This unified approach creates greater accountability on the students' end.

> "In schools where teaching teams in small learning communities take the time to problem-solve at the student level, students usually respond to the knowledge that teachers are communicating with each other about them. When they realize that their behavior and progress are a concern to a number of teachers, they often respond in a positive manner. For many adolescents who feel lost in a world of thousands of teenagers, the knowledge that an entire team of teachers has a concern or is working together to help them be successful is motivating."

The Why of Collaborative Teaming

Just as there are many different types of collaborative teams, collaborative teaming has many purposes. Collaboration is a process used to reach common goals that cannot be achieved singly or at a minimum cannot be reached efficiently without collaborative conversation. Education today has many goals, and that is why collaboration at times does not seem focused or productive. A common goal and vision needs to drive all collaboration time. Without a common goal in collaboration, some party in the collaborative process will leave having his or her needs unmet. When needs are unmet, the team member will no longer feel a need to continue to participate on the collaborative team. Without clear expectations, the collaborative team will fall apart and will be far from effective. What is the role of the collaborative team in an RTI structure?

The rampant confusion about collaboration comes from the fact that there are many roles of collaborative teaming in the RTI process. Despite the many purposes, each of these teams and purposes must be driven by a common goal. The common belief that needs to be embraced *before* moving ahead to develop an RTI framework is that the underlying focus of all decisions needs to go back to the foundation of "Academic Achievement for *All* Students." Achievement for all needs to be the goal that girds up every collaborative meeting. That is why there is no place for the admiration of problems or the degradation of particular students or teachers. That does not fit into the paradigm of academic achievement for all. When all discussion and decisions in collaborative meetings focus on academic achievement, the purpose of meetings becomes clear, and *no one* should leave feeling as if has or her own needs or agenda have not been met.

With academic achievement as the goal for all collaborative teaming, it becomes clear that even if meetings have different purposes, they are all still working toward the common goal. Within the realm of providing effective instruction and intervention in an RTI framework, the collaborative team needs time to analyze data to inform instruction, to plan instruction and interventions with a grade- level or content area team, and to plan for accommodations and instructional supports for struggling learners and students with special needs. Additionally, from time to time a collaborative team will need to make time to problem-solve specifically around particular students who have presented with challenges either behaviorally or academically.

Collaborative teaming purposes often include:

- Data discussion and goal setting
- Instructional planning based on data
- Student problem solving

Data Discussions

Creating the conditions for effective data discussions is a tall order. While it is common knowledge that teachers make better use of data when they work together than when they go it alone, there are many challenges that get in the way of effective data discussions.[7] Working collaboratively around data runs against the norm of isolation and individualistic approaches to teaching. While teachers may break out of their comfort zones to plan instruction, sharing data that reflect a teacher's own instructional practice is very risky. Without specific training, teachers struggle with this effective use of data. They must receive coaching and support in how to collect data, make sense of it, and determine the implications of the data before they can attempt to use it to drive instruction. Despite the difficulties faced in this process, a growing body of evidence suggests that when teachers collaborate to pose and answer questions informed by data on the performance of their students, their knowledge grows and their practice changes.[8]

> A growing body of evidence suggests that when teachers collaborate to pose and answer questions informed by data on the performance of their students, their knowledge grows and their practice changes.

Goal Setting

The SMART goals process is a systematic process that teachers can use to collaboratively use data to drive instructional practice.[9] The SMART goal process uses data so that teachers can focus on specific, measurable, achievable goals based on data. The data become the foundation for setting the SMART goal.

The SMART Goal Process

The SMART goals process includes the following elements:

S = Strategic and Specific

M = Measurable

A = Attainable

R = Results-based

T = Time-bound

- Strategic and Specific
  - Schools using the SMART goal process focus on the "vital few" that are considered the high-leverage areas. These high-leverage areas are often identified in the essential standards process, and goal setting and instruction are focused on essential components of the grade-level or content area standards. Other areas targeted for SMART goal development are the areas where the greatest gaps persist.
  - Specificity based on data creates the tangible evidence of improvement that propels motivation. Developing specific targets for improvement allow teachers to recognize their progress toward and the attainment of these specific targets. By targeting students and skills, teachers become very focused on their instructional practices that benefit all students.[10]

- Measurable
  - Being able to measure progress on goals is critical to the SMART goal process, as we all tend to focus our efforts on what gets measured. The SMART goals process encourages teachers to think in multiple measures or multiple parts of each goal. These are both formative and summative goals; that teachers can recognize progress toward the goals in a variety of ways. These multiple measures allow for a more complete picture of student learning.

- Attainable
  - Attainable goals are those that are almost, but not quite, within our reach. Attainable goals require teachers to stretch their current practices and thinking on how to close the gaps that persist with their current time and resources. When goals are not attainable, it is difficult to sustain the energy needed to persist.

- Results-based
  - Result-based goals are motivating because they are concrete benchmarks against which to measure efforts. When teachers receive positive results, the feedback motivates them to continue their efforts.

- Time-bound
  - Setting goals that have a specific time frame is critical, as it builds internal accountability and commitment. All teams work with greater efficiency when they have timelines and deadlines, and without these, it is highly likely that teams would put off the tasks necessary to meet the goals.

The SMART goals process is a very effective process for collaborative teaming in the grade levels and content areas. More information on the process and process tools can be found at the Solution Tree Web site at www.solution-tree.com.

The SMART goal process is built upon the professional learning community concept of multiple stakeholders adhering to a shared vision, mission, values, and goals. The PLC creates the structure for teams to improve student learning through collaborative ongoing data analysis. This collaborative team works interdependently to achieve the common goal linked to the purpose of learning for all. In a PLC, collaboration represents a systematic process in which teachers work together interdependently to affect their classroom practices in ways that will lead to better results for their students, their teams, and their schools.[11]

Instructional Planning Based on Data

In the PLC process, teachers reflect on data as they plan their instruction. In order to ensure that their instruction is data aligned, they reflect on the following questions:

◆ What do we want students to know?
This first question is addressed in the essential standard identification process and the development of instructional pacing.

◆ How will we know they know it?
This question is addressed in the development of common assessments and during the instructional planning for formative and summative curriculum-based measures.

◆ What will we do when students experience difficulty?
Teams collaboratively problem-solve, using data to determine who will receive Tier I, Tier II, and Tier III interventions based on the data.

Student Problem Solving

The student problem-solving process encompasses several layers of teaming. The first level is the small learning community approach. This collaboration occurs when the team of teachers who provide the instruction for a particular student meet to problem-solve around the needs on one student. This meeting is not intended as a time to cast blame. Teachers need to come to this meeting prepared with both academic and behavioral data that will help the team recognize patterns of strengths or weaknesses and to brainstorm instructional strategies that might meet the student's academic needs. The outcome of this type of collaborative meeting should be specific common strategies and practices that will be applied across all classes for the target student. Close monitoring of progress both academically and behaviorally should be included in the plan, with a specific timeline for implementation and follow-up. When this level of problem solving has occurred over time, and progress on goals has not been achieved, a referral to the student study or child study team is appropriate.

The How of Collaborative Teaming

Effective collaboration should be explicitly
structured to improve classroom practice of
teachers—individually and collectively.

Rick DuFour

Effective collaborative teams just don't happen. These teams need training and time to learn to become effective teams. They need to recognize that different teams have different purposes and that collaborative team meetings are only successful when a structure is applied to the process.

Integral to effective collaborative meetings is an agenda that defines the purpose. Each team member should have a role in the meeting and should come prepared, since time is at a premium. The agenda or purpose of the meeting will determine what tools will be needed: data for data meetings, instructional materials for instructional planning, and individual student data and information for student-level meetings.

The question that surfaces most often is, How can teachers cover all this ground in one hour a week? One process is to have teams work on only one type of collaborative process each week. During a month, one week can be focused specifically on data and goal setting, one week on instructional planning, one week on student-level problem solving, and the other week can be used for a variety of purposes that may rotate each month. With an agenda and planning, four hours a month can be enough time for effective teaming (see Table 10.1). The forms in Appendix H can be used to drive the discussion for each type of meeting.

Collaborative Accountability

While collaborative teams rely on their meeting times as an essential part of their job, administrators and teaching teams need to recognize the threat of the "tyranny of the urgent" that sometimes draws people away from the importance of collaborative time. With so many different things vying for the attention of teachers, one more meeting can seem like just one too many! To support teachers in the accountability that is necessary for successful collaboration and an effective RTI structure, it is best practice that teachers spend their collaboration time together in one room. Some will complain that this is demeaning and that they do not have their materials at hand, like they would in their own classroom, but too many distractions that can occur when teams are sent out to their own ends of the campus to do their planning and collaboration.

The benefits of collaboration in one space are numerous and far outweigh the reasons voiced against it. Initially, being in one room allows the administrator to play a role in each team's discussions and problem solving. The administrator, as the instructional expert, should be available (in the room and moving from group to group) during the entire collaboration time. This provides the administrator with firsthand knowledge of the instruction planned for the coming week and allows him or her to keep abreast of the current status of the data and the problem-solving discussions about individual

Table 10.1   Weekly Collaborative Meeting Schedule

	Purpose	Materials
Week 1	PLC: Data discussion and goal setting	Curriculum-based data
Week 2	PLC: Instructional planning	Curriculum materials
Week 3	SLC: Student-level meeting	Student-level data
Week 4	Other: Schoolwide professional development, Behavior data meetings, Curricular adaptations	Behavior data strategies and accommodations

students. For powerful, effective collaboration, it is essential that the site administrator, curriculum coaches, vice principal or assistant principal, counselors, behavior specialists, interventionists, Title I, Title III, special educators, and other reading specialists be present. The fact that all the teams meet in one space facilitates the support that these specialists can provide.

Exhibit 10.1 is an example of a curricular adaptation meeting process. The example focuses primarily on adaptations and accommodations for students with disabilities and other at-risk students. The form leads the grade-level or content area team through the instructional planning for the week but also identifies those students who will need additional special education supports within the core to be successful. This type of planning can only occur when it is intentionally planned and all planning teams are in the same room. It is impossible for the special educators to attend all the planning meetings and have an influence when meetings are held all over campus during instructional planning time. Having all teams working together in one space allows the expertise of all the specialists to be available to team members at all times. The process takes data discussions and instructional planning even further out of the silos and makes everyone's work transparent to others.

Enhancing Special Education Service Delivery Through Collaboration

The different types of special education collaborative teaming were discussed in Chapter Four. For effective service delivery of specially designed academic instruction to occur, special educators and general educators must have the opportunity to plan effectively to meet the specific needs of students with disabilities. If the students are in a consultative model or collaborative model, the special education teacher must ensure regular planning time to support the student with instructional accommodations and adaptations. If the special educator is not aware of what is being taught, she or he is not able to support individualized education program (IEP) students in his or her core classes. This usually creates a situation in which the general education teacher feels "dumped on" and feels unsupported by the specialists. Doing instructional planning on the fly or teaming without the special educator is usually the cause. Collaborative planning time is *not* a time for special educators to meet together as a department and discuss special education issues. It is a time for special educators and general education teaching partners to collaborate. Since special education students are served in general education, it is the special educator's role to ensure that the general educator is supported in providing the special education services within that setting. Some schools have dealt with this issue by giving special educators an additional collaboration period to work with their colleagues on special education planning and for meetings. Again, having the whole staff work together in one room aids the special educator in becoming part of more data and planning meetings.

Special educators can collaborate even more effectively when they are fully aware of the curriculum maps and the common assessment schedule for all the students on their caseloads. This allows them to develop an instructional pacing plan that gives them advance notice and ample time to collect materials and strategies that will support the needs of their students in the core classroom while also working on IEP goals.

Exhibit 10.1 Curricular Adaptation Meeting Process

Strategies and Accommodations Tool Example

Grade Level: 7th

Week of: October 1st

Content Area: Social Studies

Standard Area/s to be addressed: 7.1. Cause and Effect of Expansion of Roman Empire: Establishment of Constantinople

Students who need specific accommodations or more focused strategies:

1. Steven Osgood   2. Anthony Anderson
3. Shelby Smith   4. Austin Spahr
5. Jessica Fulmer   6. _____

Which specific research-based strategies will support the needs of some/all of these students? Target strategies for this week:

Note taking: Guided notes for all students (cloze technique)

Identifying similarities and differences using graphic organizer: Venn diagram and concept maps for the differences between the Eastern Orthodox Church and the Roman Catholic Church

What previous strategies have been attempted?

Identifying similarities and differences, note-taking guides, graphic organizers (concept maps, Venn diagrams, drawing maps)

How effective were these strategies?

Note taking (cloze technique): Most students did have correct information on guided notes pages and used this information on exit slip. Graphic organizers were effective in helping students answer check for understanding questions during class.

These/this student(s) need these additional accommodations or adaptations:

Austin Spahr: Needs fewer spots to fill in on the cloze notes. He lost his place and had the wrong information in the wrong place. Having a partner check to see if he has the correct work in each slot would help.

Jessica Fulmer: Verbal quiz or a scribe to write her answers to the daily exit slip. She knows the content but is resistant to writing.

How will the team know if these students have met the standard(s)?

If they can answer four out of five questions on the daily exit quiz with the support of their notes and a scribe to write the answers on the slip.

How will the input for these students look different?

Austin's notes will have some of the blanks filled in, but the entire class will benefit from the cloze notes strategies.

How will the content be adjusted for these students?

No adjustment.

How will the output differ for these students?

Jessica will have her daily exit quiz answers dictated to another student to write on her slip or give the teacher/aide answers verbally before leaving class

What additional instructional or supplemental support is needed for these/this student(s) to participate effectively to reach the standards?

Jessica, Anthony, and Shelby would benefit from the adapted Social Studies "Parent Alert" notes and study guides and vocabulary support at the accommodated level.

Austin would benefit from the adapted Social Studies summaries and study guide at the modified level.

Which members of the team have the expertise and skills to provide these supports?

Michele Smith: Provide adapted notes

Michael Powers: Create/use cloze notes from core curriculum, provide Venn diagram

What additional adaptations are needed from the special education case managers to support progress in these standards?

Provide Austin with cloze notes that have some of the blanks filled in ahead of time. (Michael will get copies of notes to Michele by Friday.)

How will these supports be provided?

X Consultative/Collaborative (materials, adapted homework, other: notes)

X Team Teaching: (schedule): Monday, Wednesday, Friday, second period in Michael's room)

☐ Small-group supplemental support: (schedule _____)

X Resource/Special Ed. Room support: (schedule) Tuesday, Thursday re-teaching as needed second half of second period (10:45–11:18)

☐ Other _____

Next steps/Agenda item for next meeting:

Materials for next unit, scheduling time for vocabulary preview. Who has a good video or pictures to support Islam unit?

> "For effective service delivery of specially designed academic instruction to occur, special educators and general educators must have the opportunity to plan effectively to meet the specific needs of students with disabilities. . . . Special educators can collaborate even more effectively when they are fully aware of the curriculum maps and the common assessment schedule for all the students on their caseloads. This allows them to develop an instructional pacing plan that gives them advance notice and ample time to collect materials and strategies that will support the needs of their students in the core classroom."

If the special educator is aware that the fifth-grade class is doing persuasive essays in November, she will have plenty of time to identify a graphic organizer or sentence frames that will help the fifth graders to develop their essays, even if she is not providing the direct instruction. As the strategy specialist, the special educator can help the students with special needs, and very often these same scaffolds help other students in class as well. It is very difficult for a special educator to provide scaffolded support when she is notified the day before the project is due that the student needs help. Collaboration and planning are essential for successful inclusive service delivery models.

Co-teaching Collaboration

While all collaborative teams are essential, it is the co-teaching collaborative team that needs the most nurturing. Weekly planning time might be sufficient for most collaborative teams, but the co-teaching team, especially in the initial years of implementation, needs to meet more frequently. All instructional planning for the co-teaching period should be done jointly. Finding the time to do this is difficult, but some schools have felt strongly enough about the need for nurturing and support that they allow the co-teaching teams an additional preparation period each day to plan for the co-taught period. The co-teaching team is the best combination of content expertise and instructional strategy expertise, and it is a waste of these resources to put these teachers into a classroom together without allowing them the time to determine how each will use his or her expertise in the most productive manner. The critical component of time cannot be underestimated! Once co-teaching teams have one year of instruction in a content area under their belt, they may need only a common preparation period when they can meet together once a week to plan their co-taught instruction.

Time for Collaboration

Finding time for collaboration is one of the greatest challenges that schools face. Since collaboration is central to the development of an RTI framework, administrators must work together with the staff to find solutions to the time problem. Some schools periodically repurpose their weekly staff meeting time to include a very short staff meeting and use most of the meeting time for collaborative purposes described. Some schools bank minutes during the instructional day so that they can have a longer collaboration period once a month when they can focus on professional development and instructional planning. Some schools supplement regular meeting times with quarterly release time, with the support of substitutes, to allow for extended data discussions and instructional planning opportunities. Some schools use other funding sources to pay for after-school or weekend meeting times so that teachers can develop long-term plans based on the vision, mission, and goals of the school. Some elementary school principals hold schoolwide assemblies on a regular basis to allow teachers time to meet with each other while students are at these all-school events. It may take some creative problem solving, but when teachers feel supported with the gift of time, the collaboration becomes effective at furthering the mission, vision, and goals of the school.

Collaboration is an essential element of RTI implementation. Without collaboration, the other process steps discussed in the previous chapters could not occur. Collaboration is not just an important aspect of instructional planning; it is necessary for even the first implementation steps to occur. Infrastructure building and consensus building cannot occur without collaborative agreements. Only when a school has come to common collaborative agreements is it ready to move ahead with the process steps of identifying evidence-based practices and developing standards-aligned curriculum maps. These practices are the backbone of the RTI structure and cannot occur in isolation. Once the programmatic decisions have been made, teachers can then reflect collaboratively on the data—both academic and behavioral—to adjust and inform their instruction and practice and ultimately improve student outcomes.

Wrapping Up the Main Points

The importance of collaboration in an RTI framework is fundamental. The time allocated to collaboration is indispensable. It is only through the time given to teachers to do the hard work of data analysis and goal development, instructional planning, and student-level problem solving can the monumental changes required in an RTI framework occur. As the RTI leadership team determines its action steps, it must resolve to determine how and when they will provide this essential ingredient. They also need to determine which teams to nurture first and how to provide the professional development that will allow teams the tools needed to use their time most effectively. Collaboration is a necessary ingredient to RTI implementation; determining how much and how often needs to be considered carefully in order to create a collaborative process that moves a school forward and to ensure results in improved academic achievement for all students.

Conclusion: Promising Achievement for All

For those school and district teams that have taken the challenge and are working through the arduous process steps described in this book, this chapter provides the encouragement that will keep you going when the task seems daunting. While in the throes of implementation, where each step is a step of faith, it is essential that teams are nourished with the success stories of schools that have taken these pioneering steps before them. This chapter presents national success stories as well as success stories from schools that I have worked with personally in the RTI implementation process.

It is important to note at this juncture that not one of them has "made it" yet. The process is ongoing, and the tweaking of programs, data, instruction, cut points, assessments, and instructional practices continues, but it is an invigorating adventure that none of them would leave behind. Why? Because it is about kids learning! The success stories include high school students who could not read and now have the gift of reading, of students who struggled as fourth graders, with significant gaps in reading skills, and were brought up to grade level and did not need intervention in middle school. Of students who had known only remedial instruction and had no hope of ever getting out of special education remedial programs who are scoring in the top 5 percent of the class and on their way out of special education. Persisting through the first year is the most difficult, like growing a crop, waiting for the "harvest" of data that proves that improvement has occurred, takes patience and a vision beyond the current circumstances. For those visionaries whose vision may be growing dim, this chapter is for you.

Keeping a Firm Footing on the Common Ground: Academic Achievement for *All* Students

Keeping the mantra of "academic achievement for *all* students" gets wearisome. There are so many other needs that vie for an administrator's attention and the time and energy of the leadership team and the teachers in the trenches. Data may not be as available as needed, staff members may find that working together takes some work, and the safe retreat back to the "kingdom of classroom" seems comfortable and assuring. Disagreements and a lack of common practice begin to tear some teams apart. Some students will not respond to the intervention, and despite the heroic effort on the teacher's part the achievement gap continues to persist. Cut points have created intervention groups that are too large, and the maladaptive behaviors of all students have not disappeared. RTI has not produced the Utopia it promised! It is at this point that many become

175

disillusioned and want to throw in the towel and quit … but wait. Take a moment, step back, and begin to look at the changes that have taken place, starting with data.

Let the Data Do the Talking

Data will provide a clear picture that, yes, some students have improved. It may not be that the tiers now are a perfect 80-15-5, but students have followed the arrow down from more intensive intervention to less intensity. A check of office referrals reveals that fewer students have been referred for classroom-level disruptive behavior. Benchmark assessments, while far from perfect, reveal that English learners and students with disabilities are scoring in similar ranges as their peers. And there will be some shining story of success that needs to heralded schoolwide. You may need to be a talent scout to find it, but search until you do, because this one point of light in a dark and wearisome world of schoolwide reform will bring about the renewed vigor and enthusiasm necessary to persist.

Naysayers will often identify their particular groups of students as the ones beyond any help. They will claim that no one else has worked with this kind of kid, this kind of family, this kind of poverty, this kind of unreasonable expectations. The schools presented in this chapter all had teachers and even some administrators who felt this way. These schools come from rural areas on distant islands, from inner-city schools with 100 percent free lunch and 98 percent English learners, from neighborhoods where gangs reign and violence is a way of life, yet these schools had a vision of better lives for their students and left the naysayers behind.

Implementation Research

The Center on Instruction studied implementation processes across several states and found common implementation practices that schools can use in their decision making around the difficult task of beginning the implementation process.[1] They found that, prior to implementation, all of the sites carefully examined their current practices to identify which components of RTI were already in place on their campuses. Based on the needs assessment data, all of these schools began their implementation process in phases. No sites in the study attempted a schoolwide implementation simultaneously at the beginning of year one. Some of them piloted the RTI framework at the lower elementary grades to determine what worked among screening, progress monitoring, and instructional practice. This pilot project helped them realize what did not work and what additional resources might be needed for further roll-out. This allowed them to strike a balance between not moving at all and moving too quickly.

" The Center on Instruction studied implementation processes across several states and found common implementation practices that schools can use in their decision making around the difficult task of beginning the implementation process. They found that, prior to implementation, all of the sites carefully examined their current practices to identify which components of RTI were already in place on their campuses. Based on the needs assessment data, all of these schools began their implementation process in phases. "

This pilot project roll-out allowed those resistant to change to see their successes. Many schools reported struggling with scheduling issues and teacher buy-in. Some of the sites reported that teacher buy-in increased once they saw students making progress based on data, and others brought the staff along by including all teachers in data discussions.

Each of the schools perceived RTI to have benefited their schools by enabling them to better serve their students. Several of the schools cited that the RTI interventions allowed fewer students to slip through the cracks; another often-cited benefit of RTI was increased collaboration among teachers and the sense that all staff members were on the same page, so that all students could benefit from all teachers. One of the schools reported an increase in student motivation as students became actively engaged in discussions regarding their own progress.

Based on the data collected in the research, Mohammed, Roberts, and Tackett found that all sites implemented RTI in phases, recognizing that schools and districts at the beginning implementation phase might determine to master one RTI element at a time: at the school level, implementing one grade level at a time, or at the district level, piloting one school before implementing more widely.[2]

They found that all the sites relied on creative scheduling and flexible use of funding and teachers. The schools recommended realigning teacher and staff responsibilities to fit the framework and acknowledged that some of these changes required tough choices. All of the schools found that implementation is a dynamic process and requires making changes throughout the year.

This research reaffirms that RTI implementation is not a quick fix but is an ongoing variable process that takes time in small incremental steps.

Stories of Success

The schools presented following are just a sampling of the schools that have worked through some of the process steps of implementing an RTI framework. None of them has successfully and completely implemented each and every process step but bullets identify the process steps implemented by each school. The RTI implementation process takes many years and is a continuous change process. The schools mentioned here have been in the implementation process for several years, and some have only just begun to see the result of their labors. The success stories will, I hope, allow others who are in the middle of the process steps to recognize similarities and find encouragement and practical support to persist through the process.

Union Middle School

- Collaborative models of special education
- Curriculum alignment
- Tiered interventions
- Evidence-based practices

The principal of Union Middle School in the Union Elementary School District recognized that while his school was not likely to end up in program improvement because of its high ranking in the statewide accountability system and its ability to meet all adequate yearly progress (AYP) targets, he recognized that students with disabilities were not receiving the same equitable and challenging education as their peers. The vision of an integrated RTI approach, including collaborative instruction for all learners at the school, was born. Through professional development, coaching around curriculum mapping, and evidence-based practices, the staff soon recognized that with the support of scaffolding and collaboration, students with disabilities could achieve in rigorous general education classes such as algebra and geometry, even at the middle school level.

Parents shared at the individualized education program (IEP) meeting the changes in their own children's motivation to do well in school when special education and general education teachers, with the support of effective instructional assistants, created a strong co-teaching and collaborative model that provided scaffolded support at each grade level in each content area. The vision of an energetic, strong-minded, committed principal with the support of a strong leadership team created a lasting impact on the families and students of Union Middle School.

Lillian J. Rice Elementary School

- Data-based decision making
- Evidence-based practices
- Tiered interventions

Many educators have worked in schools like Lillian J. Rice Elementary. At this school, English learners make up 36 percent of the district's population, and the focus of instruction is often on the needs of these English learners. Students at Rice benefit from an RTI framework that was adopted in the 2004–2005 school year. Since that time, the RTI framework has helped the district dramatically raise their test scores in mathematics and reading for the English learners, with the district meeting its AYP targets every year![3]

Teachers have changed their thinking from "I taught it and it's their fault if they got it or not" to "I need to keep teaching and supporting students." The instructional practice at Rice, as in many school districts across the nation, provides instruction at different intensity, frequency, and duration for different students. Here general education teachers meet the needs of students in their regular instruction in Tier I; small-group support in the classroom with some pull-out into a reading clinic characterizes Tier II; and intensive one-on-one instruction is provided to those students who need a Tier III intervention. In Tier II, Fernando, a first grader with limited ability to sound out words, was provided a one-hour intensive reading clinic four days a week. Within seventeen weeks of the start of the intervention, Fernando learned to read. His teacher noted that "he started putting the pieces together, and before we knew it, he was reading fluently."[4] With a strong focus on quality core instruction that incorporates strategies that support English learners, and an effective intensive Tier II instruction, Fernando will never need a special education referral due to reading failure. RTI fulfilled its promise of prevention in Fernando's life.

Ray Wiltsey Middle School

- Data-based decision making
- Collaborative models of special education service delivery
- Tiered interventions
- Collaborative practices

For the students in the Resource Program at Ray Wiltsey Middle School, it did not seem that an RTI framework was going to come through on its promise to prevent special education referral and special education processes. RTI at a middle school did not seem like an effective initiative, especially since many of the students in the Resource and Special Day Classes had been in special education since early elementary school. This did not stop the special education resource teacher and the school administration from embracing the vision of academic achievement for all students.

The vision included small learning communities to provide cross-curricular supports to all students; screening and placement of all students, including students with disabilities and English learners, in leveled English and math classes; and extensive instructional supports at each level based on need. Special education students were not segregated into separate classes but were included in the schoolwide tiers based on assessment data in the benchmark, strategic, or intensive classes.

Instructional support at the intensive level included co-taught classes with special educators in which content specialists and strategy specialists were able to share their expertise in a synergistic manner. These intensive classes in English language arts (ELA) were highly scaffolded to meet the needs of students with disabilities and English learners. Students in strategic classes were given instruction in the core and an additional period of instruction in general education with support from either a special educator or a trained instructional assistant. Benchmark classes received support for students with disabilities from trained instructional assistants.

This framework was initially met with some resistance from the staff. There was not yet the common belief that all students *can* learn, but the vision and passion of the vanguard group led the charge. Professional development and coaching supported the teams that took on the challenge, but the greatest change in attitude was made by data. At Ray Wiltsey, all students, including English learners and students with disabilities, participate in the district benchmark assessments. The results of the first assessment confirmed that *all* students can learn and students with disabilities are capable individuals. Figure C.1 is an example of a benchmark assessment that identifies

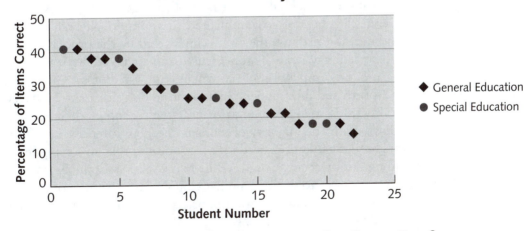

Figure C.1 Special Education Students Perform in the Top 5 Percent of the Class

two special education students in the top 5 percent of the class. Subsequent benchmark assessment proved the same to be true. Students with disabilities were able to score in the same range as their peers and often were at the top of the class. This data alone prompted an expansion of the model to include more teachers each year. Within two years, many of the students were back into strategic and benchmark classes, and the special educators at Ray Wiltsey were not working on special education referrals but were developing exit criteria *from* special education programs for their students.

Jefferson Elementary School

- Curriculum alignment
- Data-based decision making
- Multi-tiered interventions
- Evidence-based practices
- Collaborative practices

In an elementary school district directly beneath one of the busiest international airports in the world, the roar of airplanes every few minutes was the only common occurrence across the district and school sites. "Private practice" was the modus operandi. Due to the poor performance of the district for a number of years on overall scores in math and language arts for their 64 percent English language learner population, the rationale for implementing change was determined by the state.

The district had several options for improving its academic achievement and, not unlike the schools in the Center on Instruction implementation study, determined that one school would pilot an RTI model to determine the process for later roll-out districtwide. Upon completing the Standards Aligned Needs Assessment Tool, the staff identified a commonly paced and regularly assessed language arts curriculum as their greatest area of need with the highest priority. Teachers identified Tier I, or good first teaching, as needing the most attention.

The identification of essential standards, the first part of this process, was described in Chapter Seven. Teachers often commented that, despite the exhausting hours of discussion and decision making, they were empowered by the process and found that their current instruction was much more focused and aligned to what was assessed.

Screening and the compilation of placement data was discouraging. More than 60 percent of the fourth and fifth graders were found to be at least two grade levels below in reading ability. Most were reading at or near the second-grade level. The pyramid was upside down, with the majority of students needing intensive intervention! This shocking news brought about the need for collaborative problem solving that could not focus on staffing but on student need. While many schools in the beginning stages of RTI implementation are faced with a similar configuration because of the time it takes to build a strong Tier I, this building was not prepared with intervention staffing to meet the instructional needs of these students.

Exhibit C.1 Celebrating Our ELA/RTI Data and Program

Grade	Beginning of School Year	Middle of School Year (Current)	End of School Year (Projected)	Progress
4th	348 Lexile (2.0 GL)	507 Lexile (2.8 GL)	650 Lexile (3.7 GL)	1.75 yrs. in 1 year
5th	463 Lexile (2.5 GL)	639 Lexile (3.6 GL)	800 Lexile* (5.0 GL)	2+ yrs. in 1 year

38 students (20 percent) have *exited intervention*

Looking at student need alone, the grade-level team determined that the only way to meet the needs of all students was to become trained in the alternate core curriculum. They determined that they would provide instruction to all students in need rather than dole out intervention only to the bottom 3 to 5 percent. As teachers began to look at student-level data, they realized that combining the two grade levels for reading intervention instruction allowed them to provide a more precisely leveled instruction without duplication of services or levels between the two grade levels. Only the core classes were kept grade-level specific. This allowed this new combined grade-level team to provide several different levels of the intervention program across the two grade levels. This collaboration across grade levels was previously unknown, and teachers were amazed at how much they benefited from each other and the common instructional practices they were able to share. Members of the pioneering intervention team had to give up their own schedules, their own lessons, their own planning times, and their known curricula, yet the payoff at the end of the first trimester was well worth the effort! The results are shown in Exhibit C.1.

On the Scholastic Reading Inventory screening midyear, nearly forty students who had previously been more than two grade levels below scored at or near grade level. These students moved from the intensive program and were now in need of a strategic intervention to scaffold them back into the core curriculum. The staff again worked with amazing flexibility to reshuffle students and create two new strategic hybrid core classes at each grade level. Teachers worked together to develop common practices for these hybrid classes in collaboration with the core teachers to support future transitions. Teachers discovered that changing students and curriculum midyear wasn't as difficult as it seemed and that students were very flexible in joining new classes and learning new routines.

The progress made at Jefferson Elementary is not only about reading scores but also about a staff that learned that working together collaboratively is a powerful strategy for improvement.

Lennox Middle School 6

- Data-based decision making
- Collaborative models of special education services

- Tiered interventions
- Evidence-based practices
- Collaborative processes

Creating an inclusive environment in which all students achieve was the goal of the Lennox Middle School 6 principal, curriculum coach, and learning center team. With administrative support and success with a research-based reading intervention program in special education already in place, this innovative team wanted to expand the use of these practices to the at-risk populations in both language arts and math. They recognized their unique position as a sixth-grade school to provide targeted interventions to prepare their students for the rigors of middle school and high school.

The team recognized the need for current screening data and that they could not rely on state assessment data that were more than a year old. Screening of all incoming students at the end of the fifth grade year provided the foundation for a multi-tiered model of interventions regardless of student labels. Some members of the intensive intervention group indeed were special education students, but a considerable number were not. The district provided training to both general education and special education staff in the research-based instructional programs and ensured fidelity to the program with the correct number of instructional minutes and the appropriate class sizes.

After participating in periodic standards-based assessments, progress-monitoring data were used to develop cut points for exit and movement between tiers. At the end of the first trimester, nearly forty students in math and reading were exited from intensive interventions. In this school, joint ownership of all students allowed *all* students to be served based on need and not based on labels. A greater proportion of LMS 6 students will be prepared to move on to LMS 7–8 with the skills needed to be successful.

Albert Einstein Middle School

- Positive school climate
- Collaborative practices

Procedures and common expectations are the norm at Albert Einstein Middle School. It is not unusual to see teachers leading their classes outside the door and practicing entry procedures during the middle of the school year. Teachers at Einstein recognize that consistency and practice of procedures is what allows processes to become routines. As a school, they have collaboratively developed routines that describe in detail how students enter classes, turn in homework, head their papers, move about the classroom for cooperative group work, and look like when they're "paying attention." Teachers explicitly teach these behaviors and model them as frequently as necessary, using examples and non-examples to make their point. Students do not quickly forget the teacher walking across the room with a chair over his head as the non-example of how to move their chairs into cooperative groups. Teachers explicitly explain and model that "paying attention" means sitting upright in their seats with their pencils in the groove on their desks and their eyes on the teacher. Students know that this behavior will be positively reinforced. The teachers work on ensuring that they give five positive comments for each negative or redirecting comment. Some teachers have the word *Positive* written across the back wall to remind them that their task is to be positive and reinforce positive behaviors. Teachers and students know that rules and procedures are enforced in the same way across all classrooms and that consequences are consistently applied. It is a learning environment in which there are no surprises about behavioral and academic expectations and in which students feel safe and more readily able to learn.

> " The teachers work on ensuring that they give five positive comments for each negative or redirecting comment. Some teachers have the word *Positive* written across the back wall to remind them that their task is to be positive and reinforce positive behaviors. "

Putting the Pieces Together

These schools recognized the need for a strong vision of equity and academic achievement for *all*. They recognized the benefit of collaborative models of special education and services to English learners. They realized the importance of data and their alignment to instruction and the effective use of curriculum to focus instruction. They recognized the strength that comes from collaboration and the development of small learning communities to improve instruction to individual students and professional learning communities to improve instruction in content areas. They recognized that evidence-based practices and integrated inclusionary practices produced positive outcomes, even for those students who had formerly been served in segregated settings. They recognized the need for common behavioral expectations so that students can feel safe and ready to learn.

Wrapping Up the Main Points

Moving from theory to practice brings us to the place where real lives are changed. Students' futures are affected and teaching practices are forever changed by the response to intervention framework. No more silos, no more private practice, all for equitable education for all students.

Part IV

Appendixes

Appendix A: Response to Intervention Planning Questions: Assessing Current Programs

		CORE	
☐		**1. Is our core program sufficient?**	
		Step 1. Identify screening tools.	
		Step 2. Identify proficiency cut points for identified tools.	
		Step 3. Collect universal screening data.	
		Step 4. Enter, organize, and summarize data.	
		Step 5. Establish what percentage of proficiency is acceptable.	
		Step 6. Determine what percentage of the students are proficient and not proficient.	
		Step 7. Make comparison.	
		Step 8. What work, if any, do we need to do with our core program?	
☐		**2. If the core is not sufficient, why isn't it sufficient?**	
		Step 1. Review assessment.	
		Step 2. Review instruction.	
		Step 3. Review curriculum or standards.	
		Step 4. Review curriculum alignment.	
		Step 5. Consider other distal factors.	
☐		**3. How will needs identified in core be addressed?**	
		Step 1. Determine needs.	
		Step 2. Identify resources and/or training needed to address identified needs.	
		Step 3. Develop an action plan.	
		Step 4. Implement the plan.	
		Step 5. Evaluate the impact of the plan on your core program.	
☐		**4. How will the sufficiency and effectiveness of the core program be monitored over time?**	
		Step 1. What are the key indicators of success?	
		Step 2. What is the baseline performance?	
		Step 3. What is the desired goal?	
		Step 4. Determine your data collection plan.	
		Step 5. Make decisions about the sufficiency and effectiveness of core.	
☐		**5. Have improvements to the core been effective?**	
		Step 1. Consider student achievement data (screening).	
		Step 2. Compare current performance with baseline data.	
		Step 3. Consider implementation data.	
		Step 4. Make decision about effectiveness.	
		Step 5. Begin needs assessment again.	

	SUPPLEMENTAL AND INTENSIVE
☐	**6. For which students is the core instruction sufficient (or not sufficient), and why?**
	Step 1. List students for whom the core is not sufficient (significantly exceeding or less than proficient).
	Step 2. Determine diagnostic assessment tool(s) or process to identify instructional needs.
	Step 3. Determine expectations of performance for the diagnostic tool(s) or process.
	Step 4. Plan logistics and collect diagnostic data.
	Step 5. Organize, summarize, and display results.
☐	**7. What specific supplemental and intensive instruction is needed?**
	Step 1. Identify resources district currently has to match instructional needs.
	Step 2. Identify additional resources needed to match instructional needs.
☐	**8. How will specific supplemental and intensive instruction be delivered? (steps listed in no particular order)**
	Step 1. Review materials/strategies/processes selected for instructional groups.
	Step 2. Determine who will provide instruction.
	Step 3. Establish when, where, and how often instruction will occur.
	Step 4. Determine how you will monitor treatment integrity.
	Step 5. Document on a written intervention form.
☐	**9. How will the effectiveness of supplemental and intensive instruction be monitored?**
	Step 1. Select progress monitoring/formative assessments.
	Step 2. Set goals for student performance using baseline data.
	Step 3. Organize materials for ongoing data collection.
	Step 4. Determine who will collect the data and how often.
	Step 5. Determine decision-making rule.
	Step 6. Provide instruction as designed and monitor student performance and implementation integrity.
☐	**10. Which students need to move to a different level of instruction?**
	Step 1. Review progress monitoring/formative assessment data.
	Step 2. Plan for and document instructional changes if needed.

Source: Adapted from Iowa Department of Education.

Appendix B: Tier–Aligned RTI Readiness Tool

Readiness Elements	Implementation Level 1 (None)	Implementation Level 2 (Some or Beginning)	Implementation Level 3 (Most or Advanced)	Implementation Level 4 (All or Complete)	Comments
A district-level RTI implementation team has been developed					
A site-level RTI implementation team has been developed					
Grade-level or content area intervention teams have been developed					
Schoolwide Data-Based Elements					
School or district has identified universal screening tools to be utilized for all incoming students					
School or district has identified progress-monitoring tools, and teachers are trained in use of the tools					
Teachers utilize benchmark assessments based on curriculum map and standards taught to adjust instructional delivery and strategies					
Tier I Elements					
Essential standards for ELA have been identified					
Curriculum maps have been developed that are aligned to the essential standards for the grade level in ELA					

(Continued)

Readiness Elements	Implementation Level 1 (None)	Implementation Level 2 (Some or Beginning)	Implementation Level 3 (Most or Advanced)	Implementation Level 4 (All or Complete)	Comments
Curriculum maps are used to drive instructional pacing to ensure assessed standards are taught in ELA					
Weekly planning reflects standards aligned instruction identified by the curriculum map					
Teachers have regularly scheduled collaboration time to meet as a grade level					
Teachers use regularly scheduled collaboration time to plan weekly grade-level lessons in ELA					
Teachers utilize data from curriculum-based measures to plan instruction					
Teachers organize daily instruction to reflect high expectations through the use and display of daily agendas and learning goals/standards					
All teachers are trained in the curriculum materials and standards for ELA at their grade level					
Teachers use the core curriculum materials to support the instruction of the grade-level content standards					

	Implementation Level 1 (None)	Implementation Level 2 (Some or Beginning)	Implementation Level 3 (Most or Advanced)	Implementation Level 4 (All or Complete)	Comments
Readiness Elements					
Teachers have a thorough understanding and knowledge of the principles and strategies of differentiated instruction and student engagement					
Teachers are trained in the appropriate instructional accommodations for students with disabilities and English learners in ELA core					
Teachers have been involved in the development of a schoolwide positive behavior plan					
Teachers have directly taught positive behavioral expectations to students					
Tier II Elements					
Teachers use ongoing progress monitoring data and curriculum-based measures to determine student need for supplemental instruction					
Teachers analyze data as a grade level to determine which students need additional supplemental intervention					
Teachers use data to determine homogenous groupings for supplemental targeted instruction					
As a grade level, teachers identify what instructional supplemental interventions will be provided to target students					

(*Continued*)

Readiness Elements	Implementation Level 1 (None)	Implementation Level 2 (Some or Beginning)	Implementation Level 3 (Most or Advanced)	Implementation Level 4 (All or Complete)	Comments
As a grade level, teachers identify which teacher(s) will provide the supplemental instruction in their grade level					
The schedule allows for flexible scheduling to allow grade-level teams to provide supplemental instruction					
As a grade-level team, teachers will determine how to provide supplemental instruction to students within their grade level					
Students with disabilities and English learners are included in these supplemental instruction groups					
Teachers monitor student behavior using data to make decisions about supplemental behavior support					
Teachers implement supplemental behavior support strategies for students in need of extra support					
Teachers use data to make decisions about continuing or discontinuing supplemental instructional support					
Tier III Elements					
The school has intensive interventions in place designed to address common and/or frequent reading problems					

Readiness Elements	Implementation Level 1 (None)	Implementation Level 2 (Some or Beginning)	Implementation Level 3 (Most or Advanced)	Implementation Level 4 (All or Complete)	Comments
Decisions on participation in intensive interventions are based on screening and progress-monitoring data					
Frequent progress monitoring is utilized during the intensive intervention period					
Entry and exit criteria have been established for students in need of intensive interventions					
Teachers have been trained with fidelity in the implementation of the intervention program					
Intensive interventions are designed to accelerate, not remediate, reading problems					
Teachers frequently assess student progress during the reading intervention period to determine the effectiveness of the intervention					
Teachers work in collaboration and provide essential data to specialists while implementing intensive behavior supports					

Appendix C: RTI Action Plan Draft Template

School _____

Planning Team _____

Date _____

Task	Detailed Actions	Resources	Timeline	Lead(s)	Evidence of Change

Source: Adapted from Response to Intervention Readiness and Implementation: Self-Assessment Tool. Pennsylvania Department of Education, November 2007 revised.

Copyright © 2010 by WestEd. From Silvia DeRuvo's *The Essential Guide to RTI*, Jossey-Bass, 2010.

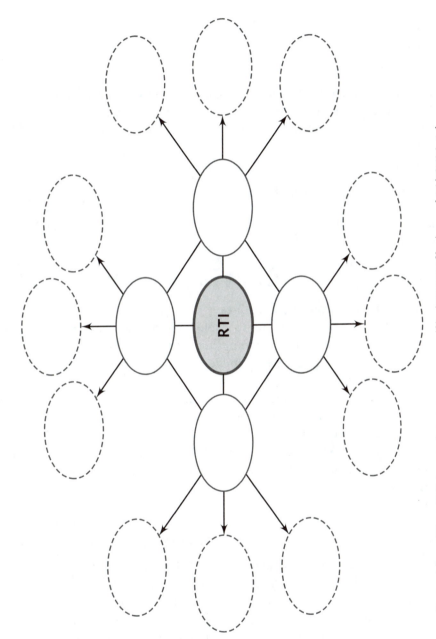

Source: Adapted from ICT Approaches, www.vcta.asn.au/files/2006%20files/compak06/ICT06_4.doc.

Appendix D: Evidence-Based Practices Check Sheet

Use this check sheet when making decisions about Tier I, Tier II, and Tier III instruction and intervention materials and practices.

Early Reading Essential Elements
- ☐ Phonemic awareness
- ☐ Phonics
- ☐ Fluency
- ☐ Vocabulary
- ☐ Comprehension

Essential Elements of Early Reading Instruction and Intervention
- ☐ Training in phonological awareness, decoding, and word study
- ☐ Guided and independent reading of progressively more difficult text
- ☐ Writing exercises
- ☐ Engaging students in comprehension practice

Secondary Reading Essential Elements
- ☐ Word study
- ☐ Fluency
- ☐ Vocabulary
- ☐ Comprehension
- ☐ Motivation

Math Essential Elements and Practices
- ☐ Balanced approach between number sense and problem-solving strategies
- ☐ Opportunities to engage in meaningful practice
- ☐ Mathematically enriched environment
    - ☐ Visible math vocabulary
    - ☐ References and explanation of abstract symbols
    - ☐ Use of manipulatives and tools
    - ☐ Use of calculators
- ☐ Explicit instruction to teach procedural knowledge
- ☐ Questioning strategies that require explanations and descriptions
- ☐ Progress-monitoring practices
- ☐ Problem-solving practice

Evidence-Based Practices for English Learners

Evidence-Based English Language Arts Instruction Practices
- ☐ Early explicit intensive instruction in phonological awareness and phonics
- ☐ Increase opportunities to develop sophisticated vocabulary
- ☐ Instruction on strategies to comprehend and analyze narrative and expository text
- ☐ Focus reading fluency on vocabulary and increased exposure to print
- ☐ Provide opportunities to engage in structured academic talk
- ☐ Structure independent reading to be purposeful, providing a good reader-text match

Evidence-Based Math Instruction and Practices
- ☐ Early explicit and intensive instruction in basic math concepts and skill
- ☐ Systematic academic language instruction of math vocabulary
- ☐ Academic language instruction to support solving of work problems

Appendix E: Pacing Guide Tools

Core Content Area: _____   Grade Level: _____

Standard Area:	Standard Area:	Standard Area:
Materials	Materials	Materials
Assignments	Assignments	Assignments
Projects	Projects	Projects
Assessments	Assessments	Assessments
Adaptations	Adaptations	Adaptations
Month:	Month:	Month:
Materials	Materials	Materials
Assignments	Assignments	Assignments
Projects	Projects	Projects
Assessments	Assessments	Assessments
Adaptations	Adaptations	Adaptations
Month:	Month:	Month:

CURRICULUM PLANNING DEVELOPMENT

Standard Area:

Materials:

Assignments:

Essential Learning Topics:

Projects:

Assessments:

Academic Vocabulary:

Adaptations:

Core Content Standards-Driven Pacing Guide

Core Content Area: _____   Grade Level: _____

August Standards Addressed	September Standards Addressed	October Standards Addressed	November Standards Addressed

Core Content Standards-Driven Pacing Guide

Core Content Area: _____   Grade Level: _____

December Standards Addressed	January Standards Addressed	February Standards Addressed	March Standards Addressed

Core Content Standards-Driven Pacing Guide

Core Content Area: _____

Grade Level: _____

April Standards Addressed	May Standards Addressed	June Standards Addressed	July Standards Addressed

Appendix F: Tracking Student Learning

Tracking My Own Learning:
Student

Student Name ______________________________ Date __________

Learning Goal

____

____

My score at beginning: __________ My goal: ________ By __________

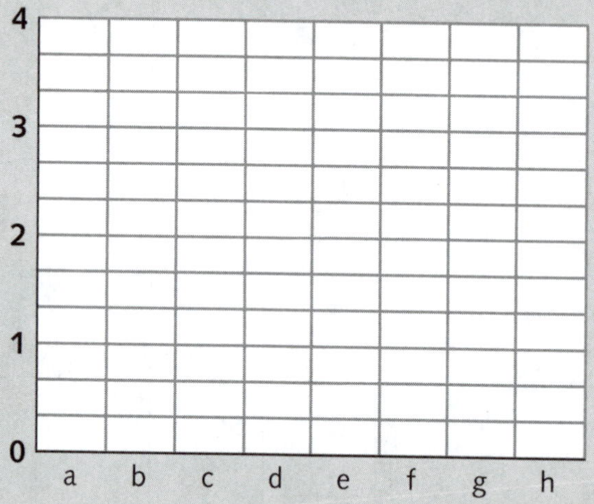

a ______________

b ______________

c ______________

d ______________

e ______________

f ______________

g ______________

h ______________

4

3

2

1

Tracking Student Learning:
Classroom

Teacher _____ Grade/Subject _____

Grading Period/Time Span _____

Learning Goal

_____

_____

Number of students represented by this graph _____

Percent Proficient and Above

100
90
80
70
60
50
40
30
20
10
0

a   b   c   d   e   f   g   h

a _____

b _____

c _____

d _____

e _____

f _____

g _____

h _____

Tracking Student Progress:
School

School _____

Grade/Subject _____   Grading Period/Time Span _____

Learning Goal

_____

_____

Number of students represented by this graph _____   *Number of teachers* _____

Percent Proficient and Above

100								
90								
80								
70								
60								
50								
40								
30								
20								
10								
0	a	b	c	d	e	f	g	h

a _____

b _____

c _____

d _____

e _____

f _____

g _____

h _____

Appendix G: Schoolwide Positive Behavior Supports Check Sheet

Primary Tier Readiness Requirements: Systems
☐ Establish a representative schoolwide positive behavior supports (SWPBS) team.
☐ Identify a team member to serve as coach.
☐ Secure 80 percent buy-in from the school staff.
☐ Employ a data system that facilitates data entry and meaningful visual displays (graphs).
☐ Participate as a team in SWPBS training.

Implementing Primary SWPBS Interventions: Practices
☐ Establish a small number of positively stated expectations.
☐ Define the expectations in the context of routines and settings.
☐ Develop scripted lesson plans to teach expectations.
☐ Increase active supervision in classroom and nonclassroom settings.
☐ Establish a continuum of strategies to acknowledge appropriate behavior.
☐ Establish a continuum of strategies to respond to inappropriate behavior.
☐ Develop a staff reinforcement plan.
☐ Develop an action plan to guide roll-out and implementation.

Monitoring Implementation Effectiveness and Fidelity: Data
☐ Review data at every SWPBS team meeting and use data to make decisions.
☐ Share data with the faculty and model data-based decision making.
☐ Celebrate successes with students and staff.
☐ Share successes with parents and other community members.

Other:

_____

_____

_____

_____

_____

_____

Check-In, Check-Out Daily Progress Report

Student's Name_____   Date_____

Teachers: Please use the following rubric to reflect student's progress on the following goals:

Mostly (5)   *Sometimes (3)*   *Never (1)*

Goals	*1*			*2*			*3*			*4*			*5*			*6*		
On Time	5	3	1	5	3	1	5	3	1	5	3	1	5	3	1	5	3	1
Prepared for Class	5	3	1	5	3	1	5	3	1	5	3	1	5	3	1	5	3	1
Followed Directions	5	3	1	5	3	1	5	3	1	5	3	1	5	3	1	5	3	1
Completed Tasks	5	3	1	5	3	1	5	3	1	5	3	1	5	3	1	5	3	1
Respectful to Others	5	3	1	5	3	1	5	3	1	5	3	1	5	3	1	5	3	1
TOTAL POINTS																		
TEACHER'S INITIALS																		

Daily Goal: (30/150)   Daily Score: (30/150)

Student Signature_____
Provide brief comments or observations

Period 1 _____

Period 2 _____

Period 3 _____

Period 4 _____

Period 5 _____

Period 6 _____

Parent/Guardian Signature _____

Parent/Guardian Comments _____

Appendix H: Collaboration Tools

Data Review Tool

Grade level:
Week of:
Content area:
Grade:

Standard area(s) to be addressed:

_____

_____

_____

Data reviewed: ☐ Assessments   ☐ Student Work   ☐ Other

_____

_____

The data show   ☐ improvement   ☐ no change   ☐ decline in student performance

Explanation of results and variations:

_____

_____

The data show the most need of improvement in the following areas:

_____

_____

Strategies for addressing the areas that need improvement:

_____

_____

_____

Effectiveness of previous strategies used:

_____

_____

Evidence of effectiveness (or noneffectiveness):

_____

_____

Next steps—agenda item for next meeting:

_____

_____

Instructional Planning Tool

Grade level:
Week of:
Content area:
Grade:

Standard area(s) to be addressed:

_____

_____

_____

Lessons addressed:

_____

_____

_____

Materials:

_____

_____

Assignments:

_____

_____

Projects:

_____

_____

Assessments (how will the attainment of the standard be measured?):

_____

_____

Adaptations:

_____

_____

Possible problems:

_____

_____

Possible solutions:

_____

_____

Possible strategies:

_____

_____

_____

Responsibilities:

_____   _____

_____   _____

_____   _____

_____   _____

_____   _____

Next steps—agenda item for next meeting:

_____

_____

Strategies and Accommodations Tool

Grade level:
Week of:
Content area:
Grade:

Standard area(s) to be addressed:

_____

_____

_____

Students who need specific accommodations or more focused strategies:

_____ _____

_____ _____

_____ _____

_____ _____

Which specific research based strategies will support the needs of some (or all) of these students? Target strategies for this week:

_____

_____

_____

What previous strategies have been attempted?

_____

_____

How effective were these strategies?

_____

_____

What is the evidence that these strategies have been (or have not been) successful?

_____

_____

These student(s) need these additional accommodations or adaptations:

_____ _____

_____ _____

_____ _____

_____ _____

_____ _____

How will the team know if these students have met the standard(s)?

_____

How will the input for these students look different?

_____

How will the content be adjusted for these students?

_____

How will the output differ for these students?

_____

What additional instructional or supplemental support is needed for these student(s) to be able to participate effectively and reach the standards?

_____   _____

_____   _____

_____   _____

_____   _____

_____   _____

Which members of the team have the expertise and skills to provide these supports?

_____   _____

_____   _____

_____   _____

_____   _____

_____   _____

What additional adaptations are needed from the special education case managers to support progress in these standards?

_____

_____

_____

How will these supports be provided?

☐ Consultative or collaborative (materials, adapted homework, other _____)

☐ Team teaching: (schedule: _____)

☐ Small-group supplemental support: (schedule _____)

☐ Resource or special ed. room support: (schedule _____)

☐ Other_____

Next steps—agenda item for next meeting:

_____

_____

Student: _____ Teacher(s): _____ Grade: _____

School: _____ Date: _____ Parents: _____

Strengths	Relevant Information	Concerns	Current or Past Interventions	Intervention Strategies: Action Plan	By Who	When
Academic:	Academic info: Assessment data:	Academic or behavioral	Instructional ____ shortened assignments ____ vary mode of presentation ____ small-group instruction ____ use of manipulatives ____ use of graphic organizers Instructional supports: Tier I ____ small group ____ peer tutoring Tier II ____ small homogenous group ____ reading tutor ____ supplemental instruction Tier III ____ alternate core instruction ____ extra supplemental instruction Type or Tier III instruction :	1. 2. 3. 4. 5. Next meeting date:		
	English language proficiency:					
	Attendance:					
	Additional assessments:		Behavioral interventions: ____ daily/weekly notes home ____ behavior contract ____ token economy ____ data monitoring of behavior ____ adult mentoring ____ counseling			
Other:	Other:		Other:			

Notes

Introduction

1. L. Kongshem, *Failure Is Not an Option: An Interview with U.S. Secretary Rod Paige,* n.d. Retrieved May 14, 2009, from *Scholastic Administrator* Web site: www2.scholastic.com/browse/srticle .jsp?id=75.

Chapter One

1. National Center on Response to Intervention, "What Is RTI?" n.d. Retrieved January 17, 2010, from www.rti4success.org.

2. Ibid.

3. J. Echevarria and J. Hasbrouck, *Response to Intervention and English Learners.* Center for Research on the Educational Achievement and Teaching of English Language Learners, 2009. Available at www.cal.org/create.

4. G. Batsche, J. Elliot, J. Graden, J. Grimes, J. Kovaleski, D. Prasse, D. Reschly, J. Schrag, and D. Tilly, *Response to Intervention: Policy Considerations and Implementation.* Alexandria, VA: National Association of State Directors of Special Education, 2005.

5. L. Fox, J. U. Carta, P. Strain, G. Dunlap, and M. L. Hemmeter, *Response to Intervention and the Pyramid Model.* Tampa: University of South Florida, Technical Assistance Center on Social Emotional Intervention for Young Children, June 2009.

6. S. Rishi, *Response to Instruction and Intervention: A Systematic Approach to Closing the Achievement Gap.* Presentation to the California Regional Consortia Statewide Meeting, California Department of Education, October 28, 2009.

7. M. C. Reynolds, "Reaction to the JLD Special Series on the Regular Education Initiative." *Journal of Learning Disabilities* 21 (1988), 352–356.

8. G. Glass, "Effectiveness of Special Education." *Policy Studies Review* 2 (1983), 65–78, p. 69.

9. National Research Center on Learning Disabilities, *RTI Manual.* Washington, DC: Author, 2006.

10. No Child Left Behind Act of 2001, Public Law 107–110, 5, 115 Stat.1427 et seq. (2002).

11. Individuals with Disabilities Education Improvement Act, 20 U.S.C., Sec. 1400 (2004).

12. D. F. Mellard and E. Johnson, *RTI: A Practitioner's Guide to Implementing Response to Intervention.* Thousand Oaks, CA: Corwin Press, 2008.

13. G. R. Lyon, J. M. Fletcher, S. E. Shaywitz, B. A. Shaywitz, J. K. Torgesen, F. B. Wood, A. Schulte, and R. Olson, *Rethinking Learning Disabilities.* Washington, DC: Hudson Institute, 2001.

14. D. F. Mellard and E. Johnson, *RTI: A Practitioner's Guide to Implementing Response to Intervention.* Thousand Oaks, CA: Corwin Press, 2008.

15. Individuals with Disabilities Education Improvement Act, 20 U.S.C.1400, Sec. 614(b)6B (2004).

16. K. K. Tackett, G., Roberts, S. Baker, and N. Scammaca, *Implementing Response to Intervention: Practices and Perspectives from Five Schools. Frequently Asked Questions.* Portsmouth, NH: RMC Research Corporation, Center on Instruction, 2009.

17. David Tilly, *Diagnosing the Learning Enabled: Response to Intervention Provisions of IDEA '04.* California State Board of Education Seminar, July 6, 2005.

18. L. S. Fuchs and D. Fuchs, "A Model for Implementing Responsiveness to Intervention." *Teaching Exceptional Children* 39:5 (2007), 14–20.

19. K. Futernick, *A Possible Dream: Retaining California Teachers So All Students Can Learn.* Sacramento: California State University, 2007.

Chapter Two

1. IDEA Partnership, "RtI: Glossary of Terms," n.d. Retrieved September 2, 2009, from www.ideapartnership.org.

2. G. Batsche, J. Elliot, J. Graden, J. Grimes, J. Kovaleski, D. Prasse, D. Reschly, J. Schrag, and D. Tilly, *Response to Intervention: Policy Considerations and Implementation.* Alexandria, VA: National Association of State Directors of Special Education, 2005.

3. S. Mohammed, G. Roberts, and K. Tackett, *Implementing RTI: Practices and Perspectives.* Schools Moving Up webinar, May 7, 2008. Retrieved January 23, 2010, from www.schoolsmovingup.net/cs/smu/view/e/2818.

4. Center for Educational Networking, "NASDSE Explains Response to Intervention." *Focus on Results: Guidance and Technical Assistance for Special Education Stakeholders* 2:7 (August 2006). Retrieved December 12, 2009, from www.cenmi.org on.

5. P. Rutherford, *Instruction for All Students.* Alexandria, VA: Just Ask Publications and Professional Development, 2008.

6. R. Horner, *Response to Intervention and School-Wide Positive Behavior Supports.* Webinar presented at the National Center on Response to Intervention, January 14, 2010. Retrieved January 23, 2010 from http://rti4success.org.

7. G. Sugai, R. Horner, G. Dunlap, M. Hieneman, T. J. Lewis, C. M. Nelson, T. Scott, C. Liaupsin, W. Sailor, A. P. Turnbull, H. R. Turnbull, D. Wickham, M. Reuf, and B. Wilcox, "Applying Positive Behavior Support and Functional Assessment in Schools." *Journal of Positive Interventions* 2 (2001), 131–143.

8. Horner, *Response to Intervention.*

9. S. Fairbanks, B. Simonsen, and G. Sugai, "Classwide Secondary and Tertiary Tier Practices and Systems." *Teaching Exceptional Children* 40:6 (2008), 44–52.

10. D. Cheney, K. Breen, and J. Rose, *Universal School-Wide Screening to Identify Students for Tier 2/ Tier 3 Interventions.* Presentation from National Forum for Implementers of School-Wide PBS, 2008.

11. Fairbanks et al., "Classwide Secondary and Tertiary Tier Practices."

Chapter Three

1. L. Danielson, From opening remarks by Lou Danielson, PhD, Director, Research to Practice Division, Office of Special Education Programs to the National SEA Conference on SLD Determination, Kansas City, MO, April 21, 2006.

2. U.S. Department of Education, Office of Special Education Programs, Data Analysis System, 2002–03.

3. Title 34, *Code of Federal Regulations* (August 6, 2006).

4. Individuals with Disabilities Education Improvement Act, 20 U.S.C., Sec. 1400 [b][6]). (2004).

5. Title 34, *Code of Federal Regulations,* Sections 300. 304–300.306 (August 6, 2006).

6. *Determining Specific Learning Disability Using Response to Instruction and Intervention (RtI²).* Sacramento: California Department of Education, CDE Press, 2009.

7. K. Hettleman, *The Road to Nowhere: The Illusion and Broken Promises of Special Education in the Baltimore City and Other Public School Systems.* Baltimore, MD: Abell Foundation, 2004.

Chapter Four

1. Center for Educational Networking, "NASDSE Explains Response to Intervention." *Focus on Results: Guidance and Technical Assistance for Special Education Stakeholders* 7:2 (August 2006). Retrieved December 12, 2009, from www.cenmi.org.

2. D. D. Smith, *Introduction to Special Education: Making a Difference.* Boston: Allyn & Bacon, 2007.

3. M. Seastrom, C. Chapman, R. Stillwell, D. McGrath, P. Peltola, R. Dinkes, and Z. Xu, *User's Guide to Computing High School Graduation Rates. Volume 2: Technical Evaluation of Proxy Graduation Indicators* (NCES 2006-605). Washington, DC: U.S. Department of Education, National Center for Education Statistics, 2006, p 27.

4. President's Commission on Excellence in Special Education. *A New Era: Revitalizing Special Education for Children And Their Families.* Washington, DC: Author, 2002.

5. Smith, *Introduction to Special Education.*

6. K. S. McGrew and J. Evans, *Expectations for Students with Cognitive Disabilities: Is the Cup Half Empty or Half Full? Can the Cup Flow Over?* (Synthesis Report 55). Minneapolis: University of Minnesota, National Center on Educational Outcomes, 2003. Retrieved May 6, 2007, from http://cehd.umn.edu/nceo/OnlinePubs/Synthesis55.html.

7. K. Hettleman, *The Road to Nowhere: The Illusion and Broken Promises of Special Education in the Baltimore City and Other Public School Systems.* Baltimore, MD: Abell Foundation, 2004.

8. M. Friend and L. Cook, *Collaboration for School Professionals.* Boston: Pearson Education, 2007.

9. Ibid.

10. Ibid.

11. The Access Center, Improving Outcomes for All Students K–8, *Improving Access to the General Curriculum for Students with Disabilities Through Collaborative Teaching—For Teachers,* n.d. Retrieved January 15, 2010, from www.k8accesscenter.org/index.php/category/co-teaching.

Chapter Five

1. S. Mohammed, G. Roberts, and K. Tackett, *Implementing RTI: Practices and Perspectives*. Schools Moving Up webinar, May 7, 2008. Retrieved January 23, 2010, from www.schoolsmovingup.net/cs/smu/view/e/2818.

2. S. Kurns and D. Tilly, *Response to Intervention: Blueprints for Implementation — School Building Level*. Alexandria, VA: National Association of State Directors of Special Education, 2008.

3. S. Mohammed, G. Roberts, and K. Tackett, *Implementing RTI: Practices and Perspectives*. Schools Moving Up webinar, May 7, 2008. Retrieved January 23, 2010, from www.schoolsmovingup.net/cs/smu/view/e/2818.

4. Kurns and Tilly, *Response to Intervention*.

Chapter Six

1. R. Newman-Gonchar, B. Clarke, and R. Gersten, *A Summary of Nine Key Studies: Multi-Tiered Intervention and Response to Interventions for Students Struggling in Mathematics*. Portsmouth, NH: RMC Research Corporation, Center on Instruction, 2009.

2. A. Griffiths, L. Parson, M. Burns, A. VanDerHeyden, and D. Tilly, *Response to Intervention: Research for Practice*. Alexandria, VA: National Association of State Directors of Special Education, 2007.

3. Center on Instruction, *Intensive Reading Interventions for Struggling Readers in Early Elementary School: A Principal's Guide*. Portsmouth, NH: RMC Research Corporation, Center on Instruction, 2006.

4. Florida Center for Reading Research, *Summary Table of FCRR Reports*. Retrieved February 2, 2010, from www.fcrr.org/FCRRReports.

5. S. Vaughn and G. Roberts, "Secondary Interventions for Reading: Providing Additional Instruction for Students At Risk." *Teaching Exceptional Children* 39:5 (2007), 40–46.

6. Center on Instruction, *Intensive Reading Interventions*.

7. Ibid.

8. A. G. Boardman, G. Roberts, S. Vaughn, J. Wexler, C. S. Murray, and M. Kosanovich, *Effective Instruction for Adolescent Struggling Readers: A Practice Brief*. Portsmouth, NH: RMC Research Corporation, Center on Instruction, 2008.

9. Ibid.

10. Ibid.

11. Ibid.

12. Ibid.

13. Ibid.

14. F. M. Graves, *The Vocabulary Book: Learning and Instruction*. Urbana, IL: Teachers College Press, 2006.

15. I. L. Beck, M. G. McKeown, and L. Kucan, *Bringing Words to Life: Robust Vocabulary Instruction*. New York: Guilford Press, 2002.

16. J. Wood, "Can Software Support Children's Vocabulary Development?" *Language Learning and Technology* 5 (2001), 166–201.

17. J. T. Guthrie and N. M. Humenick, "Motivating Students to Read: Evidence for Classroom Practices That Increase Reading Motivation and Achievement." In P. McCardle and V. Chabra (Eds.), *The Voice of Evidence in Reading Research* (pp. 329–354). Baltimore: Brookes, 2004.

18. Newman-Gonchar et al., *Summary of Nine Key Studies*.

19. Ibid.

20. L. S. Fuchs, D. Fuchs, and K. H. Hollenbeck, "Extending Responsiveness to Intervention to Mathematics at First and Third Grades." *Learning Disabilities Research and Practice* 22 (2007), 13–24.

21. M. Jayanthi, R. Gersten, and S. Baker, *Mathematics Instruction for Students with Learning Disabilities or Difficulty Learning Mathematics: A Guide for Teachers*. Portsmouth, NH: RMC Research Corporation, Center on Instruction, 2008.

22. Ibid.

23. Newman-Gonchar et al., *Summary of Nine Key Studies*.

24. D. P. Bryant, B. R. Bryant, R. Gersten, N. Scammaca, and M. Chavez, "Mathematics Interventions for First and Second Grade Students with Mathematic Difficulties: The Effects of Tier 2 Intervention Delivered as Booster Lessons." *Remedial and Special Education* 29:1 (2008), 20–32.

25. The Access Center: Improving Outcomes for Students K-8. *Concrete-Representational-Abstract Instructional Approach,* n.d. Retrieved on November 7, 2008, from www.k8accesscenter.org/training_resources/CRA_Instructional_Approach.

26. J. Echevarria and K. Short, "Programs and Practices for Effective Sheltered Content Instruction." In D. Dolson and L. Burnham-Massey (Eds.), *Improving Education for English Learners: Research-Based Approaches* (pp. 297–374). Sacramento: California Department of Education Press, 2009.

27. J. Echevarria and J. Hasbrouck, *Response to Intervention and English Learners*. Center for Research on the Educational Achievement and Teaching of English Language Learners, 2009. Available at www.cal.org/create.

28. D. J. Francis, M. Rivera, N. Lesaux, M. Kieffer, and H. Rivera, *Practical Guidelines for the Education of English Language Learners: Research-Based Recommendations for Instruction and Academic Intervention*. Portsmouth, NH: RMC Research Corporation, Center on Instruction, 2006.

29. Francis et al., *Practical Guidelines for the Education of English Language Learners*.

30. Ibid.

31. Beck at al., *Bringing Words to Life*.

32. Francis et al., *Practical Guidelines for the Education of English Language Learners*.

33. C. Arreaga-Mayer and C. Perdomo-Rivera, "Ecobehavioral Analysis of Instruction for At-Risk Language Minority Students." *Elementary School Journal* 96 (1996), 245–258.

34. Francis et al., *Practical Guidelines for the Education of English Language Learners*.

35. Center on Instruction, *Intensive Reading Interventions*.

36. Francis et al., *Practical Guidelines for the Education of English Language Learners.*

37. Ibid.

Chapter Seven

1. P. Rutherford, *Instruction for All Students.* Alexandria, VA: Just ASK Publications & Professional Development, 2008.

2. C. Wallis and S. Steptoe, "How to Fix No Child Left Behind." *Time,* June 4, 2007.

3. E. Benadom, *Identifying the Lennox Essential Standards.* Training provided to Lennox School District Staff, February 2009.

4. I. L. Beck, M. G. McKeown, and L. Kucan, *Bringing Words to Life: Robust Vocabulary Instruction.* New York: Guilford Press, 2002.

5. P. Spycher, *English Learners and Language Arts (ELLA).* Training provided to the Lennox Unified School District, July 2009.

Chapter Eight

1. D. Reeves, "Looking Deeper into Data." *Educational Leadership* 66:4 (2009), 89–90.

2. F. M. Hess, "The New Stupid." *Educational Leadership* 66:4 (2009), 12–17.

3. J. R. Jenkins, R. F. Hudson, and E. S. Johnson, "Screening for At-Risk Readers in a Response to Intervention Framework." *School Psychology Review* 36 (2007), 582–600.

4. J. R. Jenkins, *Candidate Measures for Screening At-Risk Students.* Paper presented at the National Research Center on Learning Disabilities Responsiveness-to-Intervention symposium, Kansas City, MO, December 2003. Retrieved May 15, 2008, from www.nrcld.org/symposium2003/jenkins/index.html.

5. P. M. Stecker and J. M. Hintz, *Data-Based Decision Making.* Presented at the 2006 Institute on Student Progress Monitoring, Kansas City, MO, July 13, 2006.

6. M. L. Thurlow, J. L. Elliot, and J. E. Ysseldyke, *Testing Students with Disabilities: Practical Strategies for Complying with District and State Standards.* Thousand Oaks, CA: Corwin Press, 2006.

7. R. Marzano, *Classroom Assessment and Grading That Work.* Alexandria, VA: Association for Supervision and Curriculum Development, 2006.

8. Ibid.

9. Council of Chief State School Officers (CCSSO), *Glossary of Assessment Terms and Acronyms Used in Assessing Special Education Students.* Policy to Practice Study Group: Assessing Special Education Students (ASES), Collaborative on Assessment and Student Standards (SCASS). 2003. Retrieved on December 10, 2009, from http://www.ccsso.org/publications/details.cfm?PublicationID=222.

10. Thurlow et al., *Testing Students with Disabilities.*

11. Hess, "The New Stupid."

12. D. F. Mellard and E. Johnson, *RTI: A Practitioner's Guide to Implementing Response to Intervention.* Thousand Oaks, CA: Corwin, 2008.

Notes

13. Center on Instruction, *An Introduction to Progress Monitoring in Math, Center on Instruction Mathematics Strand*, 2009. Retrieved December 1, 2009, from www.centeroninstruction.org.

14. D. Cheney, K. Breen, and J. Rose, *Universal School-Wide Screening to Identify Students for Tier 2/Tier 3 Interventions.* Presentation from National Forum for Implementers of School-Wide PBS, 2008.

15. W. J. Popham, "Anchoring Down the Data." *Educational Leadership* 66:4 (2009), 85–86.

16. G. Batsche, J. Elliot, J. Graden, J. Grimes, J. Kovaleski, D. Prasse, D. Reschly, J. Schrag, and D. Tilly, *Response to Intervention: Policy Considerations and Implementation.* Alexandria, VA: National Association of State Directors of Special Education, 2005.

17. L. B. Hauerwas and K. Matthes, *National Progress Monitoring Summer Institute Seminar.* May 31, 2006. Retrieved December 13, 2009, from www.studentprogress.org.

18. C. Lagares, "Facing High Stakes in High School: Twenty-Five Successful Strategies from an Inclusive Social Studies Classroom." *Teaching Exceptional Children* 40:2 (2007), 18–27.

19. D. Pickering, "Dimensions of Learning." Failure Is Not an Option Conference, San Diego, CA, December 6, 2007.

20. D. Ronka, M. A. Lachat, R. Slaughter, and J. Meltzer, "Answering the Questions That Count." *Educational Leadership* 66:4 (2009), 18–24.

21. R. Buhle and C. Blachowicz, "The Assessment Double Play." *Educational Leadership* 66:4 (2009), 42–46.

22. M. Schmoker, "Measuring What Matters." *Educational Leadership*, 66:4 (2009), 70–74.

Chapter Nine

1. R. Skiba and J. Sprague, "Safety Without Suspensions." *Educational Leadership* 66:1 (2008), 38–43.

2. Ibid.

3. B. Simonsen, G. Sugai, and M. Negron, "Schoolwide Positive Behavior Supports: Primary Systems and Practices." *Teaching Exceptional Children* 40:6 (2008), 32–40.

4. Ibid.

5. Ibid.

6. R. H. Horner, *Discipline Prevention Data.* Eugene, OR: University of Oregon, OSEP Center on Positive Behavioral Interventions and Supports, 2007.

7. S. Fairbanks, B. Simonsen, and G. Sugai, "Classwide Secondary and Tertiary Tier Practices and Systems." *Teaching Exceptional Children* 40:6 (2008), 44–52.

8. Ibid.

9. D. A. Crone, R. H. Horner, and L. S. Hawken, *Responding to Problem Behaviors in School: The Behavior Education Program.* New York: Guilford Press, 2004.

10. Ibid.

11. Fairbanks et al., "Classwide Secondary and Tertiary Tier Practices."

12. Simonsen et al., "Schoolwide Positive Behavior Supports."

13. Fairbanks et al., "Classwide Secondary and Tertiary Tier Practices."

14. Horner, *Discipline Prevention Data*.

15. Fairbanks et al., "Classwide Secondary and Tertiary Tier Practices."

16. L. Eber, K. Breen, J. Rose, R. M. Unizycki, and T. H London, "Wraparound as a Tertiary Level Intervention for Students with Emotional/Behavioral Needs." *Teaching Exceptional Children* 14:6 (2008), 16–22.

17. Skiba and Sprague, "Safety Without Suspensions."

Chapter Ten

1. M. Friend and L. Cook, *Collaboration for School Professionals*. Boston: Pearson Education, 2007.

2. Ibid., 7.

3. Friend and Cook, *Collaboration for School Professionals*.

4. R. DuFour, R. DuFour, R. Eaker, and T. Many, *Learning by Doing: A Handbook for Professional Learning Communities at Work*. Bloomington IN: Solution Tree, 2006.

5. G. Roberts, California RTI Guidance Technical Workgroup Meeting, June 15, 2006. Sacramento: California Department of Education, 2006.

6. K. Tackett, G. Roberts, S. Baker, and N. Scammaca, *Implementing Response to Intervention: Practices and Perspectives from Five Schools. Frequently Asked Questions*. Portsmouth, NH: RMC Research Corporation, Center on Instruction, 2009.

7. J. L. David, "Collaborative Inquiry." *Educational Leadership* 6:4 (2009), 87–88.

8. H. Borko, "Professional Development and Teacher Training: Mapping the Terrain." *Educational Researcher* 33:8 (2004), 3–15.

9. J. O'Neill, A. Conzemius, C. Commodore, and C. Pulsfus, *The Power of SMART Goals: Using Goals to Improve Student Learning*. Bloomington, IN: Solution Tree, 2006.

10. Ibid.

11. DuFour et al., *Learning by Doing*.

Conclusion

1. S. Mohammed, G. Roberts, and K. Tackett, *Implementing RTI: Practices and Perspectives*. Center on Instruction, Special Education Strand. Webinar presented at Schools Moving Up, May 7, 2008.

2. Ibid.

3. M. A. Zehr, "RTI Said to Pay Off in Gains for English Learners." *Education Week*, January 22, 2010. Retrieved January 22, 2010, from www.edweek.org/ew/articles/2010/01/22/19rtiells_ep.h29.html.

4. Ibid.

Index

Social studies, 105, 107

Software, graphing, 143

Solution Tree, 167

Sopris West Publishing, 131

Speaking, 98

Special education: accountability and, 12–13, 62; behavior plans and, 37; challenges of, 61; collaborative models for, 63–67; curriculum maps and, 117, 170; definition of, 63; disjointed programs in, 10–12; effectiveness of, 11; eligibility for, 15–16, 43–52, 85; evaluation for, 49–52; graduation rates and, 57; handicapping conditions in, 57–59; history of remedial instruction in, 11; labeling students for, 11; location of, 63; makeup of, 44; movement within RTI and, 4; origin of, 55; overidentification of students for, 12; percent of population in, 60–61; referrals to, 21, 48, 49, 85; *versus* RTI, 16, 67–68; RTI implementation and, 78, 79; RTI rationale and, 1–2, 52–53; standards for, 102; success stories of, 177–179; teaming and, 170–172; in Tier III, 32

Special education funding. *See* Funding

Special educators, 117, 119, 170, 172

Specific goals, 167

Specific learning disability: characteristics of, 59–60; definition of, 59; eligibility for, 15–16, 43–52; graduation rates and, 57; standards and, 102

Speech impairment, 59, 60

Spelling, 135

Spreadsheet programs, 143

SSBD. *See* Systematic Screening for Behavior Disorders

Staff liaisons, 76

Stakeholders, 74

Standard treatment approach: in combination with problem-solving approach, 21; description of, 20; screening and, 130

Standards: essential types of, 103–104, 106; focus on, 101; in good first teaching, 29; IEP goals and, 62; instructional decisions and, 103; pacing of, 105, 107–108; purpose of, 102; RTI implementation and, 78, 79; in special education evaluations, 50; in state assessment blueprints, 103; textbooks and, 29; Tier I and, 29

Standards Aligned Needs Assessment Tool, 180

Standards mapping: assessment and, 109–111, 117; collaboration for, 116–119; determining essential standards in, 103–104; English learners and, 104–105, 108, 117; function of, 101, 103; instructional materials and, 109; instructional plans and, 109–111; process of, 115–116; scaffolded instruction and, 117; school calendars and, 105, 108–109, 112; special education and, 117, 170; textbooks and, 109, 115, 116; tools for, 199–203; vertical alignment and, 104–105

Standards movement, 102

Standards-based assessments, 123

State standards. *See* Standards

State-level data, 124

Station teaching, 66

Stigmatizing students, 128

Strategic groups: behavioral interventions for, 37, 38–39, 40; characteristics of, 32, 33; in collaborative special education models, 67; description of, 31; frequency of progress monitoring for, 127

Student-level teaming, 164–165

Subjective data, 73

Suffixes, 90

Sugai, G., 150

Summarizing, 91, 97

Summary of Nine Key Studies: Multi-Tier Interventions and Response to Intervention for Students Struggling in Mathematics, 94

Summative assessments, 117, 123

Summer school, 93

Supervision, of students, 153

Supplemental programs: for adolescents, 89, 93; for English learners, 96, 99; in mathematics instruction, 95; placement in, 130; purpose of, 87; in reading instruction, 88; standards mapping and, 117

Supplemental support model: description of, 67; in RTI implementation, 79–80

Support networks, 158

Surveys, 74

Suspension, 147

SWPBS. *See* Schoolwide positive behavior supports

Syllables, 90

Symbols, 94

Systematic Screening for Behavior Disorders (SSBD), 128

T

Tackett, K., 73, 177

Targeted instruction: content area teams and, 163–164; data analysis for, 79; grade-level teams and, 162–163; specific learning disability eligibility and, 46; in Tier II, 31, 32

Teaming: accountability and, 169–170; data discussions in, 166; description of, 65–66; goal of, 165; for instructional plans, 161–162, 170–172; professional development for, 168; rationale for, 165–166; special education delivery and, 170–172; success stories of, 177–183; tools for, 211–216. *See also* Collaboration, among teachers; *specific teams*

Teams, leadership. *See* Leadership teams

Technology, 91, 143

Tertiary interventions: of behavioral supports, 148, 149–154, 157–159; description of, 28, 36

Text selection, 98

Textbooks: curriculum maps and, 109, 115, 116; standards movement and, 102; Tier I and, 29; Tier III and, 34

Think-alouds, 95

Three-tiered model, of RTI: academic tiers in, 28–34; behavioral tiers in, 34–40; concurrent implementation of, 82; description of, 25–26; flexibility within, 27–28; goal of, 40, 85; illustration of, 35; *versus* tracking, 27. *See also specific tiers*

Tier Aligned RTI Readiness Tool, 75, 76, 82, 101, 189

Tier I: behavioral interventions in, 37–38, 149–154; content area teams and, 164; definition of, 29; description of, 29–31; English learners in, 96, 98; implementation of, 78–79; mathematics instruction in, 94, 95; vocabulary instruction in, 90

Tier II: behavioral interventions in, 38–39, 128, 149, 154–157; content area teams and, 164; description of, 31–32, 33; English learners in, 96, 98; goal of, 32; implementation of, 79–80; mathematics instruction in, 94, 95; shadow classes in, 93; vocabulary instruction in, 90

Tier III: addressing skill gaps in, 48; attendance in, 128; behavioral interventions in, 39–40, 128, 149, 157–158; description of, 32–34, 35; English learners in, 96, 98; goal of, 34; implementation of, 80–82; mathematics in, 95–96; secondary school schedules and, 93; vocabulary instruction in, 90

Time-bound goals, 167

Topic sentences, 91

Tracking students, 16, 27, 122

Transient students, 128

Trust, 161

Tutoring, 95

U

Unemployed people, 57

Union Middle School, 177–178

Unit, instructional, 118, 127

Universal access time, 31

Universal interventions: of behavioral supports, 148, 149; description of, 28, 36

Universal screening, 123

University of Oregon, 131

V

Vertical alignment, 104–105

Vision assessments, 52

Vision, RTI, 72, 74, 75

Visual impairment, 52, 58, 59

Vocabulary instruction: in curriculum maps, 116; definition of, 87; for English learners, 96, 97–98; in mathematics, 94; in secondary instruction, 90–91

Volunteers, 75

von Goethe, J. W., 57

W

Walk and read time, 31

Web-based graphing programs, 143

Word consciousness, 90

Word problems, 99

Word study, 89–90

Word-learning strategies, 91

Working memory, 97

Worksheets, 95

Workshop classes, 67

Wraparound process, 157–158

Writing skill, 51, 135

Z

Zero tolerance policies, 36, 147